Radio and Television: A Selected, Annotated Bibliography

Supplement Two: 1982-1986

by
PETER K. PRINGLE
and
HELEN H. CLINTON

The Scarecrow Press, Inc.
Metuchen, N.J., & London
1989

This work is based on the following books compiled by William E. McCavitt:

Radio and Television: A Selected, Annotated Bibliography (Scarecrow, 1978), covering 1920 to 1976.

Radio and Television: A Selected, Annotated Bibliography; Supplement One: 1977-1981 (Scarecrow, 1982).

British Library Cataloguing-in-Publication data available

Library of Congress Cataloging-in-Publication Data

Pringle, Peter K.
    Radio and television : a selected, annotated bibliography.
Supplement two, 1982-1986 / by Peter K. Pringle and
Helen E. Clinton.
        p.   cm.
    Supplement 2 to: Radio and television / compiled by
W.E. McCavitt.
    Includes index.
    ISBN 0-8108-2158-3
    1. Broadcasting--Bibliography. I. Clinton, Helen E.,
1951- . II. McCavitt, William E., 1932- Radio and tele-
vision. III. Title.
Z7221.M23   Suppl. 2
[PN1990.8]
016.38454--dc19   88-23968

In Memoriam
  Dr. William E. McCavitt
    1932-1985

To Debbi,
For whom the pursuit of knowledge
is its own reward

CONTENTS

Preface   xii

PART I: BROADCASTING   1

A.   REFERENCES   1

     1. Bibliographies   1
     2. Dictionaries   4
     3. Directories and Guides   4
     4. Encyclopedias   8
     5. Surveys   8

B.   AUDIENCES AND RATINGS   9

C.   AUTOBIOGRAPHIES AND BIOGRAPHIES   10

D.   BUSINESS   13

E.   CAREERS   14

F.   COMMENTARY AND CRITICISM   16

G.   COMPARATIVE, FOREIGN, AND INTERNATIONAL   17

     1. Comparative   17
     2. Foreign   20
         (a) Africa   20
         (b) Asia and the Pacific   21
         (c) Australia   21
         (d) Canada   22
         (e) Europe   23
         (f) Ireland   23
         (g) Middle East   23
         (h) South America   23
         (i) Third World   24
         (j) United Kingdom   24
     3. International   28

H. HISTORY   30

I. IN SOCIETY   33

    1. General   33
    2. Education and Instruction   34
    3. Government and Politics   35
    4. Religion   38

J. LAW, REGULATION, AND POLICY   39

    1. Law and Regulation   39
        (a) General   39
        (b) Contests, Lotteries, and Promotions   42
        (c) Copyright   43
        (d) Elections and Politics   43
        (e) Entertainment   44
        (f) Equal Employment Opportunity   44
        (g) Fairness Doctrine   44
        (h) First Amendment and Freedom   45
        (i) Libel and Privacy   47
        (j) Licenses   48
        (k) Ownership   49
        (l) Process   49
        (m) Public Broadcasting   49
        (n) Remedies   49
        (o) Satellites   50
        (p) Taxation   50
    2. Policy   50

K. PROGRAMS AND CONTENT   52

    1. Entertainment   52
    2. Information   53
    3. Portrayals   53

L. PUBLIC   54

M. TECHNIQUE AND TECHNOLOGY   54

    1. Advertising, Marketing, and Promotion   54
    2. Audio   56
    3. Engineering   57
    4. Management   58
    5. News and Documentary   60
    6. Performance   63
    7. Production   63
    8. Programming   64
    9. Research   64
   10. Writing   65

PART II: RADIO   67

A.   REFERENCES: DIRECTORIES AND GUIDES   67

B.   AUDIENCES   68

C.   BUSINESS   68

D.   CAREERS   69

E.   FOREIGN AND INTERNATIONAL   70

    1.   Foreign   70
        (a)   Australia   70
        (b)   Canada   70
        (c)   United Kingdom   71
    2.   International   72

F.   HISTORY   73

G.   PROGRAMS AND CONTENT   75

    1.   Entertainment   75
    2.   Information   76
    3.   Scripts   76

H.   PUBLIC AND COMMUNITY   77

I.   TECHNIQUE AND TECHNOLOGY   78

    1.   General   78
    2.   Advertising, Marketing, and Promotion   78
    3.   Copywriting   79
    4.   Engineering   79
    5.   Management   80
    6.   News   80
    7.   Performance   81
    8.   Production   81
    9.   Programming   81
  10.   Research   82

PART III: TELEVISION   83

A.   REFERENCES   83

    1.   Bibliographies   83
    2.   Dictionaries   84
    3.   Directories and Guides   85
    4.   Encyclopedias   88

	5.	Indexes	89
	6.	Program Guides	89
	7.	Survey	92
	8.	Trivia	92
	9.	Who's Who	92

B.   AUDIENCES   93

C.   BUSINESS   93

D.   CAREERS   95

E.   COMMENTARY AND CRITICISM   96

F.   COMPARATIVE, FOREIGN, AND INTERNATIONAL   99

    1.   Comparative   99
    2.   Foreign   101
        (a)   Australia   101
        (b)   Brazil   102
        (c)   Canada   102
        (d)   Europe   103
        (e)   Ireland   104
        (f)   Singapore   104
        (g)   United Kingdom   104
    3.   International   111

G.   HISTORY   112

H.   IN SOCIETY   115

    1.   General   115
    2.   Children and Youth   120
    3.   Education and Instruction   124
    4.   Government and Politics   126
    5.   Religion   129
    6.   Sports   129

I.   LAW, REGULATION, AND POLICY   130

    1.   Law and Regulation   130
    2.   Policy   131

J.   PROGRAMS AND CONTENT   132

    1.   Children's   132
    2.   Entertainment   132
    3.   Information   138
    4.   Portrayals   143
    5.   Scripts   145

K.   PUBLIC AND COMMUNITY   146

L. PUBLICATION   147

M. TECHNIQUE AND TECHNOLOGY   147

    1. Advertising, Marketing, and Promotion   147
    2. Engineering   149
    3. Management   149
    4. News   150
    5. Performance   150
    6. Production and Direction   151
        (a) General   151
        (b) Budgets   156
        (c) Editing   157
        (d) Graphics   157
        (e) Lighting   157
        (f) Staging   158
    7. Writing   158

PART IV: CABLE   160

A. REFERENCES   160

    1. Bibliography   160
    2. Dictionary   160
    3. Directories and Guides   160
    4. Surveys   161
    5. Who's Who   162

B. AUDIO   162

C. BUSINESS   163

D. CAREERS   164

E. COMPARATIVE AND FOREIGN   165

    1. Comparative   165
    2. Foreign   166

F. HISTORY   166

G. IN SOCIETY   166

H. LAW, REGULATION, AND POLICY   167

I. PROGRAMS AND CONTENT   170

J. PUBLICATION   171

K. TECHNIQUE AND TECHNOLOGY   171

    1. Advertising, Marketing, and Promotion   171
    2. Engineering   172
    3. Management   172
    4. News   173
    5. Production   173
    6. Programming   173

PART V: NEW TECHNOLOGIES   174

A. GENERAL   174

B. CELLULAR RADIO   178

C. ELECTRONIC PUBLISHING AND INSTRUCTION   178

D. HIGH-DEFINITION TELEVISION   180

E. LOW-POWER TELEVISION   181

F. MULTIPOINT DISTRIBUTION SERVICE   181

G. RADIO SUBCARRIERS   182

H. SATELLITE MASTER ANTENNA TELEVISION   182

I. SATELLITES   183

J. SUBSCRIPTION TELEVISION   187

PART VI: HOME VIDEO   188

PART VII: PERIODICALS   194

A. BROADCASTING   194

B. RADIO   195

C. TELEVISION   196

D. CABLE   196

E. NEW TECHNOLOGIES   197

F. HOME VIDEO   197

Author Index   199

Title Index   211

PREFACE

This volume lists almost one thousand publications devoted entirely or substantially to broadcasting and related technologies, or whose contents are relevant to several media, including electronic.

Selections were made from books, booklets, and reports published in English in the years 1982 through 1986. They have been organized in six parts: Broadcasting, Radio, Television, Cable, New Technologies, and Home Video. The Broadcasting section comprises works that deal with both radio and television. It lists, also, all autobiographies and biographies. Part VII lists periodical titles, subdivided by the same six part subjects listed above.

To assist the user, cross-references are employed throughout, and author and title indexes are included.

Thanks are extended to those whose efforts have made this compilation possible: publishers who made available copies of their works; the staff of the Lupton Library at The University of Tennessee at Chattanooga, and especially Fay L. Verburg, interlibrary loan and database services coordinator; the staff of the Library of Congress and of the National Association of Broadcasters' Library and Information Center, and especially its director, Susan M. Hill; the staffs of the Rohrbach Library at Kutztown University, the Carlson Library at Clarion University of Pennsylvania, and the Pattee Library at the Pennsylvania State University; the libraries that provided publications through the interlibrary loan service; and to Florence Clinton, Charlene Jacobs, Ruth Leinart, and Cara Schollenberger for the variety of assistance they rendered.

Finally, thanks are owed to the late Bill McCavitt, a colleague and friend, who compiled two earlier bibliographies--Radio and Television: A Selected, Annotated Bibliography (Scarecrow Press, 1978), and Radio and Television: A Selected, Annotated Bibliography. Supplement One: 1977-1981 (Scarecrow Press, 1982). They represent two of his many contributions to the broadcast and broadcast education professions. He is missed by those who had the privilege to know him and to work with him.

Peter K. Pringle
Helen E. Clinton

PART I: BROADCASTING

A. REFERENCES

1. Bibliographies

1. Bibliography of CRTC Studies. Ottawa: Canadian Radio-Television and Telecommunications Commission, 1982. 75p.
   More than 350 reports, studies, and working papers prepared by or for the commission and organized by topic. Each listing contains the title, description, date, and number of pages. Text in English and French.

2. Broadcasting Bibliography: A Guide to the Literature of Radio and Television. 2d ed. Washington, DC: National Association of Broadcasters, 1984. 66p.
   Lists 360 books, most published after 1975, in seven categories: fundamentals, business, law, technology and technique, broadcasting and society, comparative, and related technologies. Name, address, brief description, and frequency of publication of trade periodicals, newsletters, and journals, and name and address of publishers/distributors. Author/title index.

3. Dorn, Nicholas, and Nigel South. Message in a Bottle: Theoretical Overview and Annotated Bibliography on the Mass Media and Alcohol. Aldershot, Eng.: Gower, 1983. 178p.
   Review of literature on the relationships among the mass media, their audiences, and the images and messages they carry about alcohol, and an abstract of each of the sources reviewed.

4. Hill, George H., and Lenwood Davis. Religious Broadcasting, 1920-1983: A Selectively Annotated Bibliography. New York: Garland, 1984. 243p.
   More than 1,600 listings of books, dissertations and theses, and articles. Subject/author index, program index.

5. Lent, John A. The New World and International Information Order: A Resource Guide and Bibliography. Singapore: Asian Mass Communication Research and Information Centre, 1982. 103p.

1

Synopsis of the issues: news flows, cultural imperialism,
technology transfer, national sovereignty, and communication
rights.   Details of major meetings and publications in which the
issues have been discussed.   Bibliography contains books, monographs, theses, documents, and periodicals.

6. Lent, John A. Women and Mass Media in Asia: An Annotated
    Bibliography. Singapore: Asian Mass Communication Research
    and Information Centre, 1985.   55p.
        More than 100 works dealing with women in media, women as
    an audience, and women's media.   Index.

7. McCavitt, William E. (comp.).   Radio and Television: A Selected,
    Annotated Bibliography. Supplement One: 1977-1981.   Metuchen,
    NJ: Scarecrow Press, 1982.   155p.
        Sequel to Radio and Television: A Selected, Annotated Bib-
    liography (1978) covering the years 1920-1976.   Contains 514 an-
    notated entries on books and periodicals, and 52 without anno-
    tations.   Emphasis on broadcasting in the United States, includ-
    ing surveys, history, regulation, programming, production, and
    broadcasting in society.   Sections on international broadcasting,
    cable television, corporate and home video, videotex, and satel-
    lites.   Cross-references, index.

8. McKerns, Joseph P.   News Media and Public Policy: An Anno-
    tated Bibliography. New York: Garland, 1985.   171p.
        Total of 731 entries from journals, periodicals, books, theses,
    and dissertations, in 10 chapters: (1)   mass communication
    theory and effects research; (2)   government and the press:
    the historical framework; (3)   newsmaking and the conventions
    of journalism; (4)   the news media and the executive; (5)   the
    news media and the legislative; (6)   the news media and the bu-
    reaucracy; (7)   the news media and the judiciary; (8)   the news
    media as adversary; (9)   news management; (10)   the news
    media's agenda-setting role and public policy.   Author index,
    subject index.

9. The New World Information and Communication Order: A Selec-
    tive Bibliography. New York: United Nations, 1984.   152p.
        Arranged in two parts.   The first lists periodical articles and
    monographs, and the second, documents and publications of the
    United Nations and specialized agencies.   Entries appear under
    the following subject headings: the New World Information and
    Communication Order, communications infrastructure, freedom of
    the press, broadcasting, and bibliographies.

10. Shearer, Benjamin F., and Marilyn Huxford (comps.).   Com-
    munications and Society: A Bibliography on Communications
    Technologies and Their Social Impact. Westport, CT: Greenwood
    Press, 1983.   242p.
        Total of 2,732 entries exploring the diversity of technologies

and their impact on society from a humanistic perspective. Organized in nine subject categories: (1) theory and process of media: technologies as media and messages; (2) the history of technological development and innovation in communication; (3) the shaping of mass media content: media sociology; (4) the social effects of mass media; (5) the mass media as creators and reflectors of public opinion; (6) politics and the mass media; (7) buyer beware: advertising and the mass media; (8) glimpses beyond: the future of mass communications; (9) fine art and literature in the technologized society. Author index, subject index.

11. Snorgrass, J. William, and Gloria T. Woody. Blacks and Media: A Selected, Annotated Bibliography, 1962-1982. Tallahassee, FL: Florida A and M University Press, 1985. 150p.
    Lists 743 books, journal and magazine articles, and other printed materials on blacks in America and their relationship to mass media. Chapters cover broadcast media, print media, advertising and public relations, and film and theater. Author/title index.

12. Sterling, Christopher H. Foreign and International Communications Systems: A Survey Bibliography. Washington, DC: Center for Telecommunications Studies, George Washington University, 1983. 20p.
    Annotated listings covering broadcast and other communication media. History, surveys, regulation and policy, satellites, news flow, developed countries, Communist and Third World countries, U.S. role in international communications, propaganda, and bibliographies and glossaries.

13. Sterling, Christopher H. Mass Communication and Electronic Media: A Survey Bibliography. 9th ed. Washington, DC: Center for Telecommunications Studies, George Washington University, 1983. 22p.
    Lists more than 250 titles, with annotations. Emphasis on electronic media books presently in print or easily available in libraries. Mass communication reference, surveys, and economics, communication theory, media history, electronic media technology, media journalistic and entertainment content, educational applications, children and media, audiences and effects, and policy and regulation.

14. Wedell, George (ed.). Mass Communications in Western Europe: An Annotated Bibliography. Manchester, Eng.: European Institute for the Media, 1985. 327p.
    Almost 800 entries from 20 countries, published between 1980 and 1985. Topic index, name index.

2. Dictionaries

15. Connors, Tracy Daniel. Longman Dictionary of Mass Media and
     Communication. New York: Longman, 1982. 255p.
         Frequently used terms and area of communication in which a
     meaning is used.

16. Editor's Guide to Telecommunications Buzzwords, Terminology,
     Acronyms and Abbreviations. Washington, DC: Television Di-
     gest, 1985. 32p.
         Companion volume to Telecom Factbook (entry 38), containing
     moré than 400 definitions.

17. Penney, Edmund. A Dictionary of Media Terms. New York:
     G.P. Putnam's Sons, 1984. 160p.
         Everyday words used by professionals in film, tape, radio,
     and the new media. Cross-references.

18. Watson, James, and Anne Hill. A Dictionary of Communication
     and Media Studies. Baltimore, MD: Edward Arnold, 1984.
     183p.
         Some 1,000 entries on mass and interpersonal communication,
     many with cross-references and suggestions for further reading.

3. Directories and Guides

19. Advertising Age Yearbook. Chicago: Crain Books, annual
     (1982-84).
         Summary of events from the preceding year, most taken from
     the weekly publication Advertising Age. Illustrations, tables,
     index.

20. AVMP. Audio Video Market Place: A Multimedia Guide. New
     York: R. R. Bowker, annual.
         Producers, distributors, and services, associations, film and
     television commissions, awards and festivals, calendar, period-
     icals, and reference books. Names, addresses, and telephone
     numbers of the firms and most of the personnel listed in the
     text.

21. Broadcasting/Cablecasting Yearbook. Washington, DC: Broad-
     casting Publications, annual.
         Comprehensive directory in nine major sections: (1) the
     Fifth Estate; (2) radio; (3) television; (4) cable; (5) satel-
     lites; (6) programming; (7) advertising and marketing; (8)
     technology; (9) professional services. Illustrations, tables,
     general, section, and advertiser indices.

22. Davis, Henry B. O. Electrical and Electronic Technologies: A
     Chronology of Events and Inventors from 1900 to 1940.

Metuchen, NJ: Scarecrow Press, 1983. 208p.
A summary of each decade, followed by year-to-year developments arranged by decade. Appendices, index.

23. Davis, Henry B. O. Electrical and Electronic Technologies: A
Chronology of Events and Inventors from 1940 to 1980. Metuchen, NJ: Scarecrow Press, 1985. 313p.
A continuation of Electrical and Electronic Technologies ...
1900 to 1940 (entry 22), with one change. Developments are
listed alphabetically by topic for each year. Bibliography, appendices, index.

24. The Directory of Religious Broadcasting. Morristown, NJ:
National Religious Broadcasters, annual.
Religious radio and television stations, program producers,
and agencies and auxiliary services connected with religious
broadcasting.

25. Ehrlich, Eugene, and Raymond Hand, Jr. (revisers). NBC
Handbook of Pronunciation. 4th ed. New York: Harper and
Row, 1984. 539 p.
More than 21,000 commonly used words and proper names,
and difficult names from history and the arts. Uses respelling
system to indicate pronunciation and supplies indications of
secondary as well as primary stresses within words.

26. Fishman, Joshua H., Esther G. Lowry, William G. Milan, and
Michael H. Gertner. Language Resources in the United States
II: Guide to Non-English-Language Broadcasting. Rosslyn,
VA: National Clearinghouse for Bilingual Education, 1982.
115p.
Profiles of more than 1,400 radio and television broadcasters
that transmit programs in languages other than English. Entries
include station call letters, address, and available information
on wattage, program length, commercial or non-commercial status,
and contact person.

27. Godfrey, Donald G. (comp.). A Directory of Broadcast Archives.
Washington, DC: Broadcast Education Association, 1983. 90p.
Guide to radio and television program archives in the United
States, Canada, and the United Kingdom. Each entry includes
the title of the archive, sponsor (private, institutional, or commercial), content description (type of recording, program types,
and subject content), and accessibility of the collection. Suggestions for locating archive material.

28. International Satellite Directory. Corte Madera, CA: SFP Designs, annual.
International organizations, equipment manufacturers, providers and users of satellite services, geosynchronous satellites,
and reference materials. Bibliography, glossary, index.

29.   The Knowledge Industry 200, 1983 Edition: America's Two
      Hundred Largest Media and Information Companies. White Plains,
      NY: Knowledge Industry Publications, 1983.   411p.
         Alphabetical listing with revenue rank, officers and directors,
      major divisions, media holdings, and financial results.   Tables,
      index of secondary companies.

30.   Lent, John A.   The New World and International Information
      Order: A Resource Guide and Bibliography.   Singapore: Asian
      Mass Communication Research and Information Centre, 1982.
      103p.
         See entry 5.

31.   Levey, Jane Freundel.   If You Want Air Time.   Washington,
      DC: National Association of Broadcasters, 1983.   30p.
         Guide for nonprofit organizations wishing to use radio or
      television stations to publicize their activities.   Hints on grab-
      bing station attention, writing cover letters, press releases,
      PSA scripts, and photo captions, and on appearing on radio
      and TV.   Illustrations, glossary.

32.   Lewis, Raymond J.   Meeting Learners' Needs through Telecom-
      munications: A Directory and Guide to Programs.   Washington,
      DC: American Association for Higher Education, 1983.   264p.
         Educational applications of telecommunications technologies by
      postsecondary organizations.   The guide describes current pat-
      terns and trends, and speculates about future problems and pos-
      sibilities.   The directory contains detailed descriptions of 70
      programs that use one or more telecommunications technologies
      to serve learners.   Illustrations, tables, glossary, appendices,
      bibliography, index.

33.   Mincer, Richard, and Deanne Mincer.   The Talk Show Book: An
      Engaging Primer on How to Talk Your Way to Success.   New
      York: Facts on File Publications, 1982.   193p.
         Practical manual on selecting and obtaining a booking in
      radio or TV, preparing for the appearance, what to do before,
      during, and after the interview, and planning and carrying out
      a talk show tour.   Appendix contains titles of more than 100
      radio and television talk/interview shows, city, station or net-
      work, address, telephone number, and program time.   Index.

34.   Newsom, Iris (ed.).   Wonderful Inventions: Motion Pictures,
      Broadcasting, and Recorded Sound at the Library of Congress.
      Washington, DC: Library of Congress, 1985.   384p.
         Essays on some of the library's holdings.   The four in the
      broadcasting section cover music scoring for "Star Trek," a
      summary and listing of selected programs in the television col-
      lection, the TV and radio forums of Theodore Granik, and the
      Armed Forces Radio Service.   Illustrations, index.

35. The Satellite Directory. Coral Springs, FL: B. Klein Publica-
    tions, annual.
       Carriers and systems operators, hardware, technical ser-
    vices, programming, consultants, associations, earth stations,
    and Immarsat terminals. Indices.

36. Slide, Anthony (ed.). International Film, Radio, and Television
    Journals. Westport, CT: Greenwood Press, 1985. 428p.
       Details of more than 200 periodicals. Each entry consists of
    a general essay providing an evaluation and offering insights in-
    to the journal's critical stance and historical background. Sup-
    plemental sections include a bibliography where appropriate;
    index, reprint and location sources; and a publication history
    listing the periodical's title, with any changes indicated by date,
    volume and issue data, publisher, place of publication, and
    editor, with any changes indicated by volume and issue number
    or by date. References in the appendices to more than 100
    additional periodicals. Appendices, general bibliography, index.

37. Sterling, Christopher H. Electronic Media: A Guide to Trends
    in Broadcasting and Newer Technologies, 1920-1983. New York:
    Praeger, 1984. 337p.
       Emphasis on broadcasting and cable data, with some informa-
    tion on newer technologies. Arranged in eight subject cate-
    gories: growth, ownership, economics, employment and train-
    ing, content, audience, international aspects, and regulation.
    Tables.

38. Telecom Factbook. Washington, DC: Television Digest, annual.
       Directory of U.S. communications carriers, satellites, elec-
    tronic mail and videotex, regulatory agencies, and associations.
    International section includes the telecommunications agency for
    each country, related bureaus and departments, national/inter-
    national communications carriers, and international telecommunica-
    tions organizations. Illustrations, index.

39. The Working Press of the Nation. Vol. 3: TV and Radio Di-
    rectory. Chicago: National Research Bureau, annual.
       Listing of commercial and public stations and major networks,
    and of local programs by subject. Station information includes
    power, network affiliation, program air times, and management
    and program personnel.

40. World Radio TV Handbook. New York: Billboard Publications,
    annual.
       Guide to radio and television services around the world,
    maps, frequency lists, related organizations, and feature arti-
    cles. Illustrations, tables.

41. Wright, Gene. Horrorshows: The A-To-Z of Horror in Film,
    TV, Radio and Theater. New York: Facts on File Publications,

1986. 296p.
Entries on more than 600 TV shows, films, and radio and
theater productions arranged in 12 chapters, each devoted to
a particular type of horror production: crazies and freaks,
mad scientists, monsters, cataclysmic disasters, ghouls, ghosts,
demons and witches, vampires, mummies, werewolves and other
shape-shifters, zombies, splatter, and anthologies. All entries
include a synopsis and credits. An introduction to each chapter
traces the evolution of themes, plots, special effects, and acting
styles. The final chapter presents short biographies of actors,
actresses, directors, and producers, and other important figures
in horror entertainment. Illustrations, bibliography, index.

4. Encyclopedias

42. Taft, William H. Encyclopedia of Twentieth-Century Journalists.
New York: Garland, 1986. 408p.
Biographical sketches of broadcast and print journalists,
with emphasis on the post-World War II period. Index.

43. Wright, Gene. The Science Fiction Image: The Illustrated Encyclopedia of Science Fiction in Film, Television, Radio and the
Theater. New York: Facts on File Publications, 1983. 336p.
More than 1,000 entries on hundreds of films, radio and TV
programs, plays, and one opera. Listings include plot summary, cast and filmmaker credits, and critiques on the contribu-
tion of the production to the genre. Cross-referenced biographies of seminal science fiction authors and filmmakers, actors,
and special effects technicians; complete list of genre Academy
Award winners; discussions of major themes; biographies of the
imaginary creatures and characters of science fiction. Illustrations.

5. Surveys

44. Bittner, John R. Broadcasting and Telecommunication: An Introduction. 2d ed. Englewood Cliffs, NJ: Prentice-Hall, 1985.
526p.
Telecommunication approach to the study of electronic communication covering broadcasting, cable, computers and data
processing, teletext and videotex, emerging telecommunications
and consumer technologies, and corporate communication. History and development of telecommunication, broadcast and information technologies, systems and programming, regulatory control, economics, and evaluation. Includes five new chapters.
Illustrations, chapter bibliographies, glossary, appendix, author
and subject indices.

45. Foster, Eugene S. Understanding Broadcasting. 2d ed.

Reading, MA: Addison-Wesley, 1982. 526p.
History, development, and current operation of radio, television, and cable. Illustrations, appendices, glossary, bibliography, index.

46. Gross, Lynne Schafer. Telecommunications: An Introduction
to Radio, Television, and Other Electronic Media. 2d ed.
Dubuque, IA: Wm. C. Brown, 1986. 490p.
An overview in five parts: social implications of telecommunications, communication systems, physical characteristics, programming, regulation and business. Illustrations, glossary,
bibliography, index.

47. Head, Sydney W., with Christopher H. Sterling. Broadcasting
in America: A Survey of Television, Radio, and New Technologies. 4th ed. Boston, MA: Houghton Mifflin, 1982. 642p.
Five-part introduction to the field: management of radio energy, origin and growth of broadcasting, non-commercial and
non-broadcast systems, the business of broadcasting, and broadcasting's effects. New chapters on public broadcasting and on
the likely future of broadcasting, and expanded material on
programs and programming strategies. Illustrations, tables,
bibliography, index.

48. Sabin, Louis. Television and Radio. Mahwah, NJ: Troll Associates, 1985. 30p.
Development and technology of radio and television, written
for children. Illustrations.

49. Smith, F. Leslie. Perspectives on Radio and Television: Telecommunication in the United States. 2d ed. New York: Harper
and Row, 1985. 588p.
Survey of radio, television, and the new technologies. History, production, content, physical properties, economics, law
and ethics, and impact. Foreign radio and TV, and a new
chapter on non-commercial broadcasting. Illustrations, tables,
chapter bibliographies, index.

50. Smith, Marvin. Radio, TV and Cable: A Telecommunications
Approach. New York: Holt, Rinehart and Winston, 1985.
386p.
Theoretical and practical survey in five parts: contexts,
technology and development, economics/programming/advertising,
law/regulation/policy, and effects. Illustrations, tables, glossary, bibliography, index.

B. AUDIENCES AND RATINGS

51. Beville, Hugh Malcolm, Jr. Audience Ratings: Radio, Television,

<u>and Cable</u>.   Hillsdale, NJ: Lawrence Erlbaum Associates, 1985.
362p.
Historical development of radio and television ratings and
services.   Comparative analysis of methodologies, qualitative
and cable audience measurements, current utilization of ratings,
public and governmental concerns, and an examination of the
impact of new technologies.   Illustration, tables, appendices,
bibliography, index.

52.   Greenberg, Bradley S., Michael Burgoon, Judee K. Burgoon,
and Felipe Korzenny.   <u>Mexican Americans and the Mass Media</u>.
Norwood, NJ: Ablex, 1983.   290p.
Use of English- and Spanish-language broadcast and print
media, content preferences, perceptions of and attitudes toward
the media, and media functions for young and adult Mexican-
Americans.   Illustration, tables, bibliography, author index,
subject index.

53.   McGuire, Bernadette, and Garret J. O'Keefe.   <u>Election Year</u>
<u>1984:   NAB-Roper Poll</u>.   Washington, DC: National Association
of Broadcasters, 1984.   12p.
Report of a national survey of 2,000 Americans' use of radio
and television for political information.   Looks at two broad questions: (1) What role does broadcasting play in the election process?   (2) What does the public want from the media in terms of
political information?   Finds that a majority of the public rely
on broadcasting as a major source of information on candidates
and issues, and that candidate debates are both desired and
encouraged.   Tables, appendix.

54.   Roper, Burns W.   <u>Public Attitudes Toward Television And Other</u>
<u>Media In a Time of Change</u>.   New York: Television Information
Office, 1985.   25p.
Results of a survey of the use of and attitudes toward television and other mass media and their coverage of news, political candidates, and portrayal of groups.   Also, attitudes toward commercially-sponsored television.   Tables.

C.   AUTOBIOGRAPHIES AND BIOGRAPHIES

55.   Bacon, James.   <u>How Sweet It Is: The Jackie Gleason Story</u>.
New York: St. Martin's Press, 1985.   214p.
Gleason's life, from pool hustler to millionaire.   Illustrations,
appendix, index.

56.   Bannerman, R. LeRoy.   <u>Norman Corwin and Radio: The Golden</u>
<u>Years</u>.   University, AL: University of Alabama Press, 1986.
275p.
The rise of Norman Corwin, his accomplishments and the

stories behind them. Illustrations, appendix, bibliography, index.

57. Bilby, Kenneth. The General: David Sarnoff and the Rise of the Communications Industry. New York: Harper and Row, 1986. 326p.
     The story of the Russian-born immigrant who rose to the presidency of RCA, his managerial style, struggles, and achievements. Bibliography, index.

58. Blythe, Cheryl, and Susan Sackett. Say Goodnight, Gracie!: The Story of Burns and Allen. New York: E. P. Dutton, 1986. 304p.
     The careers of George Burns and Gracie Allen, from vaudeville through radio to the television series, "The Burns and Allen Show." Extensive treatment of their TV program, its characters, staff, and the ingredients of its success. Title, synopsis, and air date of all 299 programs in the series. Illustrations, appendices, index.

59. Bonderoff, Jason. Mary Tyler Moore. New York: St. Martin's Press, 1986. 200p.
     Insights into the personal and professional life of the television, movie, and stage actress. Illustrations, index.

60. Caesar, Sid, with Bill Davidson. Where Have I Been? An Autobiography. New York: Crown, 1982. 280p.
     His rise to stardom, the drug and alcohol addiction that followed, and the road to recovery. Illustrations.

61. Cosell, Howard, with Peter Bonventre. I Never Played the Game. New York: William Morrow, 1985. 380p.
     The veteran sports journalist reflects on his experiences and offers his opinions on the NFL, "jockocracy" in broadcasting, boxing, ABC Sports and his "Sportsbeat" television program, and on other subjects.

62. Downs, Hugh. On Camera: My 10,000 Hours on Television. New York: G. P. Putnam's Sons, 1986. 253p.
     Chronicles the author's work on "The Tonight Show," "The Today Show," "Concentration," and "20/20," and his pursuit of personal adventure through piloting, underwater exploration, race-car driving, sailing, and a trip to the South Pole. Illustrations.

63. Dynasty: The Authorized Biography of the Carringtons. Garden City, NY: Doubleday, 1984. 158p.
     Profiles of the Carrington family and their lifestyle, accompanied by color and black-and-white photographs. Illustrations.

64. Harwell, Ernie. Tuned to Baseball. South Bend, IN: Diamond

Communications, 1985.   229p.
The autobiography of the long-time baseball announcer and
Hall of Famer.   Illustrations, index.

65.   Higham, Charles.   Lucy: The Real Life of Lucille Ball.   New
York: St. Martin's Press, 1986.   261p.
The person behind the television character, her stormy rela-
tionship with Desi Arnaz, strivings for perfection, struggles
with her children, and moments of despair as well as laughter.
List of her film and television appearances.   Illustrations, index.

66.   Jewell, Geri, with Stewart Weiner.   Geri.   New York: William
Morrow, 1984.   250p.
The story of Geri Jewell's triumph over cerebral palsy and
her rise to television stardom.

67.   King, Larry, with Emily Yoffe.   Larry King.   New York: Simon
and Schuster, 1982.   207p.
The host of "The Larry King Show" recounts his life story.

68.   Lunden, Joan, with Ardy Friedberg.   Good Morning, I'm Joan
Lunden.   New York: G. P. Putnam's Sons, 1986.   255p.
The rise to fame of the co-host of ABC Television's "Good
Morning America."   A behind-the-scenes look at the program,
balancing life as a wife, mother, and TV personality, and
celebrity anecdotes.   Illustrations.

69.   MacNeil, Robert.   The Right Place at the Right Time.   Boston,
MA: Little, Brown, 1982.   333p.
Memoir of the author's more than two decades as a journalist,
the people and events he covered, his achievements, and his
blunders.

70.   Nelson, Carole.   Script for Success.   Carole Nelson: Her Story.
St. Petersburg, FL: LaFray Young, 1985.   117p.
The personal and professional story of a TV anchor in Or-
lando, Florida.   Illustrations.

71.   Nelson, Lindsey.   Hello Everybody, I'm Lindsey Nelson.   New
York: Beech Tree Books, 1985.   430p.
The life story of the long-time sports broadcaster.   Illus-
trations, index.

72.   Savitch, Jessica.   Anchorwoman.   New York: G. P. Putnam's
Sons, 1982.   191p.
The author's life, from childhood in rural Pennsylvania and
New Jersey to network anchor.   Reflections on television jour-
nalism, anchoring, and the changing role of women in TV news.

73.   Sperber, A. M.   Murrow: His Life and Times.   New York:
Freundlich Books, 1986.   795p.

The personal and professional story of America's first broadcast journalist. Illustrations, bibliography, index.

74. Tracey, Michael. A Variety of Lives: A Biography of Sir Hugh Greene. London: Bodley Head, 1983. 344p.
      The life of a former director-general of the BBC. Illustrations, index.

75. Trethowan, Ian. Split Screen. London: Hamish Hamilton, 1984. 222p.
      The autobiography of the political writer and broadcaster who became the BBC's director-general. Illustrations, index.

76. Wallace, Mike, and Gary Paul Gates. Close Encounters. New York: William Morrow, 1984. 494p.
      Mike Wallace's life in broadcasting told in alternate chapters by Wallace himself and by Gates. Illustrations, index.

77. Woodruff, Judy, with Kathleen Maxa. "This Is Judy Woodruff at the White House." Reading, MA: Addison-Wesley, 1982. 229p.
      Judy Woodruff's rise to network White House correspondent for NBC, and how she tried to combine marriage, family, and career. Reflections on the changing role of women and the influence of TV news. Illustrations, index.

D. BUSINESS

78. Bagdikian, Ben H. The Media Monopoly. Boston, MA: Beacon Press, 1983. 282p.
      The growth and impact of the control of America's print and broadcast media by 50 corporations, and the effects of mass advertising on the form and content of broadcasting, newspapers, and magazines. Index.

79. Hamburg, Morton I. Making Millions in Telecommunications: The New Way to Get Rich in the Eighties. New York: Rawson Associates, 1985. 256p.
      The role of the station owner, raising funds, what securities to purchase and why, program creation, and other topics related to ownership success. Emphasis on broadcast facilities. Appendices, glossary, index.

80. Krasnow, Erwin G., and J. Geoffrey Bentley. Buying or Building a Broadcast Station: Everything You Want--and Need--to Know, But Didn't Know Who to Ask. Washington, DC: National Association of Broadcasters, 1982. 78p.
      Broadcasting as a business venture, and steps in buying and in applying to build a station. Tables, appendices.

81. Potential International Business Opportunities for U.S. Broad-
     casters. Washington, DC: National Association of Broadcasters,
     1986. 11p.
          Summary report of an NAB forum. Globalization trends af-
     fecting today's media markets and review of key developments
     in Western European broadcasting systems. Assessment of Far
     Eastern business options, underlying worldwide economic, ad-
     vertising, and business trends, and business risks in interna-
     tional markets.

E. CAREERS

82. Bohère, G. Profession: Journalist. A Study on the Working
     Conditions of Journalists. Geneva, Switzerland: International
     Labour Office, 1984. 177p.
          Structure, employment, constraints, ethical standards, and
     problems of the journalistic profession. Consideration of work
     hours, pay, safety and health, social security, termination, and
     industrial relations. Tables, appendix.

83. Ettema, James S., and D. Charles Whitney (eds.). Individuals
     in Mass Media Organizations: Creativity and Constraint. Bever-
     ly Hills, CA: Sage Publications, 1982. 259p.
          Broadcast, print, film, and music organizations as creative
     and constraining forces on individuals in those media. Illustra-
     tions, tables.

84. Guidelines for Broadcast Internship Programs: Minorities,
     Women, College Students. Washington, DC: National Associa-
     tion of Broadcasters, 1985.
          Establishing and publicizing the program, recruiting, se-
     lecting, managing, evaluating, compensating, and retaining or
     referring interns. Sample internship application and evaluation
     forms. Appendix.

85. Hellweg, Susan A., and Raymond L. Falcione. Internships in
     the Communication Arts and Sciences. Scottsdale, AZ: Gorsuch
     Scarisbrick, 1985. 67p.
          Definition, goals and objectives, and types of internships.
     Advice on initiating the internship, making the most of it, and
     the products of the experience. Illustration, table, appendices.

86. Niven, Harold. Broadcast Programs In American Colleges and
     Universities. Washington, DC: Broadcast Education Association,
     annual.
          State-by-state listing of colleges and universities with de-
     grees or coursework in broadcasting. Each entry includes the
     name of the department, number of broadcast courses offered,
     graduate fellowships and assistantships available, broadcast

facilities used for instructional purposes, and the names of
faculty. Tables.

87. Opportunities in Communications Law. Washington, DC: National Association of Broadcasters, 1983. 54p.
    Responsibilities and career opportunities in private practice,
corporations, federal and state governments, professional and
trade associations, and citizen groups. Listing and details of
corporations and organizations that employ communication lawyers.
Appendix, index.

88. Scholarships in Radio and Television. Washington, DC: National
Association of Broadcasters, 1986. 96p.
    Assistantships, fellowships, and scholarships for students
aspiring to careers in radio and television. NAB, national, and
state-by-state awards.

89. Vahl, Rod. Exploring Careers in Broadcast Journalism. New
York: Rosen, 1983. 122p.
    Characteristics of the broadcast journalist, tips on selecting
a journalism school, and information and advice from local station and network professionals, including Jane Pauley and Joan
Lunden. Illustrations, tables, appendices, recommended reading.

90. Weaver, David H., and G. Cleveland Wilhoit. The American
Journalist: A Portrait of U.S. News People and Their Work.
Bloomington, IN: Indiana University Press, 1986. 216p.
    The backgrounds, education, career patterns, professional
values and ethics, and job conditions of journalists working for
daily and weekly newspapers, news magazines, news services,
and radio and television stations during the early 1980s. Comparisons with findings of a 1971 survey. Based mostly on telephone interviews with 1,001 full-time journalists in late 1982
and early 1983. Illustrations, tables, appendices, bibliography,
index.

91. Weinstein, Bob. Breaking into Communications. New York:
Arco, 1984. 116p.
    Job responsibilities and qualifications in radio and television
stations, cable TV systems, and newspapers. Hints on preparing for a career and applying for a position. Illustrations,
index.

92. Zacharis, John C., Frances Forde Plude, and Andrew S. Rancer.
Exploring Careers in Communications and Telecommunications.
New York: Rosen, 1985. 161p.
    Trends and opportunities in broadcasting, cable and other
electronic media, print media, advertising, public relations,
business, and education. Career preparation, and steps in the
job-search. Illustrations, appendices.

93. Zeller, Susan L. Your Career in Radio and Television Broad-
     casting. New York: Arco, 1982. 127p.
         Guidebook for young persons contemplating a career in broad-
     casting. Brief history, and description of the responsibilities
     of station departments and personnel. Tips on researching
     markets and stations, educational preparation, cover letter and
     resume writing, and job interviewing. Illustrations, appendices,
     bibliography, index.

F. COMMENTARY AND CRITICISM

94. Bolling, Landrum R. (ed.). Reporters Under Fire: U.S. Media
     Coverage of Conflicts in Lebanon and Central America. Boulder,
     CO: Westview Press, 1985. 155p.
         Seminar presentations and discussions on criticisms of media
     coverage, media responses, and the relationship of coverage to
     U.S. foreign policy.

95. Dennis, Everette E., and John C. Merrill. Basic Issues in Mass
     Communication: A Debate. New York: Macmillan, 1984. 201p.
         Challenges and responses to contemporary views on journalism,
     the media, and the press. Among the issues are freedom of
     the press, media-government relationship, public access to the
     media, media power, the quality of media content, journalistic
     objectivity, news-gathering tactics, press councils and ethical
     codes, and Western communications imperialism. Index.

96. Mosco, Vincent, and Janet Wasko (eds.). The Critical Com-
     munications Review. Vol. 1: Labor, the Working Class and the
     Media. Norwood, NJ: Ablex, 1983. 312p.
         Challenges the established approach to criticisms of the
     media's representation of the working class. History, media
     unions, media content and working people, and new communica-
     tion technologies for the workplace. Bibliography, index.

97. Schmuhl, Robert (ed.). The Responsibilities of Journalism.
     Notre Dame, IN: University of Notre Dame Press, 1984. 138p.
         Academic, business, theological, and journalistic perspectives
     on the moral dimensions of contemporary journalism, and analysis
     of a hypothetical case study. Bibliography.

98. Wattenberg, Ben J. The Good News Is The Bad News Is Wrong.
     New York: Simon and Schuster, 1984. 431p.
         Data on and analysis of the U.S. quality of life, standard of
     living, and values and politics, and assessment of ways in which
     they are reported by the electronic and print media. Argues
     that the media are missing the biggest stories of the era--those
     dealing with progress. Index.

G. COMPARATIVE, FOREIGN, AND INTERNATIONAL

1. Comparative

99. Arno, Andrew, and Wimal Dissanayake (eds.). The News
Media in National and International Conflict. Boulder, CO:
Westview Press, 1984. 250p.
Interrelationship among government, broadcast and print
news media, and the public in conflict situations. Includes
conflicts between the United States and Iran, India and Pakis-
tan, and the United States and China, and national-level studies
in Sri Lanka, Iran, Hong Kong, and the United States. Illustrations, tables, name index, subject index.

100. Burke, Richard C. Comparative Broadcasting Systems. Chi-
cago: Science Research Associates, 1984. 43p.
Organization, programming, financing, regulation, and evalua-
tion of broadcasting in the United Kingdom, Canada, Western
Europe, the Soviet Union, Japan, and the developing world.
Illustrations.

101. Curry, Jane Leftwich, and Joan R. Dassin (eds.). Press Control Around the World. New York: Praeger, 1982. 287p.
Elements, processes, and systems of censorship in Western
democracies, Communist countries, and the developing world.
Index.

102. Edelstein, Alex S. Comparative Communication Research.
Beverly Hills, CA: Sage Publications, 1982. 160p.
Topics include communication modernization, economic development communication, the new world information order, differing views of value and culture, the construction of images,
the role of the journalist, and the idea of system and information societies.

103. Edgar, Patricia, and Syed A. Rahim (eds.). Communication
Policy in Developed Countries. London: Kegan Paul International, 1983. 297p.
Methods of policy formation, and description and critical
discussion of those policies in the United States, United Kingdom, Canada, Sweden, the Federal Republic of Germany, Australia, and New Zealand. Illustrations, tables.

104. Gerbner, George, and Marsha Siefert (eds.). World Communications: A Handbook. New York: Longman, 1984. 527p.
Papers by scholars and policy makers from the United States,
Western Europe, socialist countries, including the U.S.S.R.
and Eastern Europe, and the developing world, including Africa,
Asia, and Latin America. Organized in five parts: (1) global
perspectives on information; (2) transnational communications:

the flow of news and images; (3) telecommunications: satellites and computers; (4) mass communications: development within national contexts; (5) intergovernmental systems: toward international policies. Illustrations, tables, appendices, index.

105. Hawkridge, David, and John Robinson. Organizing Educational Broadcasting. London: Croom Helm; Paris: UNESCO, 1982. 302p.

Part one offers guidelines on organizing and managing an educational radio-television system and relies heavily on the 12 case studies that constitute part two. Covers form of governance, objectives, production and distribution, utilization, effects, and finance. The case studies are drawn from Africa, Asia, Europe, and North, Central, and South America. Illustrations, tables, index.

106. Head, Sydney W. World Broadcasting Systems: A Comparative Analysis. Belmont, CA: Wadsworth, 1985. 457p.

Introduction to the worlds of broadcasting, and problem-solving approach to the politics of broadcast ownership and access, laws, regulation, economics, facilities, programs and programming, and audience research. Chapters on transborder broadcasting, and broadcasting and freedom. Illustrations, tables, glossary, index.

107. Howell, W. J., Jr. World Broadcasting in the Age of the Satellite: Comparative Systems, Policies, and Issues in Mass Telecommunication. Norwood, NJ: Ablex, 1986. 329p.

Analysis of broadcasting around the world, with emphasis on prevailing media theory, associated ownership typologies, financial support mechanisms, dominant national models, program policy orientation, programming priorities, relative operational autonomy, and organizational structure. International broadcasting via shortwave and satellite, and national comparisons and orbital trends in broadcasting, cable, and VCR. Tables, author index, subject index.

108. International Issues in Communication Technology and Policy. Washington, DC: Academy for Educational Development, 1983. 35p.

Summary of discussions at a 1983 seminar by senior broadcast, telecommunication, and development and information personnel from Africa, Asia, the Caribbean, Europe, Latin America, the Middle East, and the Pacific. Technology and policy challenges and opportunities, and implications for their own country and worldwide cooperation. Illustrations.

109. Kaye, Anthony, and Keith Harry (eds.). Using the Media for Adult Basic Education. London: Croom Helm, 1982. 255p.

Themes and issues involved in the combined use of broadcasting, distance teaching methods, and local tutorials or

counselling. Detailed case studies of seven projects in five
European countries demonstrate that the combination is a most
effective way of reaching groups that might not be reached
otherwise. Illustrations, tables, bibliography, appendices, index.

110. Kuhn, Raymond (ed.). The Politics of Broadcasting. London:
Croom Helm, 1985. 305p.
Description and analysis of problems faced by politicians
and broadcasters in the changing technological and political
environment in Great Britain, France, West Germany, Italy,
the United States, Canada, Australia, and Japan. Illustrations, tables, index.

111. Lahav, Pnina (ed.). Press Law in Modern Democracies: A
Comparative Study. New York: Longman, 1985. 366p.
Approaches to electronic and print media law. Organized
in three divisions: Anglo-American (United Kingdom and United
States), continental (France, the Federal Republic of Germany,
and Sweden), and non-Western (Israel and Japan). Easy essay introduces the general framework of press law and examines its application to government, the judicial process, and
the individual. Concluding chapter contains an outline for a
general theory of press law in a democracy. Table, index.

112. Martin, L. John, and Anju Grover Chaudhary. Comparative
Mass Media Systems. New York: Longman, 1983. 356p.
Analytical and conceptual consideration of the environment
and practices of broadcast and print media in the Western
world, Communist countries, and the Third World. Nineteen
contributors examine the systems, their educational, persuasive,
opinion-making, and entertainment functions, concepts of news
and press freedom, and media economics. Index.

113. The Media Crisis ... A Continuing Challenge. Washington, DC:
World Press Freedom Committee, 1982. 153p.
Report on the broad issue of news media freedom, or its
lack, around the globe.

114. Merrill, John C.(ed.). Global Journalism: A Survey of the
World's Mass Media. New York: Longman, 1983. 374p.
Journalistic practices, philosophical considerations, govern-
ment-press relations, and the education of journalists in Europe
and the Middle East, Asia and the Pacific, Africa, Latin America,
and North America. Illustrations, tables, bibliography, index.

115. Nimmo, Dan, and Michael W. Mansfield (eds.). Government and
the News Media· Comparative Dimensions. Waco, TX: Baylor
University Press, 1982. 306p.
Anthology of materials from the International Communication
Association's 1977 conference in Berlin. Each article discusses

the government's impact on the media, government information
systems, the nature of the news media, and the media's impact on government. Among the countries examined are France,
Italy, Japan, Mexico, Canada, Australia, and Israel.

116. Rogers, Everett M., and Francis Balle (eds.). The Media
      Revolution in America and in Western Europe. Norwood, NJ:
      Ablex, 1985. 331p.
         Comparative aspects of Euro-American mass communication
      research, covering the changing nature of the mass media,
      new technologies, and approaches to research. Illustrations,
      tables, appendices, name index, subject index.

117. Smith, Nelson, and Leonard J. Theberge (eds.). Energy
      Coverage--Media Panic: An International Perspective. New
      York: Longman, 1983. 167p.
         Analysis and discussion of media coverage of oil and nuclear
      energy issues in the United States, France, West Germany,
      Great Britain, and Japan. Illustrations, tables, index.

118. Stevenson, Robert L., and Donald Lewis Shaw (eds.). Foreign
      News and the New World Information Order. Ames, IA: Iowa
      State University Press, 1984. 243p.
         Quantitative analysis of foreign news in Western wire ser-
      vices and in broadcast newscasts and newspapers in 17 coun-
      tries in North America, Latin America, Africa, the Middle East,
      Asia, and Eastern and Western Europe. Concludes that there
      is no justification for many of the complaints about Western
      coverage of the Third World and that foreign news in Western
      media is spotty, narrowly defined, and uneven. Illustrations,
      tables, index.

                           2. Foreign

                          (a) Africa

119. Mytton, Graham. Mass Communication in Africa. London: Ed-
      ward Arnold, 1983. 159p.
         History, organization, roles, and control of radio, television,
      and newspapers, with case studies on Zambia, Tanzania, and
      Nigeria. Illustrations, tables, bibliography, index.

120. Ugboajah, Frank Okwu (ed.). Mass Communication, Culture
      and Society in West Africa. Munich: Hans Zell, 1985. 329p.
         The functions of broadcast and other media, and their role
      as cultural mediators. History of mass communication in the
      West African region, cultural programming, media language de-
      velopment, message diffusion, professionalism, and trends in
      media research. Illustrations, tables, bibliographic essay.

(b)   Asia and the Pacific

121. Bhasin, Kamla, and Bina Agarwal (eds.). Women and Media:
Analysis, Alternatives and Action. New Delhi: Kali for
Women, 1984. 132p.
The ways in which women are portrayed in broadcast and
other media, and attempts by various women's groups to pro-
test against negative portrayals and create alternatives. Articles are drawn chiefly from the Asian and Pacific regions, with
the emphasis on India. Illustrations, bibliography.

122. Lent, John A. Women and Mass Media in Asia: An Annotated
Bibliography. Singapore: Asian Mass Communication Research
and Information Centre, 1985. 55p.
See entry 6.

(c)   Australia

123. Allen, Yolanda, and Susan Spencer. The Broadcasting Chronology, 1809-1980. North Ryde, New South Wales: Australian
Film and Television School, 1983. 221p.
Significant events in the emergence and development of Australian broadcasting. Chapter one covers the nineteenth century; chapters two through nine cover 1900-1979; and chapter
ten covers the year 1980. Each chapter begins with a summary
of the period covered. Appendices, bibliography, index.

124. Armstrong, Mark. Broadcasting Law and Policy in Australia.
Sydney: Butterworth, 1982. 291p.
Description and critical examination of changes required to
meet the expressed needs of the country. Includes chapters
on the foundations of broadcasting law, the scheme of legislation, a historical outline, general rules, the Australian Broadcasting Commission and the Special Broadcasting Service, enforcement rules on ownership, control, and rebroadcasting facilities. Appendix.

125. Armstrong, Mark, Michael Blakeney, and Ray Watterson. Media
Law in Australia. Melbourne: Oxford University Press, 1983.
274p.
Defamation, copyright, obscenity, blasphemy and sedition,
access to information, advertising, and sales promotions and
competitions, accompanied by major decisions. Separate chapters on radio and television law and on press regulation. Index.

126. Inglis, K. S., assisted by Jan Brazier. This is the ABC:
The Australian Broadcasting Commission, 1932-1983. Carlton,
Victoria: Melbourne University Press, 1983. 521p.
The people, programs, and politics of the ABC, from its
beginnings. Illustrations, index.

127. Western, J. S., and Colin A. Hughes. The Mass Media in
      Australia. 2d ed. New York: University of Queensland Press,
      1983. 209p.
         Part one reports the results of a study among 992 respond-
      ents on media use, preferences, and evaluation, and shows the
      growing importance of television as the principal source of po-
      litical attitudes and information. Part two consists of three
      case studies on the interplay of politics and the mass media.
      Tables, index.

128. Windschuttle, Keith. The Media: A New Analysis of the Press,
      Television, Radio and Advertising in Australia. Ringwood, Vic-
      toria: Penguin Books, 1985. 436p.
         Covers media economics, culture, and hegemony, and ar-
      gues that a great deal of media content is functional for working-
      class audiences. Illustrations, tables, index.

                          (d) Canada

129. Balance in Broadcasting: Report on a Seminar Held 16-17
      January, 1981 in Hull, Quebec. Ottawa: Canadian Radio-
      Television and Telecommunications Commission, 1982. 21p.
         Summaries of papers and panel and floor discussions on the
      representation of women and minorities and on political, social,
      and cultural balance in Canadian broadcasting. Text in Eng-
      lish and French.

130. Bibliography of CRTC Studies. Ottawa: Canadian Radio-
      Television and Telecommunications Commission, 1982. 75p.
         See entry 1.

131. Godfrey, Donald G. (comp.). A Directory of Broadcast Ar-
      chives. Washington, DC: Broadcast Education Association,
      1983. 90p.
         See entry 27.

132. Siegel, Arthur. Politics and the Media in Canada. Toronto:
      McGraw-Hill, 1983. 258p.
         Survey of broadcast and print media. Topics include the
      maintenance of Canadian identity, restraints on the dissemina-
      tion of information, advertising, concentration of media owner-
      ship, and regulatory agencies.

133. Singer, Benjamin D. (ed.). Communications in Canadian Society.
      Reading, MA: Addison-Wesley, 1983. 342p.
         Papers examining the status of Canadian media.

134. Soderlund, Walter C., Walter I. Romanow, E. Donald Briggs,
      and Ronald H. Wagenberg. Media and Elections in Canada.
      Toronto: Holt, Rinehart and Winston of Canada, 1984. 163p.
         Overview of Canadian politics and media development, and

analysis of broadcast reporting of the 1979 and 1980 political
campaigns and of newspaper reporting of the 1979 campaign.
Government regulation of media, and major issues relating to
media and politics in Canada. Illustrations, tables, appendix,
bibliography, index.

(e) Europe

135. Roberts, Geoffrey K. Access to Political Broadcasting in the
      EEC. Dover, NH: Manchester University Press, 1984. 29p.
         Public and private radio and television, with emphasis on
      the 1984 elections to the European Parliament.

136. Wedell, George (ed.). Mass Communications in Western Europe:
      An Annotated Bibliography. Manchester, Eng.: European
      Institute for the Media, 1985. 327p.
         See entry 14.

(f) Ireland

137. Woodman, Kieran. Media Control in Ireland, 1923-1983. Car-
      bondale, IL: Southern Illinois University Press, 1985. 352p.
         The role of government in the operation and content of
      Irish media. The impact of changing censorship, and the re-
      ligious, moral, and historical implications of government in-
      volvement.

(g) Middle East

138. Bakr, Yahya Abu, Saad Labib, and Hamdy Kandil. Develop-
      ment of Communication in the Arab States: Needs and Prior-
      ities. Paris: UNESCO, 1985. 60p.
         Policies and planning priorities, facilities, and networks and
      technology. Content, information flow, personnel development,
      communication research, inter-Arab cooperation, and the mo-
      bilization of resources. Focus on broadcasting, print media,
      and news agencies. Tables, annexes.

139. Boyd, Douglas A. Broadcasting in the Arab World: A Survey
      of Radio and Television in the Middle East. Philadelphia, PA:
      Temple University Press, 1982. 306p.
         The origins, development, and operation of broadcast ser-
      vices in Egypt, the Sudan, Lebanon, Syria, Jordan, North
      Yemen, South Yemen, the Arabian Gulf states and North Africa,
      and of international radio broadcasting in Arabic. Tables, bib-
      liography, index.

(h) South America

140. Mattelart, Michèle. Women, Media and Crisis: Femininity
      and Disorder. London: Comedia, 1986. 123p.

Essays on the image of women generally promoted by the media and changes during times of crisis, with special attention to the Chilean coup d'état of 1973.

141. Murdock, Graham, and Noreene Janus, with contributions by N. N. Pillai, V. P. Shestakov, and P. P. de Win. Mass Communications and the Advertising Industry. Paris: UNESCO, 1985. 70p.
The development of advertising, advertising and the mass media system, advertising in the new media in the United Kingdom, and the control and social impact of advertising. Based primarily on studies in Britain and Latin America. Tables.

(i) Third World

142. Gibbons, Arnold. Information, Ideology and Communication: The New Nations' Perspectives on an Intellectual Revolution. Lanham, MD: University Press of America, 1985. 219p.
Third World concerns about freedom of the press, media power, and international news flow, and the promises and threats of new communication technologies. Appendices, index.

143. Graff, Robert D. Communications for National Development: Lessons from Experience. Cambridge, MA: Oelgeschlager, Gunn and Hain, 1983. 395p.
Role of traditional and mass media in national development, based on discussions at three seminars on Communications, Development, and Social Change in Salzburg, Austria, in 1979, 1980, and 1981. Illustrations, bibliography, index.

144. Hedebro, Göran. Communication and Social Change in Developing Nations: A Critical View. Ames, IA: Iowa State University Press, 1982. 142p.
Analysis of the current role, potential, and limitations of mass media and interpersonal communication in the development process. Illustrations, table, index.

145. Stover, William James. Information Technology in the Third World: Can I.T. Lead to Humane National Development? Boulder, CO: Westview Press, 1984. 183p.
Potential of radio, television, satellites, and computer and other technologies to effect economic, social, and political development. The problems posed by the new world information order and the values of political leaders, and recommendations for fulfilling the promise offered by instructional technology. Illustrations, tables, bibliography, index.

(j) United Kingdom

146. Aubrey, Crispin (ed.). Nukespeak: The Media and the Bomb. London: Comedia, 1982. 135p.

Essays on the shortcomings of the British media in reporting the nuclear arms issue, and suggestions for effecting
changes in coverage. Illustrations.

147. Briggs, Asa. The BBC: The First Fifty Years. Oxford, Eng.:
Oxford University Press, 1985. 439p.
Interpretative history covering the wireless experiments,
the founding of the British Broadcasting Company, the establishment of the British Broadcasting Corporation, the role of
John Reith, the BBC in wartime, the emergence of television,
and the advent of commercial broadcasting. Seeks to explain
why Britain chose to organize broadcasting through a particular national institution, and how that institution has changed
in size, structure, and outlook. Illustrations, appendix, bibliographical notes, index.

148. Cohen, Phil, and Carl Gardner (eds.). It Ain't Half Racist,
Mum: Fighting Racism in the Media. London: Comedia, 1982.
119p.
Points of view on various aspects of alleged racism in
Britain's broadcast and print media, and suggestions for win-
ning redress. Illustrations, appendices, bibliography.

149. Curran, James, and Jean Seaton. Power Without Responsibility: The Press and Broadcasting in Britain. 2d ed. London:
Methuen, 1985. 396p.
Broadcast and press history, critical analysis of liberal
theories of media freedom and public service broadcasting, summary of British media policy and its contradictions, an examination of the new communications revolution, and proposals
for media reform. Tables, bibliography, index.

150. Curtis, Liz. Ireland: The Propaganda War. The British
Media and the "Battle for Hearts and Minds." London: Pluto
Press, 1984. 336p.
Background to the conflict in Northern Ireland, media repre-
sentation of the participants, and the development of propa-
ganda machines. Appendix, index.

151. Godfrey, Donald G. (comp.). A Directory of Broadcast Archives. Washington, DC: Broadcast Education Association,
1983. 90p.
See entry 27.

152. Gurevitch, Michael, Tony Bennett, James Curran, and Janet
Woollacott (eds.). Culture, Society and the Media. New York:
Methuen, 1982. 317p.
Major traditions that influence media theory, the role of
media institutions, and the power of the media in control of
communications systems, politics, and in the signification and
reporting of race. Adapted from Britain's Open University

course on Mass Communication and Society.   Illustrations,
tables, appendix.

153.   Harris, Robert.   Gotcha!   The Media, the Government and the
       Falklands Crisis.   London: Faber and Faber, 1983.   158p.
          Coverage of the Falklands war by Britain's broadcast and
       print media, and the reactions of the British government, in-
       cluding the row about the BBC's handling of the crisis.   Index.

154.   Hartley, Ian.   Goodnight Children ... Everywhere.   South-
       borough, Eng.:   Midas Books, 1983.   165p.
          The evolution of children's radio and television broadcasting
       in Britain, the programs, and the personalities.   Illustration,
       further reading, index.

155.   Hoggart, Richard, and Janet Morgan (eds.).   The Future of
       Broadcasting: Essays on Authority, Style and Choice.   London:
       Macmillan, 1982.   166p.
          Eight papers presented at a 1980 conference in Britain on
       The Foundations of Broadcasting Policy, a summary of the dis-
       cussions, and closing observations.   Analysis of the aims and
       methods of persons who establish a broadcast system (author-
       ity), its temper and tone (style), and its responsiveness to
       audience needs and wishes (choice), with emphasis on the
       British experience.   Index.

156.   Hooper, Alan.   The Military and the Media.   Aldershot, Eng.:
       Gower, 1982.   247p.
          Study of the relationship between the military and the media
       in the United Kingdom.   Case studies of the news process in
       TV and radio news and current affairs programs, portrayal of
       the military in TV documentaries and TV drama, and the re-
       porting of conflict, with examples from Vietnam, Northern Ire-
       land, and the Falklands.   Illustrations, table, bibliography,
       index.

157.   Howkins, John.   New Technologies, New Policies?   A Report
       from the Broadcasting Research Unit.   London: British Film
       Institute, 1982.   74p.
          Overview of new technologies: the production process,
       satellite delivery, cables and wires, interactive systems, video
       cassettes and discs.   Discussion on the regulation of informa-
       tion communicated.

158.   May, Annabelle, and Kathryn Rowan (eds.).   Inside Information:
       British Government and the Media.   London: Constable, 1982.
       288p.
          Theory and practice of information control within the Brit-
       ish system of government.   Legal and quasi-legal framework of
       control, ways in which politicians, civil servants, journalists,
       and academics have interpreted their roles in the process of

information management, and four case studies involving a conflict between government ideology and "the public interest."
Index.

159.   Murdock, Graham, and Noreene Janus, with contributions by
       N. N. Pillai, V. P. Shestakov, and P. P. de Win. Mass Com-
       munications and the Advertising Industry. Paris: UNESCO,
       1985. 70p.
          See entry 141.

160.   Parker, Bruce, and Nigel Farrell. TV and Radio: Everybody's
       Soapbox. Poole, Eng.: Blandford Press, 1983. 192p.
          Hints on access to British radio and television. Best ways
       and times to approach the program department, how to handle
       an interview, what to wear, how to cope with the equipment,
       and consideration of legal implications. Illustrations, index.

161.   Robertson, Geoffrey, and Andrew G. L. Nicol. Media Law:
       The Rights of Journalists and Broadcasters. London: Oyez
       Longman, 1984. 403p.
          Legal rights of journalists, broadcasters, and others who
       present news or views through the media in Britain. Freedom
       of expression, libel, contempt, confidence, copyright, and ob-
       scenity. Laws applicable to reporting on the courts, Whitehall,
       parliament, local government, and commercial enterprises. Ac-
       count of practices and procedures of regulatory bodies. Table
       of cases, of statutes, and of statutory instruments; index.

162.   Robinson, John. Learning over the Air: 60 Years of Partner-
       ship in Adult Learning. London: British Broadcasting Cor-
       poration, 1982. 256p.
          Decade-by-decade developments in educative and educational
       broadcasting in the United Kingdom from 1922, and examination
       of the three-way partnership of adult educators, broadcasters,
       and learners. Illustrations, tables, bibliography, index.

163.   Taylor, Laurie, and Bob Mullan. Uninvited Guests: The In-
       timate Secrets of Television and Radio. London: Chatto and
       Windus, 1986. 218p.
          The opinions and fantasies of the audience toward broad-
       cast heroes and villains, news readers, and others brought
       into the home by the broadcast media.

164.   Tracey, Michael. A Variety of Lives: A Biography of Sir
       Hugh Greene. London: Bodley Head, 1983. 344p.
          See entry 74.

165.   Trethowan, Ian. Split Screen. London: Hamish Hamilton,
       1984. 222p.
          See entry 75.

166. Who's Who in Broadcasting. 2d ed. Ayr, Scotland: Carrick,
      1985. 210p.
      Capsule biographies of about 1,000 British radio and TV
      personnel, organized alphabetically.

167. Wolfe, Kenneth M. The Churches and the British Broadcasting
      Corporation, 1922-1956: The Politics of Broadcast Religion.
      London: SCM Press, 1984. 627p.
      Chronicles the relationship of the BBC and the churches
      from the beginning of radio broadcasting to the emergence of
      commercial television. Ways in which the two cooperated and
      how they defined their mutual policy and agreed on the output.
      Illustrations, appendices, bibliography, index.

168. Worcester, Robert M., and Martin Harrop (eds.). Political
      Communications: The General Election Campaign of 1979.
      London: George Allen and Unwin, 1982. 181p.
      Selected papers and edited versions of discussions from a
      1980 conference of academics and practitioners in the field of
      political communications. Includes news coverage, party broad-
      casts, advertising, and public opinion polls and their use by
      the media. Illustrations, tables, appendices, index.

                          3. International

169. Boyd, Douglas A. Broadcasting in the Arab World: A Survey
      of Radio and Television in the Middle East. Philadelphia, PA:
      Temple University Press, 1982. 306p.
      See entry 139.

170. Codding, George A., Jr., and Anthony M. Rutkowski. The
      International Telecommunication Union in a Changing World.
      Dedham, MA: Artech House, 1982. 414p.
      Evolution of telecommunication technologies, problems posed
      by their use, and the role of the ITU in trying to solve them.
      The union's decision-making apparatus, results of its activities,
      and a critical evaluation of its performance. Illustrations,
      tables, annexes, bibliography, index.

171. Communications in a Changing World. Vol. 2: Issues in In-
      ternational Information. Washington, DC: Media Institute,
      1983. 71p.
      Eastern and Western perceptions of the potential impact of
      UNESCO's proposed New World Information Order on news and
      journalism, program material, business, and advertising, and
      the U.S. government's response to the proposal.

172. Gerbner, George, and Marsha Siefert (eds.). World Communi-
      cations: A Handbook. New York: Longman, 1984. 527p.
      See entry 104.

173. Hamelink, Cees J. Cultural Autonomy in Global Communications:
      Planning National Information Policy. New York: Longman,
      1983. 143p.
      The role of international communication in national cultural
      development and essential elements in national communication
      planning. Proposes that developing nations sever cultural and
      informational links with the transnational corporate chain. Il-
      lustrations, tables, bibliography, index.

174. Mosco, Vincent, and Janet Wasko (eds.). The Critical Communi-
      cation Review. Vol. 2: Changing Patterns of Communications
      Control. Norwood, NJ: Ablex, 1984. 299p.
      Consequences of the restructuring of communications sys-
      tems. Information flow, international ideological battles, cul-
      tural autonomy, impact on established media, commercial in-
      fluences, and governmental policies. Tables, author index,
      subject index.

175. Mowlana, Hamid. International Flow of Information: A Global
      Report and Analysis. Paris: UNESCO, 1985. 75p.
      Synthesis of relevant research undertaken by different in-
      stitutions and organizations, and the political, cultural, eco-
      nomic, technological, legal, and professional practices affecting
      the flow. Covers news and views, broadcasting, transborder
      data, and planetary resource flow. Illustrations, selected
      bibliography.

176. Nordenstreng, Kaarle, with Lauri Hannikainen. The Mass Media
      Declaration of Unesco. Norwood, NJ: Ablex, 1984. 475p.
      The diplomatic process of formulating the 1978 Declaration
      on Fundamental Principles concerning the Contribution of the
      Mass Media to Strengthening Peace and International Under-
      standing, to the Promotion of Human Rights and to Countering
      Racialism, Apartheid and Incitement to War. Review of interna-
      tional law applicable to journalism and mass communication, and
      the social ethics and philosophical foundations of mass communi-
      cation. Tables, appendices, name index, subject index.

177. Pavlič, Breda, and Cees J. Hamelink. The New International
      Economic Order: Links Between Economics and Communications.
      Paris: UNESCO, 1985. 65p.
      The relationship between the concepts of a new international
      economic order and a new communication order, and steps taken
      toward their implementation. Attempt at defining the contribu-
      tion that information-communication methods can make towards
      the establishment of a new economic order. Tables, selected
      bibliographies.

178. Ploman, Edward W. International Law Governing Communica-
      tions and Information: A Collection of Basic Documents. West-
      port, CT: Greenwood Press, 1982. 367p.

Major legal instruments on the international movement of information and ideas through formal communication systems.
Covers general international law and law of information, telecommunications, post, and space; intellectual property rights;
informatics law; trade and customs regulation; culture and
education; and national security and law enforcement. Index.

179. Sterling, Christopher H. (ed.). International Telecommunications and Information Policy. Washington, DC: Communications Press, 1984. 496p.
Edited proceedings of a 1983 symposium based on the government report, Long-Range Goals in International Telecommunications and Information: An Outline for United States Policy,
and a facsimile of the report. Topics include the relationship
of the International Telecommunication Union and the United
States, satellite communications policy, and the free flow of
information. Illustrations.

180. Yurow, Jane H. (ed.). Issues in International Telecommunications Policy: A Sourcebook. Washington, DC: Center for
Telecommunications Studies, George Washington University,
1983. 260p.
The International Telecommunication Union, regulatory environment, transborder data flow, telecommunications and trade
policy, and intellectual property. Chapter bibliographies,
glossary, index.

H. HISTORY

181. Allen,Yolanda, and Susan Spencer. The Broadcasting Chron-
ology, 1809-1980. North Ryde, New South Wales: Australian
Film and Television School, 1983. 221p.
See entry 123.

182. Antébi, Elizabeth. The Electronic Epoch. New York: Van
Nostrand Reinhold, 1982. 256p.
Developments in electronics and their application in telecommunications, industry, defense, medicine, consumer goods,
and research. Describes the achievements of James Clerk Max-
well, Heinrich Hertz, Lee De Forest, and Marconi. Illustrations, index of people and companies, subject index.

183. Briggs, Asa. The BBC: The First Fifty Years. Oxford, Eng.:
Oxford University Press, 1985. 439p.
See entry 147.

184. Connections: Reflections on Sixty Years of Broadcasting.
New York: National Broadcasting Company, 1986. 267p.
Recollections by some of the people involved in the first 60

years of the National Broadcasting Company. Contributors are affiliate broadcasters, network executives, news correspondents, sportscasters, and entertainers. Illustrations.

185. Czitrom, Daniel J. Media and the American Mind: From Morse to McLuhan. Chapel Hill, NC: University of North Carolina Press, 1982. 254p.
Intellectual history of modern communication. Part one examines contemporary responses to the telegraph, motion picture, and radio in their formative years. Part two treats the three major traditions of thought on the impact of modern media: the Progressive Trio of Charles Horton Cooley, John Dewey, and Robert E. Park, and their inquiries into the holistic nature of communications media; the empirically-oriented researchers and their studies of behavioral "effects"; and the radical media theories of Harold Innis and Marshall McLuhan. Illustration, tables, bibliography, index.

186. The First 50 Years of Broadcasting: The Running Story of the Fifth Estate. Washington, DC: Broadcasting Publications, 1982. 297p.
Year-by-year account of major developments in broadcasting and cable from 1931 through 1981 by the editors of Broadcasting magazine. Stories, excerpts, and photographs from many of the more than 2,000 issues of the magazine. Index.

187. Hartley, Ian. Goodnight Children ... Everywhere. Southborough, Eng.: Midas Books, 1983. 165p.
See entry 154.

188. Hill, George H. Airwaves to the Soul: The Influence and Growth of Religious Broadcasting in America. Saratoga, CA: R and E, 1983. 152p.
Chronicles 60 years of radio and television religion, from the early pioneers to the era of the "electric church." Tables, appendices, index.

189. Inglis, K. S., assisted by Jan Brazier. This is the ABC: The Australian Broadcasting Commission, 1932-1983. Carlton, Victoria: Melbourne University Press, 1983. 521p.
See entry 126.

190. Jamieson, Kathleen Hall. Packaging the Presidency: A History and Criticism of Presidential Campaign Advertising. New York: Oxford University Press, 1984. 505p.
Examination of the schemes and strategies of presidential candidates and their advertising executives in each campaign from 1952 through 1980. Development and current state of presidential advertising, how it has shaped and been shaped by the candidates, and its role in the political process. Illustrations, bibliography, index.

191. Robinson, John. Learning over the Air: 60 Years of Partner-
      ship in Adult Learning. London: British Broadcasting Cor-
      poration, 1982. 256p.
          See entry 162.

192. Smart, Samuel Chipman. The Outlet Story, 1894-1984. Provi-
      dence, RI: Outlet Communications, 1984. 223p.
          History of an operation that began as a small menswear shop
      and evolved into a major retailing and group broadcasting com-
      pany. Illustrations, bibliographical essay, index.

193. Thompson, Kenneth W. (ed.). Ten Presidents and the Press.
      Washington, DC: University Press of America, 1983. 120p.
          Discussion on the relationships of ten twentieth-century
      U.S. presidents with the press. Appendix, bibliography.

194. Toll, Robert C. The Entertainment Machine: American Show
      Business in the Twentieth Century. New York: Oxford Uni-
      versity Press, 1982. 284p.
          Development, popularization, distinctive qualities, and spe-
      cial features of radio, television, phonographs, and motion pic-
      ture, and their relationships with each other. Evolution of
      the form and content of show business and comparison of the
      treatment by the different media of westerns, popular music,
      newsreels, crime, sexuality, and comedy. Illustrations, biblio-
      graphic essay, index.

195. Turner, Kathleen J. Lyndon Johnson's Dual War: Vietnam
      and the Press. Chicago: University of Chicago Press, 1985.
      358p.
          Relationship of the presidency, the news media, and Viet-
      nam, and among interpersonal, public, and mediated communi-
      cation. Ways in which Johnson's relationship with the media
      influenced his Vietnam War rhetoric. Bibliography, index.

196. Williams, Frederick. The Communications Revolution. Beverly
      Hills, CA: Sage Publications, 1982. 291p.
          The emergence and application of communication technologies,
      their impact on our lives, and the alternatives they pose for
      our future. Illustrations, index.

197. Wolfe, Kenneth M. The Churches and the British Broadcasting
      Corporation, 1922-1956: The Politics of Broadcast Religion.
      London: SCM Press, 1984. 627p.
          See entry 167.

I. IN SOCIETY

1. General

198. Arno, Andrew, and Wimal Dissanayake (eds.). The News Media
      in National and International Conflict. Boulder, CO: Westview
      Press, 1984. 250p.
      See entry 99.

199. Courtney, Alice E., and Thomas W. Whipple. Sex Stereotyping
      in Advertising. Lexington, MA: Lexington Books, 1983. 239p.
      Portrayal of the sexes in broadcast and print advertising
      and its likely effect on children and adults, sex-role stereo-
      typing and effective advertising strategy, and a discussion of
      ways to effect change. Tables, bibliography, index.

200. Czitrom, Daniel J. Media and the American Mind: From Morse
      to McLuhan. Chapel Hill, NC: University of North Carolina
      Press, 1982. 254p.
      See entry 185.

201. Greenberg, Bradley S., Michael Burgoon, Judee K. Burgoon,
      and Felipe Korzenny. Mexican Americans and the Mass Media.
      Norwood, NJ: Ablex, 1983. 290p.
      See entry 52.

202. Gurevitch, Michael, Tony Bennett, James Curran, and Janet
      Woollacott (eds.). Culture, Society and the Media. New York:
      Methuen, 1982. 317p.
      See entry 152.

203. Howitt, Dennis. The Mass Media and Social Problems. Elms-
      ford, NY: Pergamon Press, 1982. 204p.
      Review and analysis of research on the mass media and
      societal conflict, treatment of minority groups, sex, violence,
      crime and justice, education, and health and welfare. Author
      index, subject index.

204. McKenna, George. Media Voices: Debating Critical Issues in
      Mass Media. Guilford, CT: Dushkin, 1982. 228p.
      The role, influence, rights, and responsibilities of media,
      with excerpts from addresses, articles, books, legal opinions,
      and television programs. Index.

205. McQuail, Denis. Mass Communication Theory: An Introduction.
      Beverly Hills, CA: Sage Publications, 1983. 245p.
      Definitions and characteristics of mass communication, media
      institutions, content and audiences, and the processes of media
      effects. Illustrations, name index, subject index.

206. Schmid, Alex, and Janny de Graaf. Violence as Communication:

Insurgent Terrorism and the Western News Media. Beverly
Hills, CA: Sage Publications, 1982. 283p.
  Advances the notion of insurgent terrorism as a means of
communication. Examines ways in which terrorists use the
media and the media use terrorism, and the effects of news
reporting on terrorism. The role of censorship and the relationship of terrorism to the prevailing information order also
are discussed. Illustrations, tables, appendix, bibliography.

207. Taylor, Laurie, and Bob Mullan. Uninvited Guests: The Inti-
      mate Secrets of Television and Radio. London: Chatto and
      Windus, 1986. 218p.
      See entry 163.

208. Turow, Joseph. Media Industries: The Production of News
      and Entertainment. New York: Longman, 1984. 213p.
        Resource-dependence approach to the study of forces caus-
      ing continuity and change in mass media content, and the ex-
      tent to which publics can use those forces to bring about
      changes they desire. Tables, bibliography, index.

209. Williams, Frederick. The Communications Revolution. Beverly
      Hills, CA: Sage Publications, 1982. 291p.
      See entry 196.

210. Windschuttle, Keith. The Media: A New Analysis of the Press,
      Television, Radio and Advertising in Australia. Ringwood, Vic-
      toria: Penguin Books, 1985. 436p.
      See entry 128.

211. Winfield, Betty Houchin, and Lois B. DeFleur (eds.). The
      Edward R. Murrow Heritage: Challenge for the Future.
      Ames, IA: Iowa State University Press, 1986. 113p.
        Interpretive essays and edited transcripts of panel discus-
      sions at a 1983 symposium on the impact of Edward R. Murrow.
      Considers the status of public interest documentaries, quality
      of news presentations, influences on Murrow's qualities, his
      war coverage, and reporter ethics. Keynote address by Diane
      Sawyer on the responsibilities of reporters. Illustrations, in-
      dex.

2. Education and Instruction

212. Bates, A. W. (ed.). The Role of Technology in Distance Edu-
      cation. London: Croom Helm, 1984. 231p.
        Analysis of the use, strengths, and shortcomings of audio
      and video media in course design, management, and presenta-
      tion. Includes broadcast television, video cassettes, satellite
      and cable, videodiscs, radio, audio cassettes, teletext, and
      viewdata systems. Illustrations, tables.

213. Bates, Anthony W. Broadcasting in Education: An Evaluation.
      London: Constable, 1984. 272p.
      Uses and assessment of educational broadcasting, impact of
      new technologies, prospects, and recommendations. Illustra-
      tions, tables, appendix, bibliography, index.

214. Hawkridge, David, and John Robinson. Organizing Educational
      Broadcasting. London: Croom Helm; Paris: UNESCO, 1982.
      302p.
      See entry 105.

215. Kaye, Anthony, and Keith Harry (eds.). Using the Media for
      Adult Basic Education. London: Croom Helm, 1982. 255p.
      See entry 109.

216. Robinson, John. Learning over the Air: 60 Years of Part-
      nership in Adult Learning. London: British Broadcasting
      Corporation, 1982. 256p.
      See entry 162.

3. Government and Politics

217. Arterton, F. Christopher. Media Politics: The News Strate-
      gies of Presidential Campaigns. Lexington, MA: Lexington
      Books, 1984. 221p.
      Examination of the influences of broadcast and print news
      reporting on the conduct of the 1976 and 1980 election cam-
      paigns, and the consequences of those influences. Illustra-
      tions, tables, appendix, index.

218. Battle Lines: Report of the Twentieth Century Fund Task
      Force on the Military and the Media. Background Paper by
      Peter Braestrup. New York: Priority Press Publications,
      1985. 178p.
      The Report explores the nature of the conflicts between the
      military and the media, highlighted by events in Grenada in
      1983, and recommends remedies. The Background Paper pro-
      vides an overview of U.S. military-media relations in overseas
      battle zones since 1945 and includes, for comparison, the
      United Kingdom's Falklands war in 1982. Examines also rhetor-
      ical and constitutional issues of press freedom. Appendix.

219. Bennett, W. Lance. News: The Politics of Illusion. New
      York: Longman, 1983. 161p.
      Characteristics and political effects of mass media news,
      ways in which politicians attempt to control its content and
      journalists unwittingly promote political propaganda. Dangers
      to the public of illusory political images and methods by which
      concerned citizens can make better use of the information pro-
      vides by the media. Illustrations, index.

220. Bolling, Landrum R. (ed.). Reporters Under Fire: U.S.
      Media Coverage of Conflicts in Lebanon and Central America.
      Boulder, CO: Westview Press, 1985. 155p.
      See entry 94.

221. Graber, Doris A. Mass Media and American Politics. 2d ed.
      Washington, DC: CQ Press, 1984. 385p.
      Study of how electronic and print media shape America's
      political beliefs and social values. Mass media as institutions
      in the American political system, the effects of news on indi-
      viduals, and the impact of the media on elections and policy-
      making. Illustrations, tables, index.

222. Graber, Doris A. (ed.). Media Power in Politics. Washington,
      DC: CQ Press, 1984. 348p.
      Essays on mass media effects in general and their impact on
      public opinion, elections, participants within and outside the
      political power structure, and on domestic and foreign public
      policies. Introduction accompanies each topic, and a commentary
      precedes each essay. Illustrations, tables.

223. Greenfield, Jeff. The Real Campaign: How the Media Missed
      the Story of the 1980 Campaign. New York: Summit Books,
      1982. 319p.
      Contends that television and the media made almost no dif-
      ference in the outcome of the 1980 presidential campaign and
      that their failure to recognize the nature of the campaign
      stemmed largely from their fascination with themselves as a
      political force and from their fundamental view that politics is
      more image than substance. Index.

224. Harris, Robert. Gotcha! The Media, the Government and the
      Falklands Crisis. London: Faber and Faber, 1983. 158p.
      See entry 153.

225. Hooper, Alan. The Military and the Media. Aldershot, Eng.:
      Gower, 1982. 247p.
      See entry 156.

226. Jamieson, Kathleen Hall. Packaging the Presidency: A History
      and Criticism of Presidential Campaign Advertising. New York:
      Oxford University Press, 1984. 505p.
      See entry 190.

227. Joslyn, Richard. Mass Media and Elections. Reading, MA:
      Addison-Wesley, 1984. 313p.
      Development and content of candidate appeals, campaign
      coverage and its effects on citizen beliefs and attitudes, ef-
      fects of spot advertising and candidate debates, and the impact
      of campaign communication on voting behavior. Illustrations,
      tables, bibliography, index.

228. Kraus, Sidney, and Richard M. Perloff (eds.). Mass Media
     and Political Thought: An Information-Processing Approach.
     Beverly Hills, CA: Sage Publications, 1985. 350p.
        Theory and research in political information processing.
     Basic structure of political cognition, methods by which po-
     litical information is processed, and cognitive and affective in-
     fluences of political communications and the processes by which
     these effects are achieved. Also, the interface between systems-
     level variables and micropolitical cognitions, and the implications
     of knowledge of political cognition for real-world political issues.
     Illustrations, tables, name index.

229. McGuire, Bernadette, and Garret J. O'Keefe. Election Year
     1984: NAB-Roper Poll. Washington, DC: National Association
     of Broadcasters, 1984. 12p.
        See entry 53.

230. Martel, Myles. Political Campaign Debates: Images, Strategies,
     and Tactics. New York: Longman, 1983. 193p.
        Pros and cons of debating, goals and methods of attaining
     them, debate formats, and recommendations for improvements.
     Case study of the 1980 presidential debates. Illustrations, bib-
     liography, index.

231. Nimmo, Dan, and James E. Combs. Mediated Political Realities.
     New York: Longman, 1983. 240p.
        The role of mass and group communication in the creation
     of political "reality." Argues that the process results as much
     in the creation, transmission, and adoption of political fantasies
     as in realistic views of what takes place. Author index, subject
     index.

232. Nimmo, Dan, and Michael W. Mansfield (eds.). Government and
     the News Media: Comparative Dimensions. Waco, TX: Baylor
     University Press, 1982. 306p.
        See entry 115.

233. Robinson, Michael J., and Austin Ranney (eds.). The Mass
     Media in Campaign '84: Articles from Public Opinion Magazine.
     Washington, DC: American Enterprise Institute, 1985. 71p.
        Collection of writings on the role of the media in the elec-
     toral system.

234. Rubin, David M., and Ann Marie Cunningham (eds.). War,
     Peace and the News Media: Proceedings. New York: New
     York University, 1983. 285p.
        Contents of a March 1983 meeting underwritten by the Gan-
     nett Foundation. Topics include media coverage of disarmament
     talks, foreign policy, and related subjects.

235. Siegel, Arthur. Politics and the Media in Canada. Toronto:

McGraw-Hill, 1983.   258p.
See entry 132.

236. Soderlund, Walter C., Walter I. Romanow, E. Donald Briggs,
and Ronald H. Wagenberg. Media and Elections in Canada.
Toronto: Holt, Rinehart and Winston of Canada, 1984.   163p.
See entry 134.

237. Spear, Joseph C. Presidents and the Press: The Nixon Legacy. Cambridge, MA: MIT Press, 1984.   349p.
Argues that Richard Nixon created the press manipulation
strategy used by subsequent presidents to mold public percep-
tion and opinion. Illustrations, index.

238. Thompson, Kenneth W. (ed.). The Credibility of Institutions,
Policies and Leadership. Vol. 5: The Media. Lanham, MD:
University Press of America, 1985.   241p.
Essays on the role and influence of the media in relation to
politics, the presidency, and individual presidents.

239. Thompson, Kenneth W. (ed.). Ten Presidents and the Press.
Washington, DC: University Press of America, 1983.   120p.
See entry 193.

240. Thompson, Kenneth W. (ed.). Three Press Secretaries on the
Presidency and the Press. Lanham, MD: University Press of
America, 1983.   113p.
Papers and discussion on relationships between the presi-
dent and the press by former press secretaries Jody Powell,
George Reedy, and Jerry terHorst.

241. Turner, Kathleen J. Lyndon Johnson's Dual War: Vietnam
and the Press. Chicago: University of Chicago Press, 1985.
358p.
See entry 195.

242. Western, J. S., and Colin A. Hughes. The Mass Media in
Australia. 2d ed. New York: University of Queensland Press,
1983.   209p.
See entry 127.

243. Worcester, Robert M., and Martin Harrop (eds.). Political
Communications: The General Election Campaign of 1979.
London: George Allen and Unwin, 1982.   181p.
See entry 168.

4. Religion

244. Bachman, John W. Media: Wasteland or Wonderland. Opportunities and Dangers for Christians in the Electronic Age.

Minneapolis, MN: Augsburg, 1984. 175p.
Strengths and shortcomings of broadcast and other electronic media, status and prospects for religious communication, and
recommendations for reform.

245. Hill, George H. Airwaves to the Soul: The Influence and
Growth of Religious Broadcasting in America. Saratoga, CA:
R and E, 1983. 152p.
See entry 188.

246. Wolfe, Kenneth M. The Churches and the British Broadcasting
Corporation, 1922-1956: The Politics of Broadcast Religion.
London: SCM Press, 1984. 627p.
See entry 167.

J. LAW, REGULATION, AND POLICY

1. Law and Regulation

(a) General

247. Armstrong, Mark. Broadcasting Law and Policy in Australia.
Sydney: Butterworth, 1982. 291p.
See entry 124.

248. Armstrong, Mark, Michael Blakeney, and Ray Watterson.
Media Law in Australia. Melbourne: Oxford University Press,
1983. 274p.
See entry 125.

249. Bensman, Marvin R. Broadcast Regulation: Selected Cases
and Decisions. 2d ed. Lanham, MD: University Press of
America, 1985. 192p.
Total of 649 citations from court decisions, FCC reports,
various looseleaf services, and trade and copyright reporting
services. Index.

250. Bittner, John R. Broadcast Law and Regulation. Englewood
Cliffs, NJ: Prentice-Hall, 1982. 441p.
Law and regulation from the perspectives of the scholar and
the broadcaster, organized in five parts: regulatory framework, programming and policy, broadcast and cable operations,
citizens, self-regulation and legislation, and the legal system
and legal research. Excerpts from relevant law and FCC rules,
and important cases. Illustrations, index to cases and legal
citations, index to names and subjects.

251. Chronology of Telecommunications and Cable Television Regulation in the United States. Cambridge, MA: Program on

Information Resources Policy, Harvard University, 1984. 57p.
Industry developments and state and federal regulation in
telecommunications from 1835 to 1983, and in cable from 1947
to 1983.

252. Current Developments in TV and Radio. New York: Practising
Law Institute, 1982. 611p.
Emphasis on regulation, with chapters on broadcast station
acquisition and licensing, effects of radio deregulation, network
affiliation, government restraints on programming, copyright,
DBS, and STV. Illustrations.

253. Ellmore, R. Terry. Broadcasting Law and Regulation. Blue
Ridge Summit, PA: TAB Books, 1982. 496p.
Guide to obtaining and retaining a broadcast license. Selection of licensees, laws and regulations to which they must
adhere, and operational obligations. Illustrations, tables, appendix, bibliography, index.

254. Francois, William E. Mass Media Law and Regulation. 4th ed.
New York: John Wiley and Sons, 1986. 665p.
The First Amendment, prior restraint, libel, privacy, freedom of information, free press versus fair trial, news gathering
rights, pornography, advertising, access to the media, antitrust and media ownership, and copyright. Separate chapter
on radio and television, including equal time, the Fairness
Doctrine, deregulation, and anti-lottery laws. Tables, appendices, name index, subject index, table of cases.

255. Franklin, Marc A. Cases and Materials on Mass Media Law.
2d ed. Mineola, NY: Foundation Press, 1982. 946p.
Reorganization and updating of the first edition (1977).
Chapters one through four cover the development of the concept of freedom of expression, content restrictions, legal problems of gathering information, and the administration of jus-
tice. The final three chapters treat broadcasting and deal with
the spectrum and regulation of its use, licensing, and the control of content. Table of cases, index.

256. Galvin, Katherine M. Media Law: A Legal Handbook for the
Working Journalist. Berkeley, CA: Nolo Press, 1984. 229p.
Freedom of expression, censorship, libel, privacy, free
press and fair trial, privilege, newsroom searches, access to
news sources and records, and government regulation of the
electronic media. Illustrations, appendices, index.

257. Gillmor, Donald M., and Jerome A. Barron. Mass Communication Law: Cases and Comment. 4th ed. St. Paul, MN: West,
1984. 1,076p.
Case approach, covering the First Amendment, libel, privacy,
privilege, and access. Separate chapter on the regulation of
radio and television broadcasting. Glossary, index.

258. Ginsburg, Douglas H., and Mark D. Director. <u>1983 Supplement</u>
<u>to Regulation of Broadcasting: Law and Policy towards Radio,</u>
<u>Television and Cable Communications</u>. St. Paul, MN: West,
1983. 182p.
Updates the authors' 1978 casebook. Chapter on the new
video technologies replaces the chapter on cable in the main
volume. Table of cases.

259. Goodale, James C. <u>Communications Law 1985: A Course Hand-</u>
<u>book</u>. Vol. 1. New York: Practising Law Institute, 1986.
1,000p.
Developments in electronic press law, with special attention
to libel, privacy, access to information, copyright, commercial
speech, and anti-trust.

260. Kahn, Frank J. (ed.). <u>Documents of American Broadcasting</u>.
4th ed. Englewood Cliffs, NJ: Prentice-Hall, 1984. 501p.
Collection of laws, FRC and FCC materials, court decisions,
and other documents reflecting public policy on broadcasting
and related media through the years. Covers the development
of broadcast regulation, regulation of programming and broadcast journalism, and competition, the public interest, and public
broadcasting. New chapter on understanding law includes a
glossary of legal terms. Each document is accompanied by an
introduction. Index to legal decisions, general index.

261. Lahav, Pnina (ed.). <u>Press Law in Modern Democracies: A</u>
<u>Comparative Study</u>. New York: Longman, 1985. 366p.
See entry 111.

262. <u>NAB Legal Guide to FCC Broadcast Regulations</u>. 2d ed. Washington, DC: National Association of Broadcasters, 1984.
Summary and discussion of significant commission rules and
policies, and appendices with supplementary explanatory materials, forms, directories, and memoranda. Reporting requirements, applications and compliance procedures, programming
policies and practices, announcements, commercial policies and
practices, and other operating policies and practices. Also,
cable television rules governing broadcast signal carriage, regulation of non-commercial educational broadcasters, and obtaining
advice and information from the FCC. Illustrations, appendices,
topical index.

263. Nelson, Harold L., and Dwight L. Teeter, Jr. <u>Law of Mass</u>
<u>Communications: Freedom and Control of Print and Broadcast</u>
<u>Media</u>. 5th ed. Mineola, NY: Foundation Press, 1986. 792p.
Historical background, defamation, privacy, copyright, obscenity and blasphemy, and legal problems in reporting government and the courts. Also, regulation of broadcasting, cable,
and advertising; antitrust law and the mass media; taxation
and licensing. Appendices, table of cases, index.

264. Overbeck, Wayne, and Rick D. Pullen. Major Principles of
      Media Law. 2d ed. New York: Holt, Rinehart and Winston,
      1985. 438p.
           Workings of the legal system, freedom, prior restraint, li-
      bel and slander, privacy and publicity, fair trial and the free
      press, newsgatherer's privilege, freedom of information, ob-
      scenity, advertising, and the student press. Chapters on the
      special problems of broadcast and cable television and on new
      technologies. Illustrations, appendices, index.

265. Pember, Don R. Mass Media Law. 3rd ed. Dubuque, IA:
      Wm. C. Brown, 1984. 610p.
           Principles, cases, rulings, and decisions. Libel, invasion
      of privacy, access to information, protection of news sources,
      free press and fair trial, obscenity, copyright, regulation of
      advertising and of the media as a business. Chapter on broad-
      cast regulation. Overview of American legal system and history
      of press freedom. Chapter bibliographies, glossary, table of
      cases, index.

266. Ploman, Edward W. International Law Governing Communica-
      tions and Information: A Collection of Basic Documents. West-
      port, CT: Greenwood Press, 1982. 367p.
           See entry 178.

267. Zuckman, Harvey L., and Martin J. Gaynes. Mass Communica-
      tions Law in a Nutshell. 2d ed. St. Paul, MN: West, 1983.
      473p.
           Part one, "The First Amendment and Mass Communications,"
      includes defamation, privacy, newspersons' privilege, and the
      free press-fair trial conflict. Part two, "Regulation of the
      Media," treats commercial speech, FCC structure and powers,
      its licensing policies and control of broadcast operations, and
      ends with an expanded chapter on emerging technologies.
      Table of cases, index.

                (b)   Contests, Lotteries, and Promotions

268. Albert, James A. The Broadcaster's Legal Guide for Conduct-
      ing Contests and Promotions. Chicago: Bonus Books, 1985.
      237p.
           Contest law and regulations, examples of violations, and a
      checklist to avoid problems. Illustrations, general index, sta-
      tion index.

269. Lotteries and Contests: A Broadcaster's Handbook. 2d ed.
      Washington, DC: National Association of Broadcasters, 1985.
      47p.
           Designed to assist broadcasters in avoiding common prob-
      lems involved in advertising contests and promotional plans.
      Defining a lottery, federal and state lottery laws, lottery

exceptions, and sample lotteries and legal analyses. Guidelines on the conduct of contests and legal questions and
answers on sample contests. Lottery index, contest index.

(c) Copyright

270. Strong, William S. The Copyright Book: A Practical Guide.
2d ed. Cambridge, MA: MIT Press, 1984. 224p.
Ownership, transfers, registration of copyrighted materials,
infringement, and fair use. Appendices, index.

(d) Elections and Politics

271. Broadcasters and Political Debates: An Outline for Election
Year Use. Washington, DC: National Association of Broad-
casters, 1984. 20p.
The basics of broadcast station sponsorship of debates.

272. Campaign '84: Advertising and Programming Obligations of
the Electronic Media. New York: Practising Law Institute,
1983. 507p.
Eighteen papers prepared for use at a 1983 institute program. Includes reasonable access provision, lowest unit
charge, application of the Cullman principle and the Zapple
Doctrine to non-candidate advertising. Also, ballot proposi-
tion and the Fairness Doctrine, presidential speeches, political
editorializing, and the case for repeal of Sections 315 and 312
(a)(7) of the Communications Act and repeal of the Fairness
Doctrine. Appendices.

273. Krasnow, Erwin G., and John C. Quale. A Candidate's Guide
to the Law of Political Broadcasting. 3rd ed. Washington, DC:
National Association of Broadcasters, 1984. 16p.
Introduction to federal regulations governing political broadcast advertising. Summary of equal opportunities, reasonable
access, political advertising rates, the Fairness Doctrine, personal attacks, political editorializing, sponsorship identification,
and records that broadcast stations must maintain. Appendix.

274. Perry, Larry, and Barry Selvidge. Perry's Broadcast Regulation Political Primer. Knoxville: Perry Publications, 1984.
89p.
Answers to the most-asked questions about the law and
regulation of political broadcasts, in question-and-answer format. Index.

275. Political Broadcast Catechism. 11th ed. Washington, DC:
National Association of Broadcasters, 1986. 78p.
Designed to provide broadcasters with the latest rules,
regulations, and interpretations governing political broadcasting.
Includes broadcasts under Sections 312 and 315 of the

Communications Act, the Fairness Doctrine and political broadcasts, and the FCC's handling of complaints and inquiries.
Sample agreement form for political broadcasts.

276. Rowan, Ford. Broadcast Fairness: Doctrine, Practice, Prospects. A Reappraisal of the Fairness Doctrine and Equal Time
Rule. New York: Longman, 1984. 214p.
      The evolution, implementation, and impact of the Fairness
Doctrine and Equal Opportunities rule, and proposals for
changing the current system of regulation. Index.

(e) Entertainment

277. Rudell, Michael I. Behind the Scenes: Practical Entertainment
Law. New York: Law and Business/Harcourt Brace Jovano-
vich, 1984. 270p.
      Judicial decisions, statute review, elements in drafting agree-
ments or developing productions, and industry and technological trends. Includes copyright protection, names, credits,
and titles, privacy, publicity and defamation, television, new
technologies, and music. Table of cases, index.

(f) Equal Employment Opportunity

278. Brown, Stanley J., and Carol Connor Flowe. EEO Handbook:
A Practical Guide for Broadcasters. Washington, DC: National
Association of Broadcasters, 1986. 195p.
      Details of the requirements and prohibitions of federal laws
and suggestions for avoiding and defending against discrimination actions. Overview of EEO principles, EEO and the FCC,
categories of illegal discrimination and how to avoid them, the
hiring process, discrimination issues arising during the employment relationship, and terminating the relationship. Case study
of EEOC proceedings, checklist of filing and record-keeping requirements, and a review of defensive measures. Selection of
working papers, including a sample employment application, EEO
policy statement, and EEO program. Appendices.

(g) Fairness Doctrine

279. Campaign '84: Advertising and Programming Obligations of
the Electronic Media. New York: Practising Law Institute,
1983. 507p.
      See entry 272.

280. Cooper, Louis F., and Robert E. Emeritz. Pike and Fischer's
Desk Guide to the Fairness Doctrine. Bethesda, MD: Pike
and Fischer, 1985. 183p.
      The evolution of the Fairness Doctrine, current constitutional
theory and administrative practice, guide to doctrine procedure,
and its relation to the new technologies. Bibliography, appendices, index.

281.   Political Broadcast Catechism. 11th ed. Washington, DC:
       National Association of Broadcasters, 1986. 78p.
           See entry 275.

282.   Rowan, Ford. Broadcast Fairness: Doctrine, Practice, Pros-
       pects. A Reappraisal of the Fairness Doctrine and Equal Time
       Rule. New York: Longman, 1984. 214p.
           See entry 276.

283.   Singsen, Michael (ed.). Talking Back. San Francisco: Public
       Media Center, 1983. 158p.
           The rights of the public accorded by the Fairness Doctrine,
       how they can be exercised, and case studies of individuals
       and groups that have used them to obtain access. Appendices.

(h)   First Amendment and Freedom

284.   Brasch, Walter M., and Dana R. Ulloth. The Press and The
       State: Sociohistorical and Contemporary Studies. Lanham, MD:
       University Press of America, 1986. 811p.
           Focuses on the reason for the controls placed upon the
       media and events and laws as they shape the role of the state
       in controlling freedom of expression. Part one consists of a
       review of 5,000 years of controls placed by government and
       religion upon expression and of the major political philosophies
       that helped shape those controls. Part two examines the po-
       litical values and institutions the United States has established
       to assure that the press functions as a part of the society and
       not for the destruction of the state. Bibliographies, index.

285.   Brenner, Daniel L., and William L. Rivers. Free but Regulated:
       Conflicting Traditions in Media Law. Ames, IA: Iowa State
       University Press, 1982. 283p.
           Articles from general and legal periodicals addressing di-
       verse legal topics, organized by theme and with commentary.
       Includes freedom of expression, access to and distribution of
       information, "unprotected" expression, and protected speech.
       Index.

286.   Carter, T. Barton, Marc A. Franklin, and Jay B. Wright.
       The First Amendment and the Fourth Estate: The Law of Mass
       Media. 3rd ed. Mineola, NY: Foundation Press, 1985. 708p.
           Major legal doctrines, explanations of their origins and as-
       serted justifications, and evaluation of their soundness. In-
       cludes defamation, privacy, copyright, obscenity, confidentiality,
       and media ownership. Three chapters on broadcasting, and one
       on cable and the new technologies. Table of cases, appendices,
       index.

287.   Chamberlin, Bill F., and Charlene J. Brown (eds.). The First
       Amendment Reconsidered: New Perspectives on the Meaning of

Freedom of Speech and Press.   New York: Longman, 1982.
218p.
        Winning papers from the 1979-80 First Amendment theory
paper competition of the Association for Education in Journalism
and a selection of complementary papers presented at the association's 1980 convention.   Organized in three parts: the role
of the states reconsidered, the twentieth-century search for
the meaning of freedom of the press, and the First Amendment
in the 1980s.   Appendix, case index, subject index.

288.   Collins, Keith S. (ed.).   Responsibility and Freedom in the
        Press: Are They in Conflict?   Washington, DC: Citizen's
        Choice, 1985.   119p.
            Report of the Citizen's Choice National Commission on Free
        and Responsible Media, based on evidence and oral testimony
        at seven public hearings and augmented by the views of the
        commissioners.   Finds significant support for the impression
        that many Americans feel that the information media are neither
        completely free nor sufficiently responsible and that the demo-
        cratic process suffers as a result.   Illustrations, appendices,
        bibliography, index.

289.   Curry, Jane Leftwich, and Joan R. Dassin (eds.).   Press
        Control Around the World.   New York: Praeger, 1982.   287p.
            See entry 101.

290.   Devol, Kenneth S. (ed.).   Mass Media and the Supreme Court:
        The Legacy of the Warren Years.   3rd ed. revised.   New York:
        Hastings House, 1982.   463p.
            Essays and Supreme Court opinions and dissenting views on
        First Amendment issues including prior restraint, news gather-
        ing, government regulation, public access to the media, ob-
        scenity, libel, right of privacy, and trial by television.   Ap-
        pendices, glossary, index.

291.   Diamond, Edwin, Norman Sandler, and Milton Mueller.   Tele-
        communications in Crisis: The First Amendment, Technology,
        and Deregulation.   Washington, DC: Cato Institute, 1983.
        113p.
            Aspects of deregulation and their impact on telecommunica-
        tion systems.   Topics include getting government out of broad-
        casting, deregulation versus unregulation, DBS, cellular radio,
        LPTV, and AM and FM expansion.   Illustrations.

292.   Gerald, J. Edward.   News of Crime: Courts and Press in Con-
        flict.   Westport, CT: Greenwood Press, 1983.   227p.
            Differing perspectives of the judiciary and the media on the
        reporting of crime.   Suggestions for further reading, index.

293.   In the Public Interest--III: A Report by the National News
        Council, 1979-1983.   New York: National News Council, 1984.
        610p.

Complete texts of the 63 complaints considered by the council from January 1, 1979 through July 31, 1983, and its decisions. Council statements on press freedom, complaints relating to its efforts in defense of press freedom in the period, and the council's rules of procedure and by-laws. Index of complaints by subject and participant from 1973 through 1983.

294. The Media Crisis ... A Continuing Challenge. Washington, DC: World Press Freedom Committee, 1982. 153p.
See entry 113.

295. Miller, Abraham H. (ed.). Terrorism: The Media and the Law. Dobbs Ferry, NY: Transnational, 1982. 221p.
Differing perspectives on the conflict between journalists in search of a story and law enforcement agencies trying to contain terrorism. Recommendations for reporting terrorism. Appendices, bibliography, index.

296. Pool, Ithiel de Sola. Technologies of Freedom. Cambridge, MA: Belknap Press of Harvard University Press, 1983. 299p.
The impact of resource availability on freedom from regulation and control, and examination of the possibility that electronic communication resources can be as free of public regulation in the future as the platform and printing press have been in the past. Includes chapters on the development of electronic communication, broadcasting and the First Amendment, cable television, and electronic publishing. Illustrations, index.

297. Robertson, Geoffrey, and Andrew G. L. Nicol. Media Law: The Rights of Journalists and Broadcasters. London: Oyez Longman, 1984. 403p.
See entry 161.

298. Stevens, John D. Shaping the First Amendment: The Development of Free Expression. Beverly Hills, CA: Sage Publications, 1982. 157p.
Impressionistic sketch of trends in the development of First Amendment law and theory. Suggests what free expression has meant in the United States and provides a basis for evaluating the continuing controversies that touch on the First Amendment. Index.

299. Van Alstyne, William W. Interpretations of the First Amendment. Durham, NC: Duke University Press, 1984. 136p.
Judicial interpretations of speech and press freedom and of the distinction between the print and broadcast press. Illustrations and subject, person, and case indices.

(i) Libel and Privacy

300. Adler, Renata. Reckless Disregard: Westmoreland v. CBS et

al.; Sharon v. Time.   New York: Alfred A. Knopf, 1986.
243p.
    Argues that the refusal to acknowledge, or even consider,
the possibility of error caused both CBS and Time to pursue
aggressive and recklessly expensive litigation.

301. Media Insurance: Protecting Against High Judgments, Puni-
     tive Damages, and Defense Costs.   New York: Practising Law
     Institute, 1983.   514p.
    Survey of verdicts in libel cases, their disposition on ap-
peal, and media defense costs.   Public policy limitations on the
insurability of punitive and actual damages, guidelines for ne-
gotiating the libel policy, in-house procedures to reduce exposure to uninsured damage awards, and trial tactics in defending against punitive damage claims.

302. New York Times v. Sullivan: The Next Twenty Years.   New
     York: Practising Law Institute, 1984.   759p.
    Retrospective and commentaries on the case, perspectives
on libel litigation phases, and problems associated with libel
actions.   Illustrations, tables, appendices.

303. Roth, M. Patricia.   The Juror and the General.   New York:
     William Morrow, 1986.   300p.
    The diary of a juror in the Westmoreland v. CBS libel trial.

304. Sanford, Bruce W.   Libel and Privacy: The Prevention and
     Defense of Litigation.   New York: Law and Business; Wash-
     ington, DC: Harcourt Brace Jovanovich, 1985.   715p.
    Part one considers steps in preventing libel: pre-publication
review, injury to reputation, opinion versus fact, truth, public
versus private person, standard of care, damage assessment,
state law privileges, and privacy.   Litigating the libel or privacy case is the subject of part two, which covers handling
the pre-litigation complaint, litigation prior to trial, and the
trial.   Looseleaf.   Appendices, index.

305. Smolla, Rodney A.   Suing the Press: Libel, the Media, and
     Power.   New York: Oxford University Press, 1986.   277p.
    Recent libel litigation and what it reveals about American
culture, the legal system and libel law, and the way the press
operates.   Includes a chapter on Westmoreland v. CBS.   Index.

(j)   Licenses

306. Noll, Edward M.   General Radiotelephone License Handbook.
     7th ed.   Indianapolis: Howard W. Sams, 1982.   590p.
    Study guide to FCC Element III examination for a general
radiotelephone license.   Sample test and answers.   Illustrations,
index.

307.   Swearer, Harvey F., and Joseph J. Carr.   Commercial FCC
       License Handbook.   3rd ed.   Blue Ridge Summit, PA: TAB
       Books, 1982.   383p.
          Study manual for FCC General Radiotelephone Operator Li-
       cense examination.   Sample study and test questions and
       answers.   Illustrations, appendices, index.

(k)   Ownership

308.   Besen, Stanley M., and Leland L. Johnson.   An Analysis of
       the Federal Communications Commission's Group Ownership
       Rules.   Santa Monica, CA: Rand Corporation, 1984.   52p.
          Assessment of current knowledge about the effects of media
       concentration and analysis of its implications for future public
       policy toward media ownership.

309.   Besen, Stanley M., and Leland L. Johnson.   Regulation of
       Media Ownership by the Federal Communications Commission:
       An Assessment.   Santa Monica, CA: Rand Corporation, 1984.
       77p.
          Evaluation of available empirical evidence on the effects of
       media concentration to reach judgments about the desirability
       of modifying or eliminating FCC ownership regulations.   Treats
       group ownership, regional concentration rules, rules regulating
       local market concentration, and telephone-cable television cross-
       ownership.

(l)   Process

310.   Krasnow, Erwin G., Lawrence D. Longley, and Herbert A.
       Terry.   The Politics of Broadcast Regulation.   3rd ed.   New
       York: St. Martin's Press, 1982.   304p.
          The process of regulation and the role of the principal
       players: the FCC, the broadcast industry, citizen groups,
       the courts, the White House, and Congress.   Examples of the
       political environment that produces regulation through examina-
       tion of five case studies, two of them new to this edition.
       Tables, annotated bibliography, index.

(m)   Public Broadcasting

311.   Weber, Kathleen (ed.).   Public Television and Radio and State
       Governments.   Vol. 2:   State Statutes.   Washington, DC: Na-
       tional Association of Public Television Stations, 1984.   367p.
          Authorizing legislation for state government activity.   Glos-
       sary, appendices.

(n)   Remedies

312.   Media Abuses: Rights and Remedies.   A Guide to Legal Reme-
       dies.   Washington, DC: Media Institute, 1983.   103p.

Remedies available to people and commercial entities be-
lieving they have been victims of distorted coverage by the
radio and television media. Administrative relief under the
terms of the Fairness Doctrine, Personal Attack rules, and
political broadcasting law and regulations. Judicial relief under libel and right of privacy laws, newsmen's privilege, and
details of general, actual, and punitive damages. Illustration, appendices, index.

(o) Satellites

313. Matte, Nicolas Mateesco. Aerospace Law: Telecommunications
Satellites. Toronto: Butterworth, 1982. 354p.
      Satellite types, their commercial uses, agencies involved in
their regulation, issues raised, and implications for international law. Appendices, bibliography, index of cited authors.

314. Powell, Jon T. International Broadcasting by Satellite: Issues of Regulation, Barriers to Communication. Westport, CT:
Quorum Books, 1985. 300p.
      International organizations involved, and key agreements.
Perspectives on the free flow of information, the political, cultural, technological, and economic dimensions of sovereignty
occasioned by direct broadcast satellite services, and suggested
solutions to the problems raised. Appendices, recommended
readings, index.

315. Regulation of Transnational Communications: 1984 Michigan
Yearbook of International Legal Studies. New York: Clark
Boardman, 1984. 411p.
      Nineteen papers on regulation of the geostationary orbit,
satellite communications, European developments in satellite communications, the impact of national regulation on trade in international communications, and developing communication technologies. Also, U.S. participation in international regulation
and international efforts toward regulation. Illustrations, index.

(p) Taxation

316. Simpson, Steven D. A Broadcaster's Handbook on State and
Local Taxation. Washington, DC: National Association of
Broadcasters, 1984. 89p + appendices.
      Overview of state and local taxation of the broadcasting in-
dustry, analysis of tax issues frequently encountered, and
legal and factual arguments in defending a tax case. Appendices,
table of cases.

2. Policy

317. Armstrong, Mark. Broadcasting Law and Policy in Australia.

Sydney: Butterworth, 1982. 291p.
See entry 124.

318. Besen, Stanley M., and Leland L. Johnson. An Analysis of
the Federal Communications Commission's Group Ownership
Rules. Santa Monica, CA: Rand Corporation, 1984. 52p.
See entry 308.

319. Curran, James, and Jean Seaton. Power Without Responsibility:
The Press and Broadcasting in Britain. 2d ed. London:
Methuen, 1985. 396p.
See entry 149.

320. Edgar, Patricia, and Syed A. Rahim (eds.). Communication
Policy in Developed Countries. London: Kegan Paul Interna-
tional, 1983. 297p.
See entry 103.

321. Fisher, Desmond. The Right to Communicate: A Status Report. Paris: UNESCO, 1982. 55p.
The history of discussion of the concept of the right to
communicate since it was first enunciated publicly in 1969.
Present thinking on the matter and suggestions for the next
stages in defining the right. Appendices.

322. Havick, John J. (ed.). Communications Policy and the Political
Process. Westport, CT: Greenwood Press, 1983. 223p.
The role of politics in making communications policy in major policy arenas including Congress, the executive branch,
the courts, and interest groups. Among the topics covered
are reasonable access, deregulation, international telecommunications, public interest regulation, and feminism and the FCC.
Illustrations, tables, bibliography, index.

323. Hoggart, Richard, and Janet Morgan (eds.). The Future of
Broadcasting: Essays on Authority, Style and Choice. Lon-
don: Macmillan, 1982. 166p.
See entry 155.

324. Howell, W. J., Jr. World Broadcasting in the Age of the
Satellite: Comparative Systems, Policies, and Issues in Mass
Telecommunication. Norwood, NJ: Ablex, 1986. 329p.
See entry 107.

325. International Issues in Communication Technology and Policy.
Washington, DC: Academy for Educational Development, 1983.
35p.
See entry 108.

326. Kuhn, Raymond (ed.). The Politics of Broadcasting. London:
Croom Helm, 1985. 305p.
See entry 110.

327. May, Annabelle, and Kathryn Rowan (eds.). Inside Informa-
      tion: British Government and the Media. London: Constable,
      1982. 288p.
      See entry 158.

328. Mosco, Vincent (ed.). Policy Research in Telecommunications:
      Proceedings from the Eleventh Annual Telecommunications Policy
      Research Conference. Norwood, NJ: Ablex, 1984. 458p.
      Forty-five papers on the impact of research on policy deci-
      sions, the economic, technical, social, and political dimensions
      of research, and research in international telecommunications.
      Includes cable TV, the public interest standard, teletext,
      privacy, and DBS. Illustrations, tables, author index, sub-
      ject index.

329. Nordenstreng, Kaarle, with Lauri Hannikainen. The Mass Media
      Declaration of Unesco. Norwood, NJ: Ablex, 1984. 475p.
      See entry 176.

330. Pavlič, Breda, and Cees J. Hamelink. The New International
      Economic Order: Links Between Economics and Communications.
      Paris: UNESCO, 1985. 65p.
      See entry 177.

331. Sterling, Christopher H. (ed.). International Telecommunica-
      tions and Information Policy. Washington, DC: Communications
      Press, 1984. 496p.
      See entry 179.

332. Taylor, Leslie (ed.). Expanding the Orbital Arc. Washington,
      DC: International Law Institute, Georgetown University Law
      Center, 1984. 145p.
      Transcript of a 1984 conference on domestic and interna-
      tional policy issues in the expansion of satellite capacity and
      access. Appendices.

333. Yurow, Jane H. (ed.). Issues in International Telecommunica-
      tions Policy: A Sourcebook. Washington, DC: Center for
      Telecommunications Studies, George Washington University,
      1983. 260p.
      See entry 180.

K. PROGRAMS AND CONTENT

1. Entertainment

334. Andrews, Bart, and Ahrgus Juilliard. Holy Mackerel!: The
      Amos 'n' Andy Story. New York: E. P. Dutton, 1986. 188p.
      Origins, themes, characters, and controversy surrounding

the long-running radio program and the short-lived TV series.
Title and synopsis of all 78 episodes broadcast on the CBS
Television Network. Illustrations, index.

335. Cantor, Muriel G., and Suzanne Pingree. The Soap Opera.
      Beverly Hills, CA: Sage Publications, 1983. 167p.
        History, production, contents, and audiences of daytime
      serials. Includes a content analysis of radio and television
      scripts of "The Guiding Light," emphasizing the differences
      between the programs in the two media. Tables, bibliography,
      index.

2. Information

336. Rubin, Bernard (ed.). When Information Counts: Grading
      the Media. Lexington, MA: Lexington Books, 1985. 256p.
        Articles by professionals and academics on how well the
      media informed the public, the influence of media bias, and
      the fairness of treatment of the powerless.

337. Rubin, David M., and Ann Marie Cunningham (eds.). War,
      Peace and the News Media: Proceedings. New York: New
      York University, 1983. 285p.
        See entry 234.

338. Smith, Nelson, and Leonard J. Theberge (eds.). Energy
      Coverage--Media Panic: An International Perspective. New
      York: Longman, 1983. 167p.
        See entry 117.

3. Portrayals

339. Balance in Broadcasting: Report on a Seminar Held 16-17
      January, 1981 in Hull, Quebec. Ottawa: Canadian Radio-
      television and Telecommunications Commission, 1982. 21p.
        See entry 129.

340. Bhasin, Kamla, and Bina Agarwal (eds.). Women and Media:
      Analysis, Alternatives and Action. New Delhi: Kali for Women,
      1984. 132p.
        See entry 121.

341. Courtney, Alice E., and Thomas W. Whipple. Sex Stereotyping
      in Advertising. Lexington, MA: Lexington Books, 1983.
      239p.
        See entry 199.

342. Curtis, Liz. Ireland: The Propaganda War. The British Media
      and the "Battle for Hearts and Minds." London: Pluto Press,

1984. 336p.
See entry 150.

343. Dorn, Nicholas, and Nigel South. Message in a Bottle: Theoretical Overview and Annotated Bibliography on the Mass Media
and Alcohol. Aldershot, Eng.: Gower, 1983. 178p.
See entry 3.

344. Mattelart, Michèle. Women, Media and Crisis: Femininity and
Disorder. London: Comedia, 1986. 123p.
See entry 140.

345. Sreberny-Mohammadi, Annabelle, with Kaarle Nordenstreng,
Robert Stevenson, and Frank Ugboajah (eds.). Foreign News
in the Media: International Reporting in 29 Countries. Paris:
UNESCO, 1985. 96p.
Comparative study on how the media present other countries, peoples, and related issues to readers, listeners, and
viewers. Countries are organized by region. Tables, appendices.

L. PUBLIC

346. Carey, John. Telecommunications Technologies and Public
Broadcasting. Washington, DC: Corporation for Public Broadcasting, 1986. 113p.
Assessment of the possible impact of changing technology on
non-commercial radio and television stations. Sections on cable,
alternative distribution techniques, home electronic products,
and personal computers.

347. Weber, Kathleen (ed.). Public Television and Radio and State
Governments. Vol. 1: Relationship by State. Washington,
DC: National Association of Public Television Stations, 1984.
293p.
A review of state-level activity and details of the activities
of each state. Tables, glossary, appendices.

348. Weber, Kathleen (ed.). Public Television and Radio and State
Governments. Vol. 2: State Statutes. Washington, DC:
National Association of Public Television Stations, 1984. 367p.
See entry 311.

M. TECHNIQUE AND TECHNOLOGY

1. Advertising, Marketing, and Promotion

349. Bergendorff, Fred L., Charles H. Smith, and Lance Webster.

Broadcast Advertising and Promotion: A Handbook for Students and Professionals. Edited by Lance Webster. New York: Hastings House, 1983. 449p.
　　Basics of promotion and responsibilities of the broadcast station promotion director. Ten case studies. Illustrations, appendices, index.

350.　Book, Albert C., Norman D. Cary, and Stanley I. Tannenbaum. The Radio and Television Commercial. 2d ed. Chicago: Crain Books, 1984. 222p.
　　Analysis of the techniques of current radio and television commercial formats and practical guides toward producing and judging well-designed broadcast sales messages. Illustrations, glossaries, bibliography.

351.　Eastman, Susan Tyler, and Robert A. Klein (eds.). Strategies in Broadcast and Cable Promotion: Commercial Television, Radio, Cable, Pay-Television, Public Television. Belmont, CA: Wadsworth, 1982. 355p.
　　The role of promotion, audience and sales promotion practices, and public relations. Illustrations, tables, glossary, annotated bibliography, index.

352.　Eicoff, Alvin. Or Your Money Back. New York: Crown, 1982. 151p.
　　A Chicago advertising executive details his advertising challenges, actions, and results, and offers guidelines on the effective use of broadcast advertising. Illustrations, appendices, glossary, index.

353.　Heighton, Elizabeth J., and Don R. Cunningham. Advertising in the Broadcast and Cable Media. 2d ed. Belmont, CA: Wadsworth, 1984. 368p.
　　Advertiser and agency perspective, in four parts. Part one traces the history of broadcast advertising and describes its current structure. Part two deals with the development of an advertising campaign and includes chapters on marketing research, media and creative planning, and the use of talent, with case studies. Buying and selling time is the focus of the third section, and it is followed by a section on government and self-regulation. Content new to this edition includes a chapter on direct-response advertising and videotex, updated analysis of audience research methodologies, and a discussion on cable planning strategies. Illustrations, bibliography, index.

354.　Lockhart, Ron, and Dick Weissman. Audio in Advertising: A Practical Guide to Producing and Recording Music, Voiceovers, and Sound Effects. New York: Frederick Ungar, 1982. 92p.

Recording studio equipment, how it works, and how to use it to best advantage. Combining music, dialogue, and sound effects, and the uses of music in advertising. Illustrations, glossary, bibliography, index.

355. Warner, Charles. Broadcast and Cable Selling. Belmont, CA: Wadsworth, 1986. 452p.
      Concepts of selling and marketing, followed by sections on what the author labels the SKOAPP system of selling in radio, television, and cable: skills, knowledge, opportunities, attitude, preparation, and persistence. Illustrations, appendices, glossary, index.

356. Weaver, J. Clark. Broadcast Copywriting as Process: A Practical Approach to Copywriting for Radio and Television. New York: Longman, 1984. 139p.
      Skills in writing commercial copy following an established process. Use of language, attention and motivation, planning, writing, and re-writing. Illustrations, index.

357. Woodward, Walt. An Insider's Guide to Advertising Music. New York: Art Direction, 1982. 126p.
      Advice on becoming a better advertising music producer. Music's role in advertising production, the elements of a good musical commercial, selecting and working with a production house, buying media for music, and the legal aspects of music production. Appendix, glossary, index.

358. Zeigler, Sherilyn K., and Herbert H. Howard. Broadcast Advertising: A Comprehensive Working Textbook. 2d ed. Columbus, OH: Grid, 1984. 391p.
      Development of radio and television advertising, organization and advertising practices of stations, networks, cable television systems, and agencies. Writing and producing commercials, audience research, buying and selling time, ethics and regulation, and advertising plans and campaigns. Illustrations, tables, glossary, index.

                              2. Audio

359. Alten, Stanley R. Audio in Media. 2d ed. Belmont, CA: Wadsworth, 1986. 612p.
      Principles, aesthetics, techniques, and technology in radio, television, and film, and in music recording. Illustrations, glossary, bibliography, index.

360. Clifford, Martin. Microphones. 3rd ed. Blue Ridge Summit, PA: TAB Books, 1986. 341p.
      What microphones are, the different types, how they work,

and how to use them for voice and music. Illustrations, tables, appendices, glossary, index.

361. Lockhart, Ron, and Dick Weissman. Audio in Advertising: A Practical Guide to Producing and Recording Music, Voiceovers, and Sound Effects. New York: Frederick Ungar, 1982. 92p. See entry 354.

362. Nakajima, H., T. Doi, J. Fukada, and A. Iga. Digital Audio Technology. Blue Ridge Summit, PA: TAB Books, 1983. 320p.
      Principles of recording, recorders, audio discs, super hi-fi, and a look at the future, by members of the Sony Corporation. Illustrations, index.

363. Nisbett, Alec. The Use of Microphones. 2d ed. Boston, MA: Focal Press, 1983. 167p.
      The nature of sound, characteristics and uses of microphones, microphone balance in speech and music, and functions and operation of the control desk. Illustrations, suggestions for further reading, glossary.

364. Oringel, Robert S. Audio Control Handbook For Radio and Television Broadcasting. 5th ed. revised. New York: Hastings House, 1983. 313p.
      Functions and operation of studio and control room sound equipment in radio and television stations and recording company facilities. Excerpts from product manufacturers' literature. Illustrations, glossary, index.

365. Prentiss, Stan. AM Stereo and TV Stereo: New Sound Dimensions. Blue Ridge Summit, PA: TAB Books, 1985. 192p.
      Characteristics, FCC evaluations of each, and details of stereo transmitters and receivers. Illustrations, appendices, glossary, index.

366. Woodward, Walt. An Insider's Guide to Advertising Music. New York: Art Direction, 1982. 126p. See entry 357.

3. Engineering

367. Crutchfield, E. B. (ed.). National Association of Broadcasters Engineering Handbook. 7th ed. Washington, DC: National Association of Broadcasters, 1985.
      Reference for engineers and technicians in broadcast stations and related or similar facilities, organized in seven sections: procedures and practices, antennas and towers, transmitters, program transmission facilities, production facilities, remote program origination, and special systems. Illustrations, tables, index.

368. Eargle, John. The Microphone Handbook. Plainview, NY:
      Elar, 1982. 231p.
         Principles of recording engineering, transducer theory,
      microphone characteristics, proximity effects, speech and music
      reinforcement, and electrical interface. Illustrations, bibli-
      ography, index.

369. Everest, F. Alton. Acoustic Techniques for Home and Studio.
      2d ed. Blue Ridge Summit, PA: TAB Books, 1984. 344p.
         Acoustical concepts and their application to the design of
      studios and control and listening rooms. New chapters on the
      decibel and listening room. Illustrations, tables, appendix,
      index.

370. Langley, Graham. Telecommunications Primer. Chicago: Tele-
      phony, 1983. 148p.
         Introduction to 47 concepts and topics, including switching
      and signaling, cable, and digital services. Illustrations, index.

371. Noll, Edward M. Broadcast Radio and Television Handbook.
      6th ed. Indianapolis: Howard W. Sams, 1983. 478p.
         Introduction to broadcast station facilities and equipment,
      with emphasis on transmitters. Written for engineers and tech-
      nicians and assumes knowledge of solid-state and vacuum-tube
      fundamentals. Illustrations, index.

372. Proceedings of the Annual Broadcast Engineering Conference.
      Washington, DC: National Association of Broadcasters, annual.
         Conference papers covering topics of special interest to tech-
      nical personnel.

                         4. Management

373. Crutchfield, Ben. The Hiring Guidebook for Broadcast Tech-
      nical Personnel. Washington, DC: National Association of
      Broadcasters, 1982. 48p.
         Suggestions on procedures and forms to use in recruiting,
      screening, testing, and evaluating applicants for technical
      positions. Illustrations.

374. Ducey, Richard V. Telecommunications Facilities Survey.
      Washington, DC: National Association of Broadcasters, 1985.
         Broadcasters' current and planned uses of telecommunication
      facilities and information processing technologies in six general
      areas of station operations: broadcast auxiliary services, back-
      up systems, telephone services, satellite systems, other broad-
      cast and nonbroadcast applications, and computer applications.
      Tables, appendix.

375. Krasnow, Erwin G., and Jill MacNeice. 101 Ways To Cut Legal

Fees and Manage Your Lawyer. Washington, DC: Broadcasting
Publications, 1985. 98p.
Advice on selecting the right lawyer, entering the best fee
arrangement, getting the most out of the lawyer, controlling
costs, monitoring and evaluating lawyer performance, and
remedying problems. Illustrations, appendices, index.

376. McCavitt, William E., and Peter K. Pringle. Electronic Media
Management. Boston, MA: Focal Press, 1986. 325p.
Managerial responsibilities in radio and television stations
and in cable television systems. Management of finances, personnel, programming, sales, promotion, and community relations.
The influence of regulation and the development of non-
broadcast technologies. Illustrations, appendices, bibliography, index.

377. Marcus, Norman. Broadcast and Cable Management. Englewood Cliffs, NJ: Prentice-Hall, 1986. 308p.
Introduction to management issues, major management functions and problems, and career opportunities. Final chapter
contains 12 problems to develop analytic skills and test management instincts. Illustrations, tables, index.

378. Media Insurance and Risk Management, 1985. New York:
Practising Law Institute, 1985. 543p.
Reasons, and the changing marketplace, for insurance, controlling defense costs, selecting the right insurance, constructing the policy, and reducing risk. Appendices.

379. Media Insurance: Protecting Against High Judgments, Punitive
Damages, and Defense Costs. New York: Practising Law
Institute, 1983. 514p.
See entry 301.

380. Operational Guidelines and Accounting Manual for Broadcasters.
Des Plaines, IL: Broadcast Financial Management Association,
n.d.
Three-ring folder in two parts. The guidelines section contains the following BFM publications: Broadcasters Data Pro-
cessing Vendor Guide (1985): Record Retention Guideline for
Broadcasters (1983); Wage Hour Guideline for Broadcasters
(1984); Discussion of Credit, Collections and Accounts Receiv-
able for Broadcast Entities (1982); Personnel/Human Resources
Forms Guidelines for Broadcasters (1984); Internal Control
Guidelines (1985); Equal Employment Opportunity Law Guide-
lines for Broadcasters (1985); BFM Guidelines for Trade and
Barter Transactions (1979); Operations Audit Guideline for
Broadcasters (1978); Risk and Insurance Guidelines for
Broadcasters and Cable Operators (1985); Everything You Al-
ways Wanted To Know About Broadcasting/Cable Insurance--
But Were Too Busy To Ask (1985); and Cash Control Accounting

Guidelines for Cable Communications Industry (1984). The
manual includes account descriptions, financial statement forms,
accounting for film contracts, trade agreements policies and
procedures, and an appendix of reference sources.

381.   Sanford, Bruce W.   Libel and Privacy: The Prevention and
       Defense of Litigation.   New York: Law and Business; Washing-
       ton, DC: Harcourt Brace Jovanovich, 1985.   715p.
       See entry 304.

382.   Simpson, Steven D.   A Broadcaster's Handbook on State and
       Local Taxation.   Washington, DC: National Association of
       Broadcasters, 1984.   89p + appendices.
       See entry 316.

                    5.   News and Documentary

383.   Biagi, Shirley.   Interviews That Work: A Practical Guide for
       Journalists.   Belmont, CA: Wadsworth, 1986.   184p.
          Tips on preparing for and carrying out an interview, based
       on interviews with journalists and educators.   Research pro-
       cedures, interviewee selection, telephone and face-to-face in-
       terviews, note-taking, formulating questions, choosing and using
       quotes, reporting what people say, and legal and ethical con-
       siderations.   Separate chapter on broadcast interviewing.   Il-
       lustrations, bibliography, index.

384.   Broussard, E. Joseph, and Jack F. Holgate.   Writing and Re-
       porting Broadcast News.   New York: Macmillan, 1982.   191p.
          Style, organization, story development, and rewriting.   In-
       terviewing, news stories, law and ethics, and a brief history of
       broadcast news.   Glossary, index.

385.   Chancellor, John, and Walter R. Mears.   The News Business.
       New York: Harper and Row, 1983.   181p.
          Selection and writing of stories for the broadcast and print
       media, with anecdotes and personal recollections of how each
       author dealt with specific challenges.   Hints on how to get
       started in journalism.

386.   Cohler, David Keith.   Broadcast Journalism: A Guide for the
       Presentation of Radio and Television News.   Englewood Cliffs,
       NJ: Prentice-Hall, 1985.   334p.
          Verbal, mechanical, and electronic techniques in the gather-
       ing and presentation of news.   Newswriting, field reporting
       and the use of tape in radio, switching, shooting, editing, and
       presenting the TV news story, and hints on job hunting.   Il-
       lustrations, supplementary reading, index.

387.   Fang, Irving E.   Television News, Radio News.   4th ed. rev.

St. Paul, MN: Rada Press, 1985.   418p.
Writing and reporting for radio and television.   Shooting
and editing TV news, weather, sports, editorials and documentary, and history and issues surrounding broadcast news.
New chapters on writing and reporting and on a typical morning in a radio newsroom.   Illustrations, glossary, index.

388.   Garvey, Daniel E., and William L. Rivers.   Newswriting for
the Electronic Media: Principles, Examples, Applications.
Belmont, CA: Wadsworth, 1982.   250p.
Writing, reporting, and editing news for radio, television,
and cable.   Techniques of interviewing and handling straight
news, depth and interpretive reporting, features, and documentaries.   Illustrations, appendices, glossary, index.

389.   Gilbert, Bob, Larry Perry, and Tim Brady.   Perry's Broadcast News Handbook.   Knoxville: Perry Publications, 1982.
Looseleaf manual designed primarily as a policy document for
radio and television news departments.   Sections on general
policies, news gathering, news writing and editing, legal considerations, and disaster coverage.   Appendices, index.

390.   Goodwin, H. Eugene.   Groping for Ethics in Journalism.   Ames,
IA: Iowa State University Press, 1983.   336p.
Assesses the status of ethics and provides guidance on ways
in which journalists can think through dilemmas to reach a decision.   More than 150 journalists offer their insights and experiences.   Illustrations, index.

391.   Hood, James R., and Brad Kalbfeld (comps. and eds.).   The
Associated Press Broadcast News Handbook.   New York:
Associated Press, 1982.   298p.
Theory and practice of broadcast news writing with a dic-
tionary-like primer on style, starting with "abbreviations" and
ending with "zip codes."   Incorporates the AP Libel Manual
and details of the AP's broadcast services.   Index.

392.   Hulteng, John L.   The Messenger's Motives: Ethical Problems
of the News Media.   2d ed.   Englewood Cliffs, NJ: Prentice-
Hall, 1985.   272p.
Examines the changing attitudes of the public, station owners and managers, and media personnel on the responsibilities
and performance of the media.   Illustrations, annotated bibliography, index.

393.   Newsom, Doug, and James A. Wollert.   Media Writing: News
for the Mass Media.   Belmont, CA: Wadsworth, 1985.   439p.
Principles of writing for broadcast and print media, news-
gathering skills and techniques, story forms, structures, and
treatment.   Summary of mass communication law.   Illustrations,
combined glossary/index.

394. Shook, Frederick, and Dan Lattimore. The Broadcast News
      Process. 2d ed. Englewood, CO: Morton, 1982. 375p.
          Text, exercises, and assignments on writing, reporting,
      and editing. Legal and professional considerations. Illustra-
      tions, appendices, glossary.

395. Smeyak, G. Paul. Broadcast News Writing. 2d ed. Columbus,
      OH: Grid, 1983. 297p.
          Textbook-workbook on writing and reporting news for radio,
      television, and cable. Ethical and legal considerations. Il-
      lustrations, appendices, glossary, index.

396. Stephens, Mitchell. Broadcast News. 2d ed. New York:
      Holt, Rinehart and Winston, 1986. 360p.
          Text and assignments on writing, reporting, and producing
      news and public affairs for radio and television. Illustrations,
      suggested readings, index.

397. Ullmann, John, and Steve Honeyman (eds.). The Reporter's
      Handbook: An Investigator's Guide to Documents and Tech-
      niques. New York: St. Martin's Press, 1983. 504p.
          How and why to investigate individuals and institutions,
      list of most useful records and documents, where to get them,
      and how to use them. Index.

398. Ward, Hiley H. Professional Newswriting. San Diego, CA:
      Harcourt Brace Jovanovich, 1985. 615p.
          Guide to journalistic skills necessary to become a proficient
      newswriter in broadcast and print media.

399. Weaver, J. Clark. Broadcast Newswriting as Process. New
      York: Longman, 1984. 148p.
          Procedures in writing radio and television news. Identify-
      ing news, style and techniques, and a chapter on writing com-
      mentary, analysis, editorials, reviews, and interviews. Glos-
      sary, index.

400. White, Ted, Adrian J. Meppen, and Steve Young. Broadcast
      News Writing, Reporting, and Production. New York: Mac-
      millan, 1984. 314p.
          Skills in writing, reporting, and producing news for radio
      and television. Illustrations, glossary, index.

401. Wolverton, Mike. Reality on Reels: How to Make Documentaries
      for Video/Radio/Film. Houston: Gulf, 1983. 196p.
          Planning, financing, researching, scripting, producing,
      editing, and marketing the documentary. History and types
      of the documentary, and 101 ideas for documentary treatment.
      Index.

402. Wulfemeyer, K. Tim. Beginning Broadcast Newswriting: A

Self-Instructional Learning Experience. 2d ed. Ames, IA:
Iowa State University Press, 1984. 78p.
 Basic styles, principles, and techniques, with summaries
and self-tests.

403. Wulfemeyer, K. Tim. Broadcast Newswriting: A Workbook.
Ames, IA: Iowa State University Press, 1983. 115p.
 Text, examples, and exercises on style and structure for
beginning radio and television news writers. Appendix.

6. Performance

404. Dudek, Lee J. Professional Broadcast Announcing. Boston,
MA: Allyn and Bacon, 1982. 378p.
 Principles, styles, techniques, and skills. Reading on the
air, newscasting, documentary narration, interviewing, news
analyses, commentary, and editorializing. Also, hosting talk
programs, commercials, promos, PSAs, instructional, educational,
and public broadcasting, and sports announcing. Illustrations,
tables, index.

405. Hyde, Stuart W. Television and Radio Announcing. 4th ed.
Boston, MA: Houghton Mifflin, 1983. 522p.
 Communication and performance skills, and their application
in interview and talk programs, commercials and public service
announcements, radio and TV news, and music and sports programs. New chapter on performance, and new and expanded
practice exercises. Illustrations, appendices, glossary, index.

406. Prone, Terry. Just a Few Words: How to Present Yourself
in Public. London: Marion Boyars, 1985. 109p.
 Techniques for communicating effectively in radio and television news interviews, magazine programs, and variety and
talk shows. Advice on dealing with nerves and the interviewer,
writing for the spoken word, and looking good.

7. Production

407. Book, Albert C., Norman D. Cary, and Stanley I. Tannenbaum.
The Radio and Television Commercial. 2d ed. Chicago:
Crain Books, 1984. 222p.
 See entry 350.

408. Lockhart, Ron, and Dick Weissman. Audio in Advertising: A
Practical Guide to Producing and Recording Music, Voiceovers,
and Sound Effects. New York: Frederick Ungar, 1982. 92p.
 See entry 354.

409. Woodward, Walt. An Insider's Guide to Advertising Music.

New York: Art Direction, 1982.   126p.
See entry 357.

8. Programming

410. Eastman, Susan Tyler, Sydney W. Head, and Lewis Klein.
Broadcast/Cable Programming: Strategies and Practices.   2d
ed. Belmont, CA: Wadsworth, 1985. 529p.
Programming principles, methods, resources, and constraints,
and the evaluation, selection, and scheduling of programs in
cable and in commercial and public radio and television. New
chapters on the programming of cable systems, basic cable networks, premium services and local origination, program and
audience research, and on radio networks and format syndi-
cators. Illustrations, tables, glossary, annotated bibliography,
index to program titles, general index.

411. Howard, Herbert H., and Michael S. Kievman. Radio and TV
Programming. Columbus, OH: Grid, 1983. 372p.
Skills and strategies in programming commercial and public
radio and television stations. Historical overview of programming, program criticism and regulation, and prospects for the
future. Illustrations, suggested readings, index.

412. Smith, V. Jackson. Programming for Radio and Television.
Rev. ed. Washington, DC: University Press of America, 1983.
170p.
Developments in broadcast programming, current practices,
audience listening and viewing habits, program appeals, and
the role and responsibilities of the program director. Illustrations, appendix.

9. Research

413. Dominick, Joseph R., and James E. Fletcher (eds.). Broadcasting Research Methods. Boston, MA: Allyn and Bacon,
1985. 330p.
Collection of 20 original essays on research techniques and
theoretical and applied research problems. The techniques
section includes content analysis, attitude measurement, physio-
logical responses to the media, and the development of mass
communication research models. Agenda-setting, the measurement of violence in TV programming, the mass media and sex-
role socialization, and program development research are among
the essays in the problems section. Illustrations, tables, name
index, subject index.

414. Saxton, Judith. Audience Research Workbook. Washington,
DC: National Association of Broadcasters, 1983. 31p.

Step-by-step plan for conducting basic survey research
projects, to be used in conjunction with Webster's Audience
Research (entry 415). Covers study design, survey types,
questionnaire design, sampling, analyzing the survey, and applying the findings. Appendices.

415. Webster, James. Audience Research. Washington, DC: Na-
      tional Association of Broadcasters, 1983. 39p.
         Importance and applications of research. Research methods,
      selection and employment of professional firms, basic research
      concepts, and location and use of secondary research. Illus-
      trations, tables, glossary, bibliography.

416. Wimmer, Roger D., and Joseph R. Dominick. Mass Media
      Research: An Introduction. Belmont, CA: Wadsworth, 1983.
      397p.
         The research process, approaches, statistical methods, data
      analysis and results, and applications of research in the elec-
      tronic and print media and in advertising and public relations.
      Designed for a beginning research course. Illustrations, tables,
      appendices, glossary, name index, subject index.

10. Writing

417. Garvey, Daniel E., and William L. Rivers. Broadcast Writing.
      New York: Longman, 1982. 280p.
         Style, format, and techniques of writing most kinds of radio
      and TV scripts: news, commercials, public service announce-
      ments, drama, and comedy. Also, semi-scripted programs
      (music, talk, and interview shows), and special-interest pro-
      gramming (children's TV programs, radio for the blind, women's
      programming, instructional programs, and ethnic programs).
      Illustrations, glossary, bibliography, index.

418. Garvey, Daniel E., and William L. Rivers. Broadcast Writing
      Workbook. New York: Longman, 1982. 169p.
         Designed for use with the authors' Broadcast Writing (entry
      417) or by itself. Text and exercises on all topics covered in
      the textbook. Illustrations.

419. Hilliard, Robert L. Writing for Television and Radio. 4th ed.
      Belmont, CA: Wadsworth, 1984. 385p.
         Techniques and examples of writing. Commercials and an-
      nouncements; news and sports; features and documentaries;
      talk, music, variety, and comedy programs; drama. Chapters
      on children's, women's, minority and ethnic programs, on edu-
      cation and information programs, and on professional writing
      opportunities. Consideration of broadcast audiences and pro-
      duction elements. Illustrations, glossary, suggested readings,
      index.

420. Hutchison, Earl R., Sr. Writing for Mass Communication.
      New York: Longman, 1986. 474p.
         Instruction in writing to inform, entertain, and persuade
      in broadcast and print media, with examples and exercises.
      Illustrations, appendices, index.

421. Mayeux, Peter E. Writing for the Broadcast Media. Boston,
      MA: Allyn and Bacon, 1985. 368p.
         Scripting forms, approaches and techniques, the role and
      responsibility of the writer, process, and consideration of pro-
      duction and business principles. Covers commercials and an-
      nouncements; news and sports; editorials and commentaries;
      documentaries and investigative reports; talk, music, and vari-
      ety programs; dramas and comedies; and writing for spe-
      cialized audiences. Illustrations, appendices, index.

422. Orlik, Peter B. Broadcast Copywriting. 3rd ed. Boston, MA:
      Allyn and Bacon, 1986. 618p.
         Skills and methods of creating continuity for radio and tele-
      vision. IDs, station and program promos, interviews and semi-
      scripts, public service announcements, and commercials. Broad-
      cast and cross-media campaign strategies. Illustrations, ap-
      pendices, index.

423. Straczynski, J. Michael. The Complete Book of Script-Writing.
      Cincinnati, OH: Writer's Digest Books, 1982. 265p.
         Art, craft, and marketing of scripts for television, radio,
      motion pictures, and stage. Illustrations, appendices, index.

424. Weaver, J. Clark. Broadcast Copywriting as Process: A Prac-
      tical Approach to Copywriting for Radio and Television. New
      York: Longman, 1984. 139p.
         See entry 356.

PART II: RADIO

A. REFERENCES: DIRECTORIES AND GUIDES

425. Duncan, James H., Jr. Duncan's Radio Market Guide. Kalamazoo, MI: Duncan's American Radio, annual.
Market-by-market data, including revenue estimates. Tables, index.

426. Radio Is.... Washington, DC: National Association of Broadcasters, 1983. 48p.
Facts and figures on history, stations, listenership, and much more.

427. Salomonson, Terry G. G. A Radio Broadcast Log of the Western Drama Program: The Lone Ranger. Saint Charles, MO: Terry G. G. Salomonson, 1985. 106p.
Original air date and broadcast sequence number of the 3,377 programs. Recording sequence number, script synopsis or program title, and script author(s).

428. Smart, James R. (comp.). Radio Broadcasts in the Library of Congress, 1924-1941: A Catalog of Recordings. Washington, DC: Library of Congress, 1982. 149p.
Chronological list of recordings of live broadcasts of domestic and foreign origin available for study in the Library of Congress. Entries include program title and length, performers, and call letters of the station from which the program was recorded. Programs for which an exact broadcast date cannot be determined are listed separately in alphabetical order. Illustrations, index.

429. Syndicated Radio Programming Directory. Washington, DC: National Association of Broadcasters, annual.
Syndicator name and content description in the following categories: jingles, production libraries, special programs (general), special programs (music), and formats. Company index.

B. AUDIENCES

430. Reymer and Gersin Associates, Inc. Radio W.A.R.S.: How
      to Survive in the '80s. Washington, DC: National Association
      of Broadcasters, 1983. 34p.
        Findings of a study of 1,300 listeners across the country.
      Comparison of the psychology of each format's fans, charac-
      teristics of groups or segments of listeners, guide in applying
      the "segmentation" approach in marketing the station, and key
      data tables. Illustrations, tables, appendix.

431. Reymer and Gersin Associates, Inc. Radio W.A.R.S. II: How
      to Push Listeners' "Hot Buttons." Washington, DC: National
      Association of Broadcasters, 1985. 18p.
        Profiles, attitudes, preferences, and motivations of seven
      basic types of radio listeners that cut across format boundaries.
      Illustration, tables.

C. BUSINESS

432. Bortz, Paul I., and Harold Mendelsohn. Radio Today--and
      Tomorrow. Washington, DC: National Association of Broad-
      casters, 1982. 75p.
        Review of current and projected demographic and social
      trends with respect to their potential impacts on radio. Survey
      of media habits and lifestyles of 1,500 households and forecast
      on how new technology may affect the future structure and
      strategies of the radio broadcasting industry. Tables, ap-
      pendices.

433. Cheen, Bruce Bishop. Fair Market Value of Radio Stations:
      A Buyer's Guide. Washington DC: National Association of
      Broadcasters, 1986. 193p.
        The radio broadcasting industry and its operations, financial
      aspects of acquiring a radio station, and a pricing model for
      determining market value. A hypothetical station is profiled
      and the model applied. Illustrations, tables, glossary.

434. DeSonne, Marcia L. Radio New Technology and You. Washing-
      ton, DC: National Association of Broadcasters, 1982. 24p.
        Exploration of various directions radio may take in response
      to the explosion in communications technologies. Radio's growth,
      networking, satellite earth stations, digital audio, cable and
      radio, AM stereo, and AM and FM SCA opportunities. Tables.

435. Ducey, Richard V., and Mark R. Fratrik. The New Audio
      Marketplace: Challenges and Opportunities for Broadcasters.
      Washington, DC: National Association of Broadcasters, 1985.
      25p.

Profile of the new audio marketplace, cable audio and its potential impact on radio broadcasting, and action strategies for broadcasters. Tables.

436. Martin, Robin B. Broadcast Lending: A Lender's Guide to the Radio Industry. Washington, DC: National Association of Broadcasters, 1984. 14p.
   Details of broadcast industry history and regulation, economics of the advertising media and of radio, operational and competitive strategy, evaluation of radio properties, lending opportunities and considerations, and a look into the future.

437. Radio Employee Compensation and Fringe Benefits Report. Washington, DC: National Association of Broadcasters, biennial.
   Profiles, organized according to station revenue, market population, full-time AM stations, FM stations, AM/FM stations, and AM daytime stations. Tables.

438. Radio Financial Report. Washington, DC: National Association of Broadcasters, annual.
   Results of the NAB's survey of commercial radio station revenues, expenses, and profits. Tables.

D. CAREERS

439. Blume, Dan. Making It In Radio: Your Future In The Modern Medium. Hartford, CT: Continental Media Company, 1983. 175p.
   The development of commercial radio, characteristics of stations, the operation of station departments and skills needed to make them run, and advice on radio careers from 19 professionals. Illustrations, glossary, bibliography, index.

440. Careers in Radio. Washington, DC: National Association of Broadcasters, 1986. 23p.
   Divisions of a commercial radio station, employees, and their responsibilities and qualifications. Hints on obtaining an education and on job-hunting. Illustrations.

441. Lerner, Mark. Careers With A Radio Station. Minneapolis: Lerner Publications, 1983.
   Young person's guide to who does what. Illustrations.

E.   FOREIGN AND INTERNATIONAL

1.   Foreign

(a)   Australia

442.   Bridges, Nancye, with Frank Crook. Wonderful Wireless:
Reminiscences of the Stars of Australia's Live Radio. North
Ryde, New South Wales: Methuen, 1983. 144p.
Personality profiles and photographs, from the beginnings
through the early 1980s. Illustrations, index.

443.   Higgins, C. S., and P. D. Moss. Sounds Real: Radio in
Everyday Life. St. Lucia, Queensland: University of Queensland Press, 1982. 237p.
Attempt to identify the cultural functions and importance of
radio through analysis of a variety of Australian radio texts.
Focus on the language in which messages are coded, the nature
and significance of the structure of radio programs, and the
codes and conventions of radio as a genre. Illustrations, tables,
bibliography.

444.   Kent, Jacqueline. Out of the Bakelite Box: The Heyday of
Australian Radio. Sydney: Angus and Robertson, 1983.
277p.
The people and programs of Australian radio from the end
of World War II to the arrival of television. Illustrations, appendix, select bibliography, index.

445.   Muscio, Winston T. Australian Radio: The Technical Story,
1923-1983. Kenthurst: Kangaroo Press, 1984. 243p.
Developments flowing from nineteenth-century discoveries
and inventions and accounts of some of the fields of radio
transmission and reception with which the author had personal
experience. Illustrations, tables, index.

446.   Press and Television Interests in Australian Commercial Radio.
Sydney: Federation of Australian Radio Broadcasters, 1982.
21p.
Review of the extent of radio ownership by newspaper interests and by companies holding interests in commercial television licenses. Illustrations, table.

(b)   Canada

447.   Duffy, Dennis J. Imagine Please: Early Radio Broadcasting
in British Columbia. Victoria, British Columbia: Provincial
Archives of British Columbia, 1983. 92p.
Public and private broadcasting. The pioneer stations,
their financing, origins of networking, programs, and post-
World War II developments. Illustrations.

(c)   United Kingdom

448. Adams, Douglas. The Original Hitchhiker Radio Scripts.
      Edited by Geoffrey Perkins. New York: Harmony Books,
      1985. 248p.
          Complete, unedited scripts from the original BBC "Hitch-
      hiker Radio Show," as broadcast by National Public Radio.

449. Baehr, Helen, and Michèle Ryan. Shut Up and Listen! Wom-
      en and Local Radio: A View from the Inside. London: Comedia,
      1984. 64p.
          Based on the experiences of one of the authors as an em-
      ployee of an independent (commercial) station. Asserts that
      Britain's Independent Local Radio has grown out of touch with
      women of the 1980s. Offers suggestions for change and guide-
      lines for women with an interest in a radio career. Appendices.

450. Hind, John, and Stephen Mosco. Rebel Radio: The Full Story
      of British Pirate Radio. London: Pluto Press, 1985. 163p.
          The programming and methods of operation of illegal music
      and community stations. The case for and against the pirates,
      and thoughts on their function and that of radio in general.
      Illustrations, appendices.

451. Local Radio Workshop. Capital: Local Radio and Private Profit.
      London: Comedia, 1983. 128p.
          Analysis of the relationship between profit and programming
      in commercial local radio in Britain through study of Capital
      Radio, London's pop music station. Calls for reconsideration
      of the role of private finance in local radio and suggests meth-
      ods of achieving greater public control. Tables, appendices.

452. Local Radio Workshop. Nothing Local About It: London's
      Local Radio. London: Comedia, 1983. 215p.
          Monitoring and analysis of one week's programming on Lon-
      don's two commercial radio stations, Capital and London Broad-
      casting Company, and on non-commercial BBC Radio London.
      Concludes that all three stations seemed unable or unwilling
      to come to grips with London issues. Illustrations, tables, ap-
      pendices.

453. Mansell, Gerard. Let Truth Be Told: 50 Years of BBC Ex-
      ternal Broadcasting. London: Weidenfeld and Nicolson, 1982.
      300p.
          The story of BBC international broadcasting from the initial
      broadcast to Australia and New Zealand in 1932 to the early
      1980s. Illustrations, bibliography, index.

454. Partridge, Simon. Not the BBC/IBA: The Case for Community
      Radio. London: Comedia, 1982. 75p.
          The development and status of the community radio debate

in Britain, the idea in practice, and guidelines for getting a
station off the ground. Illustrations, glossary, appendices,
bibliography.

455. Pegg, Mark. Broadcasting and Society, 1918-1939. London:
      Croom Helm, 1983. 263p.
          Development and utilization of radio and its influence in
      Britain. Listening patterns, equipment and costs, listener
      organizations, methods and use of listener research, and im-
      pact on the local community and general population. Illustra-
      tions, tables, bibliography, index.

456. Stoppard, Tom. Four Plays for Radio. London: Faber and
      Faber, 1984. 150p.
          Scripts of "Artist Descending a Staircase," "Where Are
      They Now?," "If You're Glad I'll be Frank," and "Albert's
      Bridge." Date, cast, and producer of the first broadcast of
      each play on the BBC.

457. West, W. J. (ed.). Orwell: The War Broadcasts. London:
      Gerald Duckworth/British Broadcasting Corporation, 1985.
      304p.
          Scripts of 16 literary and other talks written and mostly
      broadcast by George Orwell during the two years (1941-43)
      he spent as a talks producer in the Indian section of the BBC's
      Eastern Service, and letters relating to them. Political talks,
      experimental programs, talks on famous authors and plays,
      and adaptations of stories by others. Illustrations, appendices,
      index.

458. West, W. J. (ed.). Orwell: The War Commentaries. London:
      Gerald Duckworth/British Broadcasting Corporation, 1985.
      248p.
          Scripts of weekly newstalks written by George Orwell and
      broadcast on the BBC's Eastern Service from December 1941
      through March 1943. Appendix, maps, index.

                          2. International

459. Browne, Donald R. International Radio Broadcasting: The
      Limits of the Limitless Medium. New York: Praeger, 1982.
      370p.
          The emergence and growth of international radio broad-
      casting and stations, and treatment of political, cultural, tech-
      nical, and economic constraints, content, and audiences. Chap-
      ters on Voice of America, BBC External Services, Radio Moscow
      and other Soviet and Communist services, the Third World,
      and religious broadcasting. Appendices, bibliography, index.

460. Fejes, Fred. Imperialism, Media, and the Good Neighbor: New

Deal Foreign Policy and United States Shortwave Broadcasting
to Latin America. Norwood, NJ: Ablex, 1986. 190p.
The development of communication ties between the United
States and Latin America and their interaction with U.S. foreign
policy in the region. Bibliography, author index, subject index.

461. Frederick, Howard H. Cuban-American Radio Wars: Ideology
in International Telecommunications. Norwood, NJ: Ablex,
1986. 200p.
Examination of the ideological conflict between the United
States and Cuba through a case study of the content of international newscasts of La Voz de los Estados Unidos de America
(Voice of America) and Radio Havana Cuba. Tables, bibliography, author index, subject index.

462. Kolehmainen, John I. Voice of America Calling Finland. New
York Mills, MN: Parta Printers, 1985. 128p.
Reflections on the VOA's Finnish Service from 1942 to 1945
and 1951 to 1953. Illustrations, bibliography.

463. Mansell, Gerard. Let Truth Be Told: 50 Years of BBC External Broadcasting. London: Weidenfeld and Nicolson, 1982.
300p.
See entry 453.

464. Mickelson, Sig. America's Other Voice: The Story of Radio
Free Europe and Radio Liberty. New York: Praeger, 1983.
269p.
History, accomplishments, and potential of the services, by
a former RFE/RL president. Chronology, appendix, index.

F. HISTORY

465. Aitken, Hugh G. J. The Continuous Wave: Technology and
American Radio, 1900-1932. Princeton, NJ: Princeton University Press, 1985. 588p.
Origins and development of the technology that made broadcasting possible, from Fessenden and the alternator through
the consent decree separating RCA from GE and Westinghouse.
Illustrations, appendix, index.

466. Bridges, Nancye, with Frank Crook. Wonderful Wireless:
Reminiscences of the Stars of Australia's Live Radio. North
Ryde, New South Wales: Methuen, 1983. 144p.
See entry 442.

467. Duffy, Dennis J. Imagine Please: Early Radio Broadcasting
in British Columbia. Victoria, British Columbia: Provincial

Archives of British Columbia, 1983. 92p.
See entry 447.

468. Duncan, James H., Jr. (comp. and ed.). Radio in the United
      States, 1976-1982: A Statistical History. Kalamazoo, MI: Dun-
      can Media Enterprises, 1983.
         Trends in radio station audiences, revenues and profitabil-
      ity, advertising costs, and formats, nationally and in 170
      markets. Details of station trading in those markets between
      1970 and 1982. Tables.

469. Eberly, Philip K. Music in the Air: America's Changing Tastes
      in Popular Music, 1920-1980. New York: Hastings House,
      1982. 406p.
         The evolution of music on radio stations and networks, the
      programs, and performers. Role of the disc jockey, research,
      and program consultants. Illustrations, tables, discography,
      bibliography, appendices, index.

470. Fejes, Fred. Imperialism, Media, and the Good Neighbor:
      New Deal Foreign Policy and United States Shortwave Broad-
      casting to Latin America. Norwood, NJ: Ablex, 1986. 190p.
      See entry 460.

471. Hosley, David H. As Good As Any: Foreign Correspondence
      on American Radio, 1930-1940. Westport, CT: Greenwood
      Press, 1984. 165p.
         The techniques and values of the pioneers of foreign cor-
      respondence, among them Edward R. Murrow, William L. Shirer,
      and Eric Sevareid. Illustrations, bibliography, index.

472. Kent, Jacqueline. Out of the Bakelite Box: The Heyday of
      Australian Radio. Sydney: Angus and Robertson, 1983.
      277p.
      See entry 444.

473. Kolehmainen, John I. Voice of America Calling Finland. New
      York Mills, MN: Parta Printers, 1985. 128p.
      See entry 462.

474. Mansell, Gerard. Let Truth Be Told: 50 Years of BBC Ex-
      ternal Broadcasting. London: Weidenfeld and Nicolson, 1982.
      300p.
      See entry 453.

475. Mickelson, Sig. America's Other Voice: The Story of Radio
      Free Europe and Radio Liberty. New York: Praeger, 1983.
      269p.
      See entry 464.

476. Muscio, Winston T. Australian Radio: The Technical Story,

1923-1983. Kenthurst: Kangaroo Press, 1984. 243p.
See entry 445.

477. Pegg, Mark. Broadcasting and Society, 1918-1939. London:
Croom Helm, 1983. 263p.
See entry 455.

478. Renner, Louis L. The KNOM/Father Jim Poole Story. Port-
land, OR: Binford and Mort, 1985. 150p.
The establishment and operation of the radio station broadcasting to Western Alaska, and the significance of the role
played by Father Jim Poole. Illustrations.

479. Short, K. R. M. (ed.). Film and Radio Propaganda in World
War II. Knoxville: University of Tennessee Press, 1983.
341p.
Selected and revised papers presented at a 1982 conference,
most dealing with film. The emergence of radio as an international propaganda tool is part of a paper on propaganda in
international politics between 1919 and 1939. Radio is included
in a paper on the struggle for control of French minds between
1940 and 1944, and in another on Japanese domestic propaganda from 1937 to 1945. Only two papers deal exclusively
with radio: one on propaganda at Radio Luxembourg in 1944-
1945, authored by Erik Barnouw, and the other on Japanese
overseas broadcasting by Namikawa Ryó, a member of Japan's
Cabinet Information Bureau during the war. Index.

480. Sklar, Rick. Rocking America: How the All-Hit Radio Stations
Took Over. New York: St. Martin's Press, 1984. 220p.
Remembrances of the rise of rock-and-roll radio in New
York, by a former WABC programmer. The people, stories,
and stations, especially WABC. Glimpses of the inner work-
ings of the radio business. Illustrations, index.

481. Slide, Anthony. Great Radio Personalities in Historic Photographs. New York: Dover Publications, 1982. 117p.
Photographs and capsule biographies of 235 stars of radio's
golden age, beginning with Abbott and Costello and ending with
Ed Wynn. Illustrations.

G. PROGRAMS AND CONTENT

1. Entertainment

482. Salomonson, Terry G. G. A Radio Broadcast Log of the
Western Drama Program: The Lone Ranger. Saint Charles,
MO: Terry G. G. Salomonson, 1985. 106p.
See entry 427.

483. Sklar, Rick. Rocking America: How the All-Hit Radio Stations
      Took Over. New York: St. Martin's Press, 1984. 220p.
      See entry 480.

2. Information

484. Frederick, Howard H. Cuban-American Radio Wars: Ideology
      In International Telecommunications. Norwood, NJ: Ablex,
      1986. 200p.
      See entry 461.

3. Scripts

485. Adams, Douglas. The Original Hitchhiker Radio Scripts. Edited
      by Geoffrey Perkins. New York: Harmony Books, 1985.
      248p.
      See entry 448.

486. Elliott, Bob, and Ray Goulding. From Approximately Coast to
      Coast ... It's The Bob and Ray Show. New York: Atheneum,
      1983. 216p.
         Scripts of 52 comedy sketches, most performed originally on
      radio by the authors. Illustrations.

487. Giangola, Andrew (comp. and ed.). Radio Copy Book: Ideas
      and Inspiration for Radio Copywriters. New York: Radio
      Advertising Bureau, 1986. 222p.
         Scripts containing humor, hard sell, image, item and
      straight sales copy, divided by business category.

488. Gragert, Steven K. (ed.). Radio Broadcasts of Will Rogers.
      Stillwater, OK: Oklahoma State University Press, 1983. 211p.
         Transcripts of the humorist's 12 essays for E. R. Squibb
      and Sons (April 6-June 22, 1930), Depression era talk for the
      Organization on Unemployment Relief (1931), and 16 of the 53
      shows he made for Gulf Oil Company between 1933 and 1935.
      Topics include politics, foreign relations, domestic affairs, pro-
      hibition, motion pictures, economics, and lifestyles. Illustra-
      tions, appendix, index.

489. Stamberg, Susan. Every Night at Five: Susan Stamberg's
      "All Things Considered" Book. New York: Pantheon Books,
      1982. 211p.
         Collection of scripts of favorite pieces from National Public
      Radio's "All Things Considered," selected by listeners and the
      staffs of NPR and its member stations. Topics include Water-
      gate, a memorial service for John Lennon, how to ripen pears,
      and where to find the best hamburger in America. Illustra-
      tions.

490. Stoppard, Tom. Four Plays for Radio. London: Faber and
      Faber, 1984. 150p.
          See entry 456.

491. West, W. J. (ed.). Orwell: The War Broadcasts. London:
      Gerald Duckworth/British Broadcasting Corporation, 1985.
      304p.
          See entry 457.

492. West, W. J. (ed.). Orwell: The War Commentaries. London:
      Gerald Duckworth/British Broadcasting Corporation, 1985.
      248p.
          See entry 458.

H. PUBLIC AND COMMUNITY

493. Mendel, Robin, Natan Katzman, and Solomon Katzman. Public
      Radio Programming Content by Category: Fiscal Year 1982.
      Washington, DC: Corporation for Public Broadcasting, 1984.
      54p.
          Results of a survey of the 228 CPB-qualified stations from
      October 2, 1981 through September 30, 1982. Covers music,
      news/public affairs, and informational, spoken word, instruc-
      tional, and special interest programming. Stations are cate-
      gorized by licensee type, budget, region, time zone, market
      type, AM, and FM, and programming by daypart and by NPR
      and local distribution. Illustrations, tables, appendices.

494. Milam, Lorenzo Wilson. The Radio Papers: From KRAB to
      KCHU. Essays on the Art and Practice of Radio Transmission.
      San Diego: MHO and MHO Works, 1986. 174p.
          Essays written for the program guides of five non-commercial
      "community" radio stations: KRAB (Seattle), KBOO (Portland),
      KDNA (St. Louis), KTAO (Los Gatos), and KCHU (Dallas).
      Illustrations.

495. Partridge, Simon. Not the BBC/IBA: The Case for Community
      Radio. London: Comedia, 1982. 75p.
          See entry 454.

496. Public Radio Stations' Educational Services, 1982-83. Wash-
      ington, DC: Corporation for Public Broadcasting, 1984. 51p.
          Highlights of the results of a survey of services to ele-
      mentary, secondary, and postsecondary educational institutions
      throughout the United States. Tables, appendices.

497. Stamberg, Susan. Every Night at Five: Susan Stamberg's
      "All Things Considered" Book. New York: Pantheon Books,
      1982. 211p.
          See entry 489.

I. TECHNIQUE AND TECHNOLOGY

1. General

498. Busby, Linda, and Donald Parker. The Art and Science of
      Radio. Boston: Allyn and Bacon, 1984. 214p.
        History, production, copywriting, news, programming,
      ownership and operation, sales and promotion, and government
      and other regulators. Illustrations, tables, chapter bibli-
      ographies, appendices.

499. Hilliard, Robert L. (ed.). Radio Broadcasting: An Introduc-
      to the Sound Medium. 3rd ed. New York: Longman, 1985.
      334p.
        History and regulation, management, studio and operating
      facilities, format, writing, producing and directing, and per-
      forming. Illustrations, chapter bibliographies, index.

500. Keith, Michael C., and Joseph M. Krause. The Radio Station.
      Boston, MA: Focal Press, 1986. 256p.
        Profile of the commercial radio station, its departments, and
      personnel. Station management, programming, sales, news, re-
      search, promotion, traffic and billing, production, engineering,
      and the role of consultants and syndicators. Illustrations, glos-
      sary, index.

2. Advertising, Marketing, and Promotion

501. Bunzel, Reed. Guidelines for Radio: Copywriting. Washing-
      ton, DC: National Association of Broadcasters, 1982. 63p.
        Defining the creative myth, developing an approach, writ-
      ing the commercial, and the creative use of sound. Twenty-
      two steps to better copywriting. Illustrations.

502. Dawson, James, Angela Couloumbis, and Catherine Seigerman
      (comps.). Guidelines for Radio: Promotion II. Washington,
      DC: National Association of Broadcasters, 1985. 64p.
        Collection of best promotion-related articles from NAB's
      RadioActive magazine. Covers idea exchanges, basics, TV,
      station events, outdoor, community service, print promotions,
      and jingles. Illustrations.

503. Giangola, Andrew (comp. and ed.). Radio Copy Book: Ideas
      and Inspiration for Radio Copywriters. New York: Radio
      Advertising Bureau, 1986. 222p.
        See entry 487.

504. Keith, Michael C. Production in Format Radio Handbook. Lan-
      ham, MD: University Press of America, 1984. 206p.

Analysis of copy, delivery, and mixdown of commercial messages in 10 widely-used music and information formats. Tips
on copywriting, announcing, editing, use of a sound library,
and preparation of an audition tape. Illustrations, glossary,
bibliography, index.

505. The Research Group. MegaRates: How To Get Top Dollar For
      Your Spots. Washington, DC: National Association of Broad-
      casters, 1986. 162p.
         Compilation of nine-question interviews with 51 radio sta-
      tion general managers and general sales managers known for
      their ability to get higher rates for their spots. Questions
      cover factors in getting and maintaining high rates, motivators
      and training for sales staff, overcoming rate objections, atti-
      tudes about long-term contracts, and specific sales practices.

506. Reymer and Gersin Associates, Inc. Radio W.A.R.S.: How
      to Survive in the '80s. Washington, DC: National Association
      of Broadcasters, 1983. 34p.
         See entry 430.

507. Reymer and Gersin Associates, Inc. Radio W.A.R.S. II: How
      to Push Listeners' "Hot Buttons." Washington, DC: National
      Association of Broadcasters, 1985. 18p.
         See entry 431.

508. Savage, Bob, Larry Perry, and Don Craig. Perry's Broadcast
      Promotion Sourcebook. Oak Ridge, TN: Perry Publications,
      1982. 253p.
         Total of 150 promotion ideas and mechanics for their execu-
      tion, in four categories: cume builders, quarter-hour builders,
      seasonal ideas, and charitable tie-ins. Developing a promotion-
      al game plan, contests versus promotions, promotion within the
      station, and promotion management. Looseleaf. Illustrations,
      index.

3. Copywriting

509. Bunzel, Reed. Guidelines for Radio: Copywriting. Washing-
      ton, DC: National Association of Broadcasters, 1982. 63p.
         See entry 501.

510. Giangola, Andrew (comp. and ed.). Radio Copy Book: Ideas
      and Inspiration for Radio Copywriters. New York: Radio
      Advertising Bureau, 1986. 222p.
         See entry 487.

4. Engineering

511. Carr, Joseph J. The TAB Handbook of Radio Communications.

Blue Ridge Summit, PA: TAB Books, 1984.   1,050p.
Text, diagrams, and reference materials for amateurs and
professionals.   Illustrations.

512. Klein, Harrison J. Modulation, Overmodulation, and Occupied
      Bandwidth: Recommendations for the AM Broadcast Industry.
      Washington, DC: National Association of Broadcasters, 1986.
      55p.
          Technical report for AM engineers on assuring transmission
      of a clean and full-fidelity signal, prevention of overmodulation
      and of "splatter" interference.   Conclusions and recommenda-
      tions.   Illustrations, appendices.

5. Management

513. Kirkley, Donald H., Jr. Station Policy and Procedures: A
      Guide for Radio. Washington, DC: National Association of
      Broadcasters, 1985.   83p.
          Rationale, suggested content, and language for a radio sta-
      tion employee manual.   Covers general business policies and
      procedures, programming, news and editorial, public service
      and public affairs programming, traffic and continuity, sales,
      promotion, and engineering.   Illustrations.

514. McGuire, Bernadette (ed.). Radio in Search of Excellence:
      Lessons from America's Best-Run Radio Stations. Washington,
      DC: National Association of Broadcasters, 1985.   150p.
          Detailed findings of an in-depth analysis by McKinsey and
      Company of 11 top-performing radio stations, results of an NAB
      survey of leading stations, and consultants' advice on applying
      the principles of successful management.   Illustrations, tables.

515. Wollert, James, and Catherine Seigerman. The NAB Computer
      Primer for Radio Broadcasters: A Beginner's Guide to Com-
      puters. Edited by Catherine Seigerman. Washington, DC:
      National Association of Broadcasters, 1984.   23p.
          Components and types of computer systems; software types,
      needs, and applications; the impact of a computer on the sta-
      tion.   Glossary.

6. News

516. Josephson, Larry (ed.). Telling the Story: The National
      Public Radio Guide to Radio Journalism. Dubuque, IA: Kendall/
      Hunt, 1983.   228p.
          Covering hard news and features, recording, editing and
      producing, and consideration of legal aspects.   Appendices, in-
      dex.

7. Performance

517. Drake, Harold L. Humanistic Radio Production. Washington, DC: University Press of America, 1982. 116p.
Use of radio's "Golden Age" formats and of video to teach production, announcing, and interviewing. Bibliography.

8. Production

518. Drake, Harold L. Humanistic Radio Production. Washington, DC: University Press of America, 1982. 116p.
See entry 517.

519. Keith, Michael C. Production in Format Radio Handbook. Lanham, MD: University Press of America, 1984. 206p.
See entry 504.

520. Matthews, Arthur C. Radio Production Handbook: A Beginner's Guide to Broadcasting and Cablecasting. Downers Grove, IL: Meriwether, 1982. 277p.
Basic equipment and operating skills and techniques. The interview, announcement, editorial commentary, radio drama, producing a series, news, magazine, and documentary. Illustrations.

521. O'Donnell, Lewis B., Philip Benoit, and Carl Hausman. Modern Radio Production. Belmont, CA: Wadsworth, 1986. 258p.
Radio equipment and techniques and their application in the production of drama, commercials, news and public affairs, remote, and sports broadcasts. Illustrations, appendices, suggested reading, glossary, index.

9. Programming

522. The Method to the Madness: Radio's Morning Show Manual. Bridgeport, CT: American Comedy Network, 1985. 61p.
Tips on creating a funny, creative, entertaining, and successful show, based on questionnaire responses from and interviews with 70 morning personalities. Illustration, appendix.

523. Paiva, Bob. The Program Director's Handbook. Blue Ridge Summit, PA: TAB Books, 1983. 162p.
The duties of the radio program director, entertainment and information program practices, promotion, conducting and utilizing research, and responsibility to the public. Illustrations, appendix, index.

524. Shane, Ed. Programming Dynamics: Radio's Management Guide.

Overland Park, KS: Globecom, 1984.   119p.
Program philosophy and practice, ratings, advertising, research, and a look to the future.

10.   Research

525. Fletcher, James E.   Squeezing Profits Out of Ratings: A
      Manual for Radio Managers, Sales Managers and Programmers.
      Washington, DC: National Association of Broadcasters, 1985.
      Self-instruction manual on audience measurement techniques
      based on the methods of Arbitron Ratings Company and Birch
      Radio.   Divided into seven lessons: contents of the rating
      report, accuracy of radio ratings, sales uses of ratings, use
      of ratings to improve programs, geography of rating surveys,
      samples, and ratings problems.   Each lesson has exercises on
      sales and programming.   Illustrations, tables, additional read-
      ings, appendices.

526. Hiber, Jhan.   Hibernetics: A Guide to Radio Ratings and Re-
      search.   Los Angeles: R and R Books, 1984.   251p.
      Description and utilization of focus groups, telephone
      studies, the Arbitron diary, and Birch telephone-recall.   Sales
      research tools and methods.   Illustrations, appendices, glos-
      sary.

PART III: TELEVISION

A. REFERENCES

1. Bibliographies

527. Cassata, Mary, and Thomas Skill. <u>Television: A Guide to the
Literature</u>. Phoenix, AZ: Oryx Press, 1985. 148p.
    Ten bibliographic essays, organized in three parts. Part
one covers the mass communication process, the historical development of television, and reference sources; part two, research, with special attention to children, news, and politics;
and part three, the TV industry, criticism, anthologies, and
annual reviews. Each essay concludes with a bibliography.
Indexed by author, title, and subject.

528. Hill, George H., and Sylvia Saverson Hill. <u>Blacks on Television: A Selectively Annotated Bibliography</u>. Metuchen, NJ:
Scarecrow Press, 1985. 223p.
    Total of 2,834 listings tracing black involvement in television
from 1939 through the 1983-84 season. Seventy-eight books
(32 with annotations), 26 dissertations and theses (20 with annotations), and 52 journal articles and 2,678 newspaper and
magazine articles without annotations. The newspaper and
magazine section is organized by subject matter. Appendices,
program index, subject/author index.

529. Müller, Werner, and Manfred Meyer (comps.). <u>Children and
Families Watching Television: A Bibliography of Research on
Viewing Processes</u>. New York: K. G. Saur, 1985. 159p.
    Lists 454 references published between 1975 and 1985, with
the focus on empirical studies covering children from two to
12. Organized in four parts: bibliographies and introductory
literature, reception processes, viewing situation, and media
education. Author index, subject index.

530. Schreibman, Fay C. (comp.), and Peter J. Bukalski (ed.).
<u>Broadcast Television: A Research Guide</u>. Frederick, MD:
University Publications of America, 1983. 62p.
    Sources of information on broadcast television in the United

States. Part one lists books and yearbooks, many with annotations; part two covers periodicals, news transcripts and
scripts, and catalogues; and part three, institutional sources,
including archives and private collections. Author index,
title index.

531. Signorielli, Nancy (comp. and ed.). Role Portrayal and Stereotyping on Television: An Annotated Bibliography of Studies
Relating to Women, Minorities, Aging, Sexual Behavior, Health
and Handicaps. Westport, CT: Greenwood Press, 1985. 214p.
Total of 423 listings, chiefly articles published in scholarly
journals and in books. Each annotation consists of a biblio-
graphic citation, a description of the sample used in the research if described and/or appropriate, and an abstract of the
results. Author index, subject index.

532. Smith, Myron J., Jr. (comp.). U.S. Television Network News:
A Guide to Sources in English. Jefferson, NC: McFarland,
1984. 233p.
Total of 3,215 entries from books, monographs, scholarly
papers, periodical and journal articles, government documents,
doctoral dissertations, and theses. Brief annotations for book
titles and certain periodical articles. Organized in topical
sections, each with an introduction: (1) reference works;
(2) television network news: general works, histories, audiences; (3) the television networks: news reporting and programming; (4) documentary and public affairs programming;
(5) network television news in controversy; (6) network television news and domestic affairs; (7) network television news
and United States presidents; (8) network television news and
presidential elections; (9) television network news and the
foreign affairs/defense communities; (10) bibliography. Author
index, subject index.

2. Dictionaries

533. Ensign, Lynne Naylor, and Robyn Eileen Knapton. The Complete Dictionary of Television and Film. New York: Stein and
Day, 1985. 256p.
Most common definitions of words, including slang, and
subordinate meanings in widespread use, from "A and B rolls"
to "zoom shot."

534. Oakey, Virginia. Dictionary of Film and Television Terms.
New York: Barnes and Noble Books, 1983. 206p.
About 3,000 technical, informal, artistic, and business terms,
with examples and cross-references.

3. Directories and Guides

535. Bensinger, Charles. The Video Guide. 3rd ed. Santa Fe,
NM: Video-Info Publications, 1982. 254p.
Survey of major manufacturers' large- and small-format
studio and portable video systems. Cameras, recorders, moni-
tors, and projectors. Purchasing, set-up and operational procedures, and production and editing tips. Illustrations, glossary, appendices, index.

536. Burger, Richard L. The Producers: A Descriptive Directory
of Film and Television Producers in the Los Angeles Area.
4th ed. Venice, CA: Burger Publications, 1985. 128p.
Producers of different types of content, including made-
for-television movies, feature films, series, commercials, specials, informational shorts, cable and pay TV films, and music
videos. Names, addresses, and brief descriptions of companies,
names of key personnel, types of productions undertaken, and
titles of recent works. Index.

537. Doney, Ruane L. Guide to Innovative Children's Programs for
Television. Washington, DC: National Association of Broadcasters, 1984. 35p.
Title and description of children's programs being aired at
some NAB member stations. Regularly scheduled and locally
produced, locally produced special programs, and syndicated
programs in a series. Also, children's TV PSA sharing bank,
telethons to benefit children, and successful community outreach
projects. Illustrations, appendix.

538. Franks, Don (comp.). Tony, Grammy, Emmy, Country: A
Broadway, Television and Records Awards Reference. Jeffer-
son, NC: McFarland, 1986. 202p.
Origins and short descriptions of the awards and lists of
recipients from their beginnings through 1984, except for 1983
Emmy. Index.

539. International Television Almanac. New York: Quigley, annual.
Broadcast television statistics, capsule biographies, feature
film credits and running time, and services, networks, set
manufacturers, major producers, and major group station owners. Producers-distributors of programs, commercials, feature
films, and shorts. TV channel allocations by market, with call
letters, network affiliation, and personnel, advertising agencies,
station representatives, network prime-time shows, new syndicated shows, state and national organizations, and trade publications. Cable television statistics, system operators, and program suppliers. The TV industry in Great Britain and Ireland,
and a survey of the world market. Tables.

540. Kids' Stuff: A Resource Book for Children's Television

Programming. Washington, DC: National Association of
Broadcasters, 1983.
     Legal aspects of children's television, examples of program-
ming efforts promoting reading and/or writing, the PSA sharing
bank, and community outreach projects. Details of children's
television awards, media interest groups, and syndicated program availabilities. Illustrations.

541.   Parish, James Robert, and Vincent Terrace. Actors' Televi-
       sion Credits. Supplement II: 1977-1981. Metuchen, NJ:
       Scarecrow Press, 1982. 327p.
            Alphabetical listing of performers, with details of program(s),
       type, date, and network. Also contains additions and correc-
       tions to the base volume (1973) and Supplement I (1978).

542.   Passingham, Kenneth. The Guinness Book of TV Facts and
       Feats. Enfield, Eng.: Guinness Superlatives, 1984. 298p.
            Mostly British anecdotes, statistics, "firsts," records, oddi-
       ties, achievements, and other trivia. Illustrations, index.

543.   Paterson, Richard (ed.). International TV and Video Guide.
       New York: New York Zoetrope, annual.
            Country-by-country review of entertainment from Argentina
       to Zimbabwe, articles, and television and video schools, ar-
       chives, and sources. Index.

544.   Reed, Robert M. The American Telecommunications Market:
       Commercial/Public TV, Cable, STV, MDS, LPTV, Home Video.
       Syosset, NY: National Video Clearinghouse, 1982. 202p. +
       appendices.
            Profile for non-American professionals. Financial, ownership,
       and regulatory structure, and program services. Illustrations,
       tables, appendices.

545.   Rose, Brian G. Television and the Performing Arts: A Hand-
       book and Reference Guide to American Cultural Programming.
       Westport, CT: Greenwood Press, 1986. 271p.
            Development, innovations, trials, and achievements of Ameri-
       can television and the performing arts of dance, classical mu-
       sic, opera, and theater from the 1930s through the close of
       the 1984-85 TV season. Each chapter includes a videography
       listing the production credits of a dozen or so shows cited for
       their significance and merit. Index.

546.   Rose, Brian G. (ed.). TV Genres: A Handbook and Reference
       Guide. Westport, CT: Greenwood Press, 1985. 453p.
            Essays on 19 TV genres. Eight deal with fictional pro-
       gramming: the police show, detective show, TV western, med-
       ical melodrama, science fiction and fantasy, situation comedy,
       soap opera, and American made-for-television movie, and one
       with the docudrama, a combination of fact and fiction. Six

cover genres that bear some relationship to reality: news,
documentary, sports, the game show, variety, and talk show.
Four treat genres that often include elements of fiction and nonfiction: children's, educational and cultural, and religious programming, and the commercial. Each essay includes sections
on the historical development and principal themes and issues
of the genre and, with the exception of the essay on the commercial, a videography listing examples of programs in the
genre, their network and/or syndication history, and primary
stars. Chapter bibliographies, index.

547. Sackett, Susan, and Cheryl Blythe. You Can Be a Game Show
Contestant and Win. New York: Dell, 1982. 165p.
Guidelines on applying, how to prepare for and act during
the contestant selection process and, if chosen, on the program. Details of 15 game shows: prizes, rules of play, eligibility requirements, application method, preparation, and
strategy. Reference guide to production companies. Illustrations.

548. Slide, Anthony. A Collector's Guide to TV Memorabilia. Lom-
bard, IL: Wallace-Homestead, 1985. 125p.
Hints on items worth collecting, where to find them, and
their current value. Illustrations, index.

549. Steinberg, Cobbett. TV Facts. Rev. ed. New York: Facts
On File Publications, 1985. 478p.
The story of American television from its beginnings to the
mid-1980s told in facts, figures, statistics, charts, and tables.
Programs, viewers, ratings, advertisers, awards, networks,
and stations. Tables, index.

550. Television and Cable Factbook. 2 vols. Washington, DC:
Television Digest, annual.
One volume, subtitled Stations, contains details of all U.S.,
Canadian, and international stations, low power directory,
translator stations, market rankings, CPs and applications,
and group and cross-ownership information. The other, Cable
and Services, includes a directory of cable systems, cable
group ownership, and manufacturers and suppliers of broadcast and cable equipment. Each volume carries a content index and a buyers' guide product index.

551. The Video Register. White Plains, NY: Knowledge Industry
Publications, annual.
Video users, manufacturers of video and audio hardware
and software, dealers renting or selling equipment, non-
broadcast program distributors, cable access and origination
centers, production and post-production facilities, consultants,
and production services and resources. Entries are listed alphabetically and include company name, address, and telephone
number, and a description of services provided. Indices.

552. The Video Source Book. Syosset, NY: National Video Clearing-
      house, annual.
          Title, description, running time, format, and other details
      of programs available on video in the following categories:
      business/industry, children/juvenile, fine arts, general inter-
      est/education, health/science, how-to/instruction, movies/
      entertainment, and sports/recreation. Indices to main category,
      subject category, videodisc, closed caption, and video program
      sources.

553. A Videotex/Teletext Bibliography. Bethesda, MD: Phillips,
      annual.
          Directory of services and information sources. Equipment
      suppliers, online and broadcast services, access networks,
      standards groups, business and technical services, associations
      and educational institutions, communications attorneys, and the
      regulatory environment.

                          4. Encyclopedias

554. Brown, Les. Les Brown's Encyclopedia of Television. New
      York: New York Zoetrope, 1982. 496p.
          Update of The New York Times Encyclopedia of Television
      (1977), with close to 400 new articles and hundreds of re-
      written entries. An A ("AA Rating") to Z ("Vladimir Zwory-
      kin") of people, programs, organizations, events, terminology,
      and the rest of what the author calls the "moveable parts" of
      television. Illustrations, bibliography, appendices.

555. Schemering, Christopher. The Soap Opera Encyclopedia. New
      York: Ballantine Books, 1985. 358p.
          Short history of television soap opera and background in-
      formation on every daytime and prime-time television soap opera
      broadcast on the three major networks and on a selection of
      syndicated, cable, and foreign programs. Profiles of more
      than two dozen stars who have contributed most to the genre.
      Illustrations, appendices, bibliography, index of personalities.

556. Terrace, Vincent. Encyclopedia of Television. Vol. 1: Series,
      Pilots and Specials, 1937-1973. New York: New York Zoetrope,
      1986. 480p.
          Alphabetical listing of almost 5,000 series, pilots, specials,
      and experimental programs broadcast between November 1937
      and December 1973. Program type, synopsis, cast and creative
      staff, network, program length, number of episodes, and date
      of first and last broadcast. Illustrations.

557. Terrace, Vincent. Encyclopedia of Television. Vol. 2: Series,
      Pilots and Specials, 1974-1984. New York: New York Zoetrope,
      1985. 458p.

Nearly 3,000 series, pilots, and specials broadcast on ABC, CBS, The Disney Channel, The Entertainment Channel, Home Box Office, NBC, Operation Prime Time, PBS, Showtime, and in syndication from January 1, 1974 through December 31, 1984. Each listing includes cast details, story line, credits, number of episodes, running times, and network, syndication, and/or cable information. Illustrations.

5. Indexes

558. Johnson, Catherine E. (ed.). TV Guide Index: 1978-1982 Cumulative Supplement. Radnor, PA: Triangle Publications, 1983. 176p.
    Author and subject index for virtually every article published between January 1978 and December 1982.

559. Naficy, Hamid (comp.). Iran Media Index. Westport, CT: Greenwood Press, 1984. 264p.
    Annotated topical index of nonfiction films, filmstrips, television news stories, and public affairs programs about Iran by major English-speaking countries, with emphasis on the United States. The 3,539 entries cover the period from the late nineteenth century to 1982 and include Iranian-produced films and videotapes distributed or shown in the United States and samples of important films and television programs made by filmmakers of other countries. Title index, index of producers, holders, and distributors.

6. Program Guides

560. Brooks, Tim, and Earle Marsh. The Complete Directory to Prime Time Network TV Shows, 1946-Present. 3rd ed. New York: Ballantine Books, 1985. 1,123p.
    Lists every regular series ever carried on the four commercial networks during prime time, all network series carried in the early evening and late night, and the top syndicated programs of all time that were aired primarily in the evening hours. Each entry includes the date of first and last telecast, days, times, and network on which the series aired, and regular cast members. Current through October 1, 1984. Appendices, index of personalities and performers.

561. Brooks, Tim, and Earle Marsh. TV's Greatest Hits: The 150 Most Popular TV Shows of All Time. New York: Ballantine Books, 1985. 299p.
    Alphabetical listing of top prime-time series aired on ABC, CBS, and NBC from A ("The A-Team") to Y ("Your Show of Shows"). Each entry includes dates on which the series was first and, if appropriate, last seen on a network; days, times,

and networks on which the series was broadcast; regular cast
members; and a description of the series and its principals.
Index.

562. Castleman, Harry, and Walter J. Podrazik. The TV Schedule
Book: Four Decades of Network Programming from Sign-On
to Sign-Off. New York: McGraw-Hill, 1984. 309p.
  Schedule graphs of network programs from 1944 through
1983. Each year is broken into three periods: fall (September
to December), winter (January to May), and summer (June to
August). Background narrative and chronology of events.
Text index, schedule index.

563. Eisner, Joel, and David Krinsky. Television Comedy Series:
An Episode Guide to 153 TV Sitcoms in Syndication. Jefferson, NC: McFarland, 1984. 866p.
  Details of more than 11,000 episodes of prime-time series
broadcast from 1949 to 1980 and still available for syndication.
Each series listing includes title, date of first and last broadcast, format (film or tape), number of episodes, color or black-
and-white, producer, production company and/or syndicator,
cast, writers and directors, and description. Episodes usually
are listed in order of production and carry the title and plot
summary. Illustrations, index.

564. Fischer, Stuart. Kids' TV: The First 25 Years. New York:
Facts on File Publications, 1983. 289p.
  Entries on every children's show aired on network television
from the 1946-47 season through 1972-73. Includes air day and
time, network, debut, credits, and synopsis of each program.
Illustrations, index.

565. Gianakos, Larry James. Television Drama Series Programming:
A Comprehensive Chronicle, 1980-1982. Metuchen, NJ: Scarecrow Press, 1983. 678p.
  Narrative overview of dramatic programming during the period. Days and times of network prime-time programming from
fall 1980 through summer 1982, dramatic series initiated prior
to fall 1980, drama series programming from 1980 to 1982, and
dramatic programming from 1947 to 1980. Appendices, index of
series titles.

566. McNeil, Alex. Total Television: A Comprehensive Guide to
Programming from 1948 to the Present. 2d ed. New York:
Penguin Books, 1984. 1,027p.
  Alphabetical listing and details of more than 3,900 network
and syndicated prime-time and daytime series. Chronological
list of special programs and broadcasts, fall prime-time schedules
for the three major commercial networks, Emmy and Peabody
Award winners, and top-rated series for each season. Series
index, name index.

References   91

567. Maltin, Leonard (ed.). Leonard Maltin's TV Movies, 1985-86.
New York: New American Library, 1984. 1,021p.
Alphabetical listing of more than 16,000 movies and details
of director, stars, date, color or black-and-white, original
length, key songs in musicals, and a capsule summary and review of each.

568. Marill, Alvin H. Movies Made For Television: The Telefeature
and the Mini-Series, 1964-1984. New York: New York Zoetrope, 1984. 453p.
Total of 1,693 entries listed in order of their premiere date.
Each entry is accompanied by complete cast and credit information, plot description, background notes, and pertinent awards
data. Illustrations, index of titles, casts, directors, producers,
and writers.

569. Perry, Jeb H. Universal Television: The Studio and Its Programs, 1950-1980. Metuchen, NJ: Scarecrow Press, 1983.
443p.
Title, description, cast, production credits and other data
on more than 200 series, 250 telefeatures, 20 pilots, and 20
specials. Emmy Award nominees and winners. Illustrations,
appendices, index.

570. Terrace, Vincent. Encyclopedia of Television. Vol. 1: Series,
Pilots and Specials, 1937-1973. New York: New York Zoetrope,
1986. 480p.
See entry 556.

571. Terrace, Vincent. Encyclopedia of Television. Vol. 2: Series,
Pilots and Specials, 1974-1984. New York: New York Zoe-
trope, 1985. 458p.
See entry 557.

572. Woolery, George W. Children's Television: The First Thirty-
Five Years, 1946-1981. Part I: Animated Cartoon Series.
Metuchen, NJ: Scarecrow Press, 1983. 386p.
Profiles of more than 300 series programmed on the commer-
cial networks and public television or syndicated extensively.
Each entry contains series title, network and syndicated his-
tories, production credits, principal characters and voices, and
series summary. Appendices, name index, subject index.

573. Woolery, George W. Children's Television: The First Thirty-
Five Years, 1946-1981. Part II: Live, Film, and Tape Series.
Metuchen, NJ: Scarecrow Press, 1985. 788p.
Alphabetical listing of series for children and young people
broadcast live or from film or tape on the networks and syndicated. Listings include network and syndicated histories, production credits, cast, and series description. Appendices and
name, subject, and series indices.

574. Woolley, Lynn, Robert W. Malsbary, and Robert G. Strange,
      Jr. Warner Bros. Television: Every Show of the Fifties and
      Sixties Episode-by-Episode. Jefferson, NC: McFarland, 1985.
      296p.
          Profiles of 13 series: "Cheyenne," "Sugarfoot," "Bronco,"
      "Maverick," "77 Sunset Strip," "Bourbon Street Beat," "Hawaiian
      Eye," "SurfSide 6," "Colt .45," "Lawmen," "The Gallant Men,"
      "The Alaskans," and "The Roaring 20's." Biographies of their
      stars and season-by-season series index with the title and
      synopsis of each program. Date of series debut, length, net-
      work, series format, cast, executive producer, producer, theme,
      and location. Illustrations, index.

7. Survey

575. Griffin-Beale, Christopher, and Robyn Gee. TV and Video.
      London: Usborne, 1982. 32p.
          Young person's guide to broadcasting and to equipment,
      studios, transmission and reception, recording and editing,
      electronic effects, home video equipment, TV, and computers.
      Illustrations, index.

8. Trivia

576. Andrews, Bart. The Super Official TV Trivia Quiz Book.
      New York: New American Library, 1985.
          Hundreds of questions and answers on people, programs,
      places, and events. Combines the author's The Official TV
      Trivia Quiz Book (1975), The Official TV Trivia Quiz Book
      Number 2 (1976), and The Official TV Trivia Quiz Book Num-
      ber 3 (1978). Illustrations.

577. Editors of Consumer Guide. TV Trivia: Thirty Years of
      Television. New York: Beekman House, 1984. 64p.
          Questions, answers, and photographs from 39 TV shows of
      the previous 30 years. Illustrations.

9. Who's Who

578. Lamparski, Richard. Whatever Became of ...? Tenth series.
      New York: Crown, 1986. 214p.
          Profiles of 100 TV personalities and movie stars, accompanied
      by then-and-now photographs of each. Illustrations.

579. Scheuer, Steven H. (ed.). Who's Who in Television and Cable.
      New York: Facts On File Publications, 1983. 579p.
          Biographies of more than 2,000 individuals in the TV, video,
      and cable industries. The majority of entries are devoted to

leading executives of the three commercial networks, public
television, and the major national cable services. Also includes
hundreds of on-air television journalists, actors and actresses,
and dozens of executives employed by local TV stations in
New York, Washington, and Los Angeles. Illustrations, corporate index, job title index.

B. AUDIENCES

580. Bower, Robert T. The Changing Television Audience in
America. New York: Columbia University Press, 1985. 172p.
     Trends in the composition of the audience from 1960 to 1980
and in audience attitudes toward commercial entertainment programs. The role of TV as a news medium, commercials, and
the medium's influence on children. Illustrations, tables, appendices, index.

581. Frank, Ronald E., and Marshall G. Greenberg. Audiences for
Public Television. Beverly Hills, CA: Sage Publications,
1982. 230p.
     Analysis of leisure interests and needs of a sample of more
than 2,700 Americans aged 13 and over, subdivided into 14
interest-based groups and their use of public television. Concludes that public television can reach more people without
sacrificing its standards. Tables, appendix.

582. Webster, James G. The Impact of Cable and Pay Cable Television on Local Station Audiences. Washington, DC: National
Association of Broadcasters, 1982. 108p.
     Comparison of the size and composition of audiences in
broadcast only, basic cable, and pay cable households, using
Arbitron diary data from 24 markets in February 1982. Among
the conclusions: (1) while almost every commercial station ap-
peared to lose audience shares to cable competition, the magni-
tude of loss differed from station to station; (2) local news
shares were highest in broadcast homes and lowest among pay
cable viewers; (3) prime-time access programs aired by affili-
ates evidenced a loss in audience shares; (4) heads of households and individual viewers in pay cable homes were, on aver-
age, younger than in other household categories. Tables.

C. BUSINESS

583. Bellaire, Arthur. The Bellaire Guide to TV Commercial Cost
Control. Chicago: Crain Books, 1982. 205p.
     Examines the problem of high production costs, the reasons
for them, and step-by-step methods to get the most for your
money. Glossary, index.

584. Canape, Charlene. How to Capitalize on the Video Revolution:
      A Guide to New Business Enterprises. New York: Holt, Rine-
      hart and Winston, 1984. 196p.
         Establishing and operating a video business. Buying equip-
      ment, marketing, advertising and selling, and protecting what
      is produced. Business opportunities in show business, law,
      business, dating services, and the consumer market. Tables,
      index.

585. Graham, Margaret B. W. RCA and the VideoDisc: The Busi-
      ness of Research. New York: Cambridge University Press,
      1986. 258p.
         Problems of managing research and development in a cor-
      porate setting as exemplified by the development and subse-
      quent withdrawal from the marketplace of RCA's Selectavision
      VideoDisc system. Illustrations, appendix, index.

586. Howard, Herbert H. Group and Cross-Media Ownership of
      Television Stations. Washington, DC: National Association of
      Broadcasters, annual.
         Statistical profile of TV station ownership, ownership de-
      velopments, and historical background.

587. Nadel, Mark, and Eli Noam (eds.). The Economics of Tradi-
      tional Broadcasting (VHF/UHF): An Anthology. New York:
      Graduate School of Business, Columbia University, 1983. 158p.
         Technical and cost comparisons of VHF and UHF, compara-
      tive profitability, station sales prices, growth projections, pro-
      gramming costs, and audience shares. Illustrations, tables.

588. Noam, Eli M. (ed.). Video Media Competition: Regulation,
      Economics, and Technology. New York: Columbia University
      Press, 1985. 468p.
         Empirical studies of various aspects of media rivalry in the
      United States, regulatory issues of media diversity, develop-
      ments in other industrialized countries, and the impact of the
      new technologies in the Third World. Illustrations, tables.

589. Television Employee Compensation and Fringe Benefits Report.
      Washington, DC: National Association of Broadcasters, biennial.
         Profiles for all stations, and for affiliated and independent
      stations by ADI rank. Tables.

590. Television Financial Report. Washington, DC: National Asso-
      ciation of Broadcasters, annual.
         Summary of responses of television stations to a question-
      naire requesting revenue sources, department expenses, and
      specific line items. Data organized by market rank and revenue
      size for all stations, affiliate stations, independent stations,
      UHF stations, UHF affiliate stations, UHF independent stations,
      and VHF independent stations.

591. Television Market Analysis. Washington, DC: National Association of Broadcasters, annual.
Five-year trend report of aggregate revenues, expenses, and profits. Data for more than 100 television markets with three or more stations. Tables, appendices.

D. CAREERS

592. Berlyn, David W. Exploring Careers in Cable/TV. New York: Rosen, 1985. 127p.
Career preparation and opportunities in programming, journalism, station management, engineering, sales, and promotion. Chapters on cable and public broadcasting. Illustrations, bibliography.

593. Careers in Television. Washington, DC: National Association of Broadcasters, 1986. 32p.
Division of activity in a television station, the personnel, their duties and qualifications. Illustrations.

594. Cohen, Daniel, and Susan Cohen. How to Get Started in Video. New York: Franklin Watts, 1986. 112p.
Prospects and career opportunities in stations and cable systems or as an independent, and suggested preparations. Illustrations, index.

595. Hollingsworth, T. R. Tune In To a Television Career. New York: Julian Messner, 1984. 160p.
Young person's guide, with details of opportunities and responsibilities in production, news, performing, studio work, administration, promotion, and engineering. Illustrations, glossary, index.

596. Keller, Barbara Berger. Film, Tape and TV: Where Do I Fit In? Great Neck, NY: Keller International, 1985. 124p.
Questions to ask in planning a career: required skills, where to obtain them, and how to employ them. More than 40 job descriptions and duties, résumé preparation, and details of organizations and associations that can provide information.

597. Kurtis, Bill. Bill Kurtis on Assignment. Chicago: Rand McNally, 1983. 192p.
The life of a foreign correspondent, described in words and pictures by the former co-anchor of "The CBS Morning News." Insider's look at the making of investigative reports on the effects of the defoliant Agent Orange and the plight of Amerasian children in Vietnam. Illustrations.

598. Reed, Maxine K., and Robert M. Reed. Career Opportunities

in Television, Cable, and Video.   2d ed.   New York: Facts
on File Publications, 1986.   266p.
　　Description of 100 jobs.   Seventy are in broadcast television
and cover management and administration, programming, production, news, engineering, advertising sales, advertising agency,
and performance arts and crafts.   The remainder are in non-
broadcast TV, including cable, subscription TV, multichannel
multipoint distribution service, consumer electronics and home
video, and media centers in education, private industry, government, and health.   Each description consists of a career profile and ladder, details of position duties, salary range, employment and advancement prospects, educational and experience/
skill qualifications, opportunities for minorities and women, and
union or association membership requirements.   Appendices,
bibliography, index.

599.   Whitley, Dianna, and Ray Manzella.   Soap Stars: America's
　　31 Favorite Daytime Actors Speak for Themselves.   Garden City,
　　NY: Doubleday/Dolphin, 1985.   187p.
　　　　The lives, careers, and dreams of selected stars of daytime
　　serials.   Illustrations.

E.   COMMENTARY AND CRITICISM

600.   Bennett, Tony (ed.).   Popular Television and Film: A Reader.
　　London: British Film Institute and The Open University, 1982.
　　353p.
　　　　Twenty-five essays on genre, the discourses of television,
　　popular film, and pleasure, history/politics, and narrative.

601.   Brown, Les, and Savannah Waring Walker (eds.).   Fast For-
　　ward: The New Television and American Society.   Kansas City,
　　KS: Andrews and McMeel, 1983.   213p.
　　　　Twenty-five essays from 1981 and 1982 issues of Channels
　　of Communications magazine.   Includes reflections on cable, in-
　　teractive television, the networks, the new enemies of jour-
　　nalism, the language of television, ratings, satellite dishes, the
　　New Right, Archie Bunker, soap operas, and private eyes.

602.   Conrad, Peter.   Television: The Medium and Its Manners.
　　Boston, MA: Routledge and Kegan Paul, 1982.   170p.
　　　　Critical analysis of the technology and content of television,
　　with examples from the United States and the United Kingdom.
　　Argues that TV has taken over the house, that the presence
　　of the television camera alters reality, and that its form deter-
　　mines its content.

603.   D'Agostino, Peter (ed.).   Transmission.   New York: Tanam
　　Press, 1985.   326p.

Source book of new television theory and practice, encompassing television aesthetics, social commentary, and applications of new technologies. Illustrations, videography, bibliography, index.

604. Eliot, Marc. <u>Televisions: One Season in American Television</u>.
New York: St. Martin's Press, 1983. 179p.
Reflections on the 1981-82 season. The rise of Jerry Falwell's Moral Majority, strikes that threatened to bring the entire entertainment industry to a halt, and the explosion of cable. Also, network programs and their ratings, changes in network news, independent production, and assorted other items.

605. Ellis, John. <u>Visible Fictions: Cinema, Television, Video</u>.
London: Routledge and Kegan Paul, 1982. 295p.
Argues that cinema and broadcast television are not interchangeable media in direct competition with each other. Examines differences in their social roles, forms of institutional organization, and general aesthetic procedures, and speculates about both media in the video age. Illustrations, bibliography.

606. Esslin, Martin. <u>The Age of Television</u>. San Francisco: W. H.
Freeman, 1982. 138p.
Analysis of the nature, impact, and long-term consequences of American television, by the retired head of the BBC's radio drama department. Illustrations, index.

607. Himmelstein, Hal. <u>Television Myth and the American Mind</u>.
New York: Praeger, 1984. 337p.
Critical analysis of a variety of TV content, using myth analysis to identify the constructed meanings television produces for its viewers. Among the content examined is advertising, social comedies, melodrama, news and documentary, sport, religion, and the talk show. Illustrations, index.

608. Kaminsky, Stuart M., with Jeffrey H. Mahan. <u>American Television Genres</u>. Chicago: Nelson-Hall, 1985. 220p.
Historical and structural, psychological, and sociological and anthropological approaches to the study of television content, and their application to entertainment and information genres. Illustrations, appendix, bibliography, index.

609. Kaplan, E. Ann (ed.). <u>Regarding Television: Critical Approaches--An Anthology</u>. Frederick, MD: University Publications of America, 1983. 147p.
Eleven essays on, among other topics, writing, news, sport, soap opera, commercials, made-for-television movies, and video art. Bibliography.

610. Marc, David. <u>Demographic Vistas: Television in American</u>

Culture. Philadelphia, PA: University of Pennsylvania Press,
1984. 214p.
Critical analysis using adaptations of the tools of theatrical
and literary criticism. Focus on comedy through study of a
comic auteur (Paul Henning, creator of "Beverly Hillbillies"),
genre (the crime show and late-night satirical reviews), and
personality (Jackie Gleason). Bibliography, glossary, main
index, index of TV series, index of films made for theatrical
release.

611. Newcomb, Horace (ed.). Television: The Critical View. 3rd
      ed. New York: Oxford University Press, 1982. 549p.
      Thirty analytical essays, 15 of them new to this edition, on
      programs, advertising, and the relation of television to society.
      Tables.

612. O'Connor, John E. (ed.). American History/American Tele-
      vision: Interpreting the Video Past. New York: Frederick
      Ungar, 1983. 420p.
      Fourteen original essays examining the long-range historical
      meanings of television and covering programs, series, genres,
      news, and personalities. Tables, bibliography, index.

613. Postman, Neil. Amusing Ourselves to Death: Public Discourse
      in the Age of Show Business. New York: Viking/Penguin,
      1985. 184p.
      Reflections on what the author sees as the decline of the
      Age of Typography and the ascendancy of the Age of Televi-
      sion. Argues that substance and logic have been replaced by
      the gestures, images, and formats of television as the basis for
      decision-making and policies. Bibliography, index.

614. Rowland, Willard D., Jr., and Bruce Watkins (eds.). Inter-
      preting Television: Current Research Perspectives. Beverly
      Hills, CA: Sage Publications, 1984. 293p.
      Eleven essays covering theoretical models for examining
      the meanings in television and examples of ways in which sev-
      eral of them may be applied. Illustrations, table.

615. Shales, Tom. On the Air! New York: Summit Books, 1982.
      299p.
      Selected columns on the television medium, its programs,
      and personalities, by the nationally syndicated columnist and
      chief television critic of The Washington Post.

616. Williams, Martin. TV: The Casual Art. New York: Oxford
      University Press, 1982. 161p.
      Essays, many previously published in newspapers and maga-
      zines, on the television medium, its programs, and personal-
      ities.

F. COMPARATIVE, FOREIGN, AND INTERNATIONAL

1. Comparative

617. Aldershoff-Gaemers, Lidy. New Media Developments: Satellite TV. Hilversum, Netherlands: Intomart, 1984. 152p.
Growth of satellites and their use in the U.S., Canada, Japan, and Europe. Launchers, prospects for high-definition television, receiving equipment, comparative European and U.S. costs, and anticipated consumer reactions. Illustrations, tables.

618. Buckman, Peter. All For Love: A Study in Soap Opera. Salem, NH: Salem House, 1985. 226p.
The soap opera phenomenon in the United States and Britain. Characters, plots, writers, players, directors and producers, critics, and the public. Bibliography, index.

619. The DBS Summit Conference. Washington, DC: Television Digest, 1983. 102p.
Transcript of a 1983 conference on technical, business, and policy issues posed by DBS in the United States and Europe.

620. Gould, Peter, Jeffrey Johnson, and Graham Chapman. The Structure of Television. London: Pion, 1984.
Two books in one. One, subtitled Television: The World of Structure (177 pages) treats in a non-technical way the problems of monitoring international television and examines classification, description, values, meaning, and culture in international television. It includes also a chapter on the structure of television in Sweden, Britain, the United States, Japan, and Jamaica. The other, subtitled Structure: The World of Television (135 pages), deals with the methodological and technical story and examines a mathematical "language" for describing structures, traditional classification, the algebra and structure of television programs, and graphic representation and computer processing. Television: The World of Structure contains illustrations, tables, appendices, and index. Structure: The World of Television contains illustrations, tables, and index.

621. Hilliard, Robert L. (ed.). Television and Adult Education. Cambridge, MA: Schenkman Books, 1985. 215p.
Papers from a 1983 seminar attended by U.S. and West German theorists and practitioners. Topics are target audiences, problems and cooperation, sources of materials and approaches to presentation, methods of distribution, research, and international exchange. The final chapter consists of recommendations on each topic. Illustrations, tables.

622. Huesmann, L. Rowell, and Leonard D. Eron (eds.). Television and the Aggressive Child: A Cross National Comparison. Hillsdale, NJ: Lawrence Erlbaum Associates, 1986. 326p. Studies from five nations on the relationship of television viewing and aggression in children. Bibliographies.

623. Information Systems Report. Washington, DC: American Newspaper Publishers Association, 1983. 72p. Operational or completed teletext and videotex services in the United States, Finland, France, Germany, Japan, the Netherlands, Sweden, the United Kingdom, and Venezuela. Each entry describes the service and lists its name and sponsor. Glossary, index.

624. McLean, Mick (ed.). The Information Explosion: The New Electronic Media in Japan and Europe. Westport, CT: Greenwood Press, 1985. 130p. Viewpoints on technological, economic, and social aspects by analysts and decision-makers from Europe and Japan. Includes viewdata, videotex, and satellite broadcasting. Illustrations, tables, index.

625. McQuail, Denis, and Karen Siune (eds.). New Media Politics: Comparative Perspectives in Western Europe. Beverly Hills, CA: Sage Publications, 1986. 216p. Dynamics of policy-making and development of policies for public uses of new electronic communications media, including cable, satellites, and home video. Illustrations, tables, index.

626. Paterson, Richard (ed.). International TV and Video Guide. New York: New York Zoetrope, annual. See entry 543.

627. Sigel, Efrem. The Future of Videotext: Worldwide Prospects for Home/Office Electronic Information Services. White Plains, NY: Knowledge Industry Publications, 1983. 197p. Videotext technology and its implications for consumers and business. The emergence, operations, and services of videotext in the United States, Canada, and France, and of videotext and teletext in the United Kingdom. Summary of videotext developments in a dozen other countries. Illustrations, tables, appendix, bibliography, index.

628. Syfret, Toby. Television Today and Television Tomorrow: A Guide to New Electronic Media and Trends in Commercial Television in Western Europe. London: J. Walter Thompson, 1983. 95p. Report of responses of media managers of 16 European offices of the J. Walter Thompson Company to a questionnaire about the new electronic media. Summary of domestic TV broadcasting services in each country, viewer satisfaction with

programming, receptivity of viewers to foreign programming,
and the potential for extra advertising expenditure. Penetration of video, videotext, and satellite, and country-by-country
prospects for commercial television. Tables.

629. Veith, Richard H. Television's Teletext. New York: North-
Holland, 1983. 180p.
Broadcast and cable systems and services in the United
States; formats and standards; teletext in Western Europe,
Canada, and Japan; videotex; predicted roles for teletext in
American society. Illustrations, tables, appendices, bibliogra-
phy, index.

2. Foreign

(a) Australia

630. Barr, Trevor. The Electronic Estate: New Communications
Media and Australia. Ringwood, Victoria: Penguin Books,
1985. 271p.
Social impact of the new technologies, including domestic
satellites, videotex, and cable. Illustration, tables, bibliography, index.

631. Burke, Jacinta, Susanna Agardy, Maria Fricker, and Jim
Biles. Children, Television and Food. Melbourne: Australian
Broadcasting Tribunal, 1982. 111p.
The relationships between children's television viewing and
their eating behavior and attitudes to food, based on a study
of almost 1,000 third-grade children from the Sydney metro-
politan area. Tables, appendices.

632. Moran, Albert. Making a TV Series: The "Bellamy" Project.
Woollahra, New South Wales: Currency Press, 1982. 175p.
Case study of the production of the police drama series
"Bellamy" in Sydney in 1980-81. Emphasis on the production
process. Illustrations, episode credits, synopsis and cast,
glossary, index.

633. Palmer, Patricia. The Lively Audience: A Study of Children
Around the TV Set. Sydney: Allen and Unwin, 1986. 166p.
Study of the role of television in the lives of Australian
children, and the nature of their relationship with it. Concludes that children define "television" in terms of those programs they enjoy most, that it is an important part of most
children's lives, and that, while watching, they are not usually
still and silent for long. Finds that, with friends, children do
most of their talk and acting out from TV and that children as
young as eight know the programs they like best and make de-
liberate choices. Illustrations, tables, appendices, bibliography,
index.

634. Press and Television Interests in Australian Commercial Radio.
      Sydney: Federation of Australian Radio Broadcasters, 1982.
      21p.
      See entry 446.

635. Stewart, Donald E. The Television Family: A Content Analysis
      of the Portrayal of Family Life in Prime Time Television. Mel-
      bourne: Institute of Family Studies, 1983. 66p.
      Study of overall content and values in programs broadcast
      in Melbourne in one week of September 1982. Concludes that
      programs ignore reality and give a distorted picture of mar-
      riage, the family, sex roles, work, youth, the aged, and
      ethnic groups. Illustrations, tables, appendices.

                          (b) Brazil

636. Mattos, Sérgio. The Impact of the 1964 Revolution on Brazilian
      Television. San Antonio: V. Klingensmith, 1982. 129p.
      Evolution of television in Brazil and its use by the military
      regime to promote a new social and developmental order.
      Tables, bibliography.

                          (c) Canada

637. Cultures in Collision: The Interaction of Canadian and U.S.
      Television Broadcast Policies. A Canadian-U.S. Conference on
      Communications Policies. New York: Praeger, 1984. 210p.
      Presentations from a 1983 conference addressing four princi-
      pal areas: a historical comparison of Canadian and American
      approaches to broadcast policy, sovereignty and television,
      the impact of new technologies on Canadian-U.S. broadcasting
      relationships, and the border-broadcasting dispute. Table,
      appendix.

638. Lyman, Peter. Canada's Video Revolution: Pay-TV, Home
      Video and Beyond. Toronto: James Lorimer, 1983. 173p.
      Impact of the new technologies on the evolution of Canada's
      traditional cultural media, and proposals for greater Canadian
      participation in domestic and international cultural markets.
      Illustrations, tables.

639. Murray, Catherine A. Managing Diversity: Federal-Provincial
      Collaboration and the Committee on Extension of Services to
      Northern and Remote Communities. Kingston, Ontario: Institute
      of Intergovernmental Relations, Queen's University, 1983.
      179p.
      Assessment of the experiment in federal-provincial collabora-
      tion on cultural and industrial issues raised by satellite TV in
      Canada. Exploration of prerequisites for an effective framework
      for intergovernmental collaboration on broadcasting policy and
      regulation. Appendices.

640. Tourigny, Patrick. Community Television Handbook for North-
     ern and Underserved Communities. Ottawa: Canadian Radio-
     Television and Telecommunications Commission, 1983. 35p.
     Reference tool for groups and individuals licensed to pro-
     vide new broadcasting services. Describes the rationale, goals,
     and methods of community programming, licensee and community
     responsibilities, and costs and operation of equipment. Text
     in English and French. Illustrations, appendices.

641. Williams, Tannis Macbeth. The Impact of Television: A Natu-
     ral Experiment in Three Communities. Orlando, FL: Academic
     Press, 1986. 446p.
     Study of three Canadian communities on two occasions: just
     before one of them obtained television for the first time and
     again two years later. The goal was to understand the pro-
     cesses involved in television's influence and the complexities
     of the relationships between TV and human behavior. Examines
     readings skills, cognitive development, leisure activities, use
     of other media, sex-role attitudes, children's aggressive be-
     havior, and adults' thinking, personality, and attitudes. Il-
     lustrations, tables, author index, subject index.

642. Woodrow, R. Brian, and Kenneth B. Woodside (eds.). The
     Introduction of Pay-TV in Canada: Issues and Implications.
     Montreal: Institute for Research on Public Policy, 1982. 240p.
     Essays on the history of discussions on pay television,
     technological possibilities, regulatory issues, and economic as-
     pects and their effects on the Canadian communications in-
     dustry. Commentary on the 1982 Canadian Radio-television
     and Telecommunications Commission decision on the licensing of
     pay-TV services. Illustrations, table, glossary.

(d) Europe

643. Blumler, Jay G. (ed.). Communicating to Voters: Television
     in the First European Parliamentary Elections. Beverly Hills,
     CA: Sage Publications, 1983. 389p.
     Television network activities and their role in fashioning
     the climate of the 1979 Direct Election to the European Parlia-
     ment campaign. Illustrations, tables, index.

644. Glenn, Robin Day. Legal Issues Affecting Licensing of TV
     Programs in the European Economic Community from the Per-
     spective of the U.S. Exporter. Washington, DC: International
     Law Institute, Georgetown University Law Center, 1983. 49p.
     The changing legal and economic climate for access by Ameri-
     can television program exporters, and video copyright questions
     within the framework of international treaties and domestic le-
     gal regimes. Comparison of three methods of collecting and
     distributing copyright royalties and ways in which they are
     applied in Europe.

645. Johnson-Smaragdi, Ulla. TV Use and Social Interaction in
      Adolescence: A Longitudinal Study. Stockholm, Sweden:
      Almqvist and Wiksell, 1983. 239p.
          Exploration and analysis of the use of television and other
      media, and social correlates of adolescent TV consumption in
      Sweden. Among the conclusions: television viewing seems to
      enhance family and peer activities, and, through their own view-
      ing habits, parents strongly influence the amount of their
      children's viewing. Illustrations, tables, appendix.

646. Pragnell, Anthony. Television in Europe: Quality and Values
      in a Time of Change. Manchester, Eng.: European Institute
      for the Media, 1985. 125p.
          The status of European television, its reliance on American
      programming, and the need for more local programs.

647. Ward, Scott, Tom Robertson, and Ray Brown (eds.). Commer-
      cial Television and European Children: An International Re-
      search Digest. Aldershot, Eng.: Gower, 1986. 243p.
          Papers presented at a 1984 conference in Provence, France,
      on television advertising and children from four perspectives:
      age-related differences in children's reactions to TV adver-
      tising, micro-processes of children's response to advertising,
      parent-child relationships in reference to TV advertising, and
      consumer socialization and TV advertising. Illustrations,
      tables.

(e) Ireland

648. McLoone, Martin, and John MacMahon (eds.). Television and
      Irish Society: 21 Years of Irish Television. Dublin: Radio
      Telefís Éireann, 1984. 151p.
          Essays on current affairs, drama, form and content, ideol-
      ogy, and the representation of women, family and community,
      and the urban working class. Challenges to public service
      broadcasting, and the strengths and weaknesses of Irish tele-
      vision. Illustrations, appendices.

(f) Singapore

649. Heidt, Erhard U. Television in Singapore: An Analysis of
      a Week's Viewing. Pasir Panjang, Singapore: Institute of
      Southeast Asian Studies, 1984. 71p.
          Content analysis of a representative week of programming
      on the two channels of the only television station in Singapore,
      the Singapore Broadcasting Corporation. Programs, language
      used, imported and SBC productions, serialization, and con-
      cluding observations. Tables, appendices, bibliography.

(g) United Kingdom

650. Aldrich, Michael. Videotex: Key to the Wired City. London:

Quiller Press, 1982. 115p.
Potential, implications, and issues created by videotex in
Britain. Illustrations, glossary, bibliography.

651. Alvarado, Manuel, and John Stewart. Made for Television:
Euston Films Limited. London: British Film Institute, 1985.
228p.
How Euston was formed, its production methods, and critical assessments of its series, many of them among the most
popular on British television. Illustrations, appendices.

652. Anwar, Muhammad, and Anthony Shang. Television in a Multi-
racial Society: A Research Report. London: Commission for
Racial Equality, 1982. 84p.
The portrayal of ethnic minorities in dramas, light enter-
tainment, documentaries, and current affairs programs in the
United Kingdom.

653. Barker, Martin (ed.). The Video Nasties: Freedom and Censorship in the Media. London: Pluto Press, 1984. 131p.
Responses to the campaign for the classification of videos in
Britain and to the assumption and contents of the Video Recordings Bill establishing a classification system. Illustration,
table, index.

654. Blanchard, Simon, and David Morley (eds.). What's This Channel Fo(u)r? An Alternative Report. London: Comedia, 1982.
186p.
Origins and working of Britain's two newest commercial TV
networks, Channel Four, serving England, Scotland, and
Northern Ireland, and Sianel 4 Cymru (S4C), serving Wales.
Discussion of their responsibility to provide a distinctive and
high quality service, analysis of arguments on the kind of programming they will provide, predictions for their success, and
methods by which viewers can influence their content. Illustrations, appendices.

655. Buckman, Peter. All For Love: A Study in Soap Opera. Salem, NH: Salem House, 1985. 226p.
See entry 618.

656. Conrad, Peter. Television: The Medium and Its Manners.
Boston, MA: Routledge and Kegan Paul, 1982. 170p.
See entry 602.

657. Cox, Geoffrey. See It Happen: The Making of ITN. London:
Bodley Head, 1983. 248p.
The story of Britain's Independent Television News organiza-
tion by one of its former editors. Illustrations, index.

658. Cullingford, Cedric. Children and Television. New York:

St. Martin's Press, 1984. 239p.
   What children see and what they expect, learn, and take
from television. Based on written material and responses to
questions posed to more than 5,000 children, most in Britain
and some in North America. Appendix, bibliography, index.

659. Dunkley, Christopher. Television Today and Tomorrow: Wall-
      to-Wall Dallas? Harmondsworth, Eng.: Penguin Books, 1985.
      159p.
         Technical and socio-political aspects of television in the
      United Kingdom and ways in which the British are grappling
      with them.

660. Glasgow University Media Group. Really Bad News. New York:
      Writers and Readers, 1982. 170p.
         Examination of the representation of politics on television
      and of the historical and social factors that shape television's
      view of the world. Illustrations.

661. Gunter, Barrie, Michael Svennerig, and Mallory Wober. Tele-
      vision Coverage of the 1983 General Election: Audiences, Ap-
      preciation and Public Opinion. Aldershot, Eng.: Gower, 1986.
      136p.
         Report of a study to investigate public attention and re-
      sponses to the coverage of the British election. Tables.

662. Harrison, Martin. Television News: Whose Bias? A Casebook
      Analysis of Strikes, Television and Media Studies. Hermitage,
      Eng.: Policy Journals, 1985. 400p.
         Examines the transcripts of television news coverage of the
      miners' strike of the mid-1970s and of other industrial disputes.
      Questions the accuracy of earlier analyses.

663. Hartley, John. Understanding News. London: Methuen,
      1982. 203p.
         Criteria for developing a critical understanding of news dis-
      course, based on a British study of how television and news-
      paper news works, the interests it serves, and an analysis of
      its meanings. Illustrations, tables, index.

664. Hetherington, Alastair. News, Newspapers and Television.
      London: Macmillan, 1985. 329p.
         Priorities, processes, and product of British television
      and newspapers, including chapters on coverage by the two
      media of the 1984-85 dispute between the National Union of
      Mineworkers and the National Coal Board. Illustrations, tables,
      appendices, glossary, bibliography, index.

665. Hobson, Dorothy. "Crossroads": The Drama of a Soap Opera.
      London: Methuen, 1982. 176p.
         Production, players, and audience response to the popular

British serial and the furor created by the decision to fire its
lead character. Illustration, index.

666. Hollins, Timothy. Beyond Broadcasting: Into the Cable Age.
London: British Film Institute, 1984. 385p.
The cable debate in the United Kingdom in the context of
experience and developments in Canada and the United States.
Technology, history, politics, practical implications, and plans
and prospects for cable in Britain, and chapters on cable in
Canada and the United States. Illustrations, tables, appendices,
index.

667. Hood, Stuart. On Television. 2d ed. London: Pluto Press,
1983. 134p.
Institutions, operation, and role of television in the United
Kingdom. New chapters on television coverage of the Falklands
war and on the expansion of information technology. Suggestions
for further reading.

668. Hooper, Richard. Prestel, Escher, Bach: Changes Within
Changes. Cambridge, MA: Program on Information Resources
Policy, Harvard University, 1984. 13p.
Attempts to improve sales performance by Prestel, British
Telecom's videotex service. Emphasis on the change from a
common carrier policy to a range of vertically integrated ser-
vices for targeted market sectors.

669. Hughes, Patrick, Gary Wersky, Neil McCartney, and John Ainsley. Hunt on Cable TV: Chaos or Coherence? London:
Campaign for Press and Broadcasting Freedom, 1982. 76p.
Critical appraisal of the Hunt Report on cable television
in the United Kingdom and recommendations for the intervention of the labor movement to replace bureaucratic "regulation"
with mass-based representation. Glossary.

670. Inside BBC Television: A Year Behind the Camera. Exeter,
Eng.: Webb and Bower, 1983. 224p.
Behind-the-scenes account of a variety of BBC Television
productions in the course of one year, accompanied by color
photographs. Illustrations, glossary.

671. Lambert, Stephen. Channel Four: Television with a Difference?
London: British Film Institute, 1982. 178p.
Descriptive account of developments leading to the establishment of Britain's fourth national television service. Illustration, appendices, index.

672. Leapman, Michael. Treachery? The Power Struggle at TV-am.
London: George Allen and Unwin, 1984. 211p.
The ambitions, broken ideals, and betrayed hopes of the
television professionals granted the license for Britain's commercial television breakfast-time service. Illustrations, index.

673. Look, Hugh Evison (ed.). Electronic Publishing: A Snapshot
      of the Early 1980s. Oxford, Eng.: Learned Information, 1983.
      200p.
          Historical developments and ingredients of information re-
      trieval. Online and videotex industries, telecommunications,
      present and emerging technologies, and directions for the fu-
      ture. Profile of Data-Star, The Source, and Reuters. Illus-
      tration, glossary.

674. Lusted, David, and Phillip Drummond (eds.). TV and School-
      ing. London: British Film Institute, 1985. 124p.
          Essays by critics, academics, teachers, and broadcasters
      on television and its role in relation to the education system.
      Treats several themes raised in a 1983 British government re-
      port titled Popular Television and Schoolchildren, including
      television's representation of adult life, the cultural skills of
      "reading" television, and the meaning of television for differ-
      ent social groups. Illustrations, tables, appendices, index.

675. Masterman, Len (ed.). Television Mythologies: Stars, Shows,
      and Signs. London: Comedia/MK Media Press, 1984. 143p.
          Essays attempting to unearth some of the myths perpetuated
      by British television during the summer of 1984. Illustrations.

676. Millington, Bob, and Robin Nelson. Boys from the Blackstuff:
      Making a TV Drama. London: Comedia, 1986. 192p.
          Process by which an idea in the mind of a writer ultimately
      became an acclaimed series on BBC-2. Theory on the nature
      of television, ways in which meaning is created, and how the
      audience responds. Case study of the production process,
      with the writer, actors, and production personnel explaining
      their perceptions of what they do. Illustrations, appendix,
      glossary, further reading.

677. Moulds, M. J. British Television Revealed: An Economic
      Study. Coventry, Eng.: Xray Books, 1983. 175p.
          An attempt to unravel the fundamental structure of the
      British television service and an examination of the strategies
      of the various stockholders. Illustrations.

678. Norman, Bruce. Here's Looking at You: The Story of British
      Television, 1908-1939. London: British Broadcasting Corpora-
      tion and The Royal Television Society, 1984. 224p.
          The pioneers, their alternative systems, demonstrations, pro-
      grams and production, and audience reactions. Illustrations,
      bibliography, index.

679. Nown, Graham (ed.). Coronation Street: 25 Years, 1960-1985.
      London: Ward Lock, in association with Granada Television,
      1985. 214p.
          Text and photographs marking the silver jubilee of Granada

Television's "Coronation Street," the world's longest-running
TV series. A look behind the scenes, the program's beginnings
and prospects, character profiles, and a month-by-month diary
of events in the street during its first 25 years. Illustrations.

680. Passingham, Kenneth. The Guinness Book of TV Facts and
Feats. Enfield, Eng.: Guinness Superlatives, 1984. 298p.
See entry 542.

681. Perry, George. Life of Python. Boston, MA: Little, Brown,
1983. 192p.
    The evolution of British humor in the twentieth century,
the origins and antics of Monty Python, and profiles of the
members of the group. Illustrations, "Pythonography."

682. A Report from the Working Party on the New Technologies.
London: Broadcasting Research Unit, 1983. 346p.
    Conclusions and account of deliberations on the social, cul-
tural, political, and economic implications of developments in
cable, satellite, and video in Britain. Illustrations, tables,
appendices.

683. Report on Cable Systems. London: Her Majesty's Stationery
Office, 1982. 54p.
    Potential role of cable systems in the United Kingdom and
recommendations by the government's Information Technology
Advisory Panel for a major program of cable installation. Appendices.

684. Schlesinger, Philip, Graham Murdock, and Philip Elliott. Televising "Terrorism": Political Violence in Popular Culture.
London: Comedia, 1983. 181p.
    Examination of ways in which terrorism is interpreted and
debated in Britain, and of its treatment in information and fiction programs. Censorship methods, arguments against more
censorship, and the relationship of television to the state.
Illustrations, tables.

685. Self, David. Television Drama: An Introduction. London:
Macmillan, 1984. 173p.
    The state and practice of the art of TV drama in Britain.
Genres and their providers, and the role of the producer,
writer, and director. Design, on-location and in-studio production, and audience response. Illustrations, glossary, bibliography, index.

686. Sendall, Bernard. Independent Television in Britain. Vol. 1:
Origin and Foundation, 1946-62. London: Macmillan, 1982.
418p.
    The beginning and early years of commercial television.
Legislation, selection and responsibilities of program companies,

their ownership and programming, and public concerns about
profitability. Illustrations, tables, appendices, index.

687. Sendall, Bernard. Independent Television in Britain. Vol. 2:
      Expansion and Change, 1958-68. London: Macmillan, 1983.
      429p.
         Continuing story of commercial television, covering the es-
      tablishment of regional program companies, the highly critical
      Pilkington Committee Report, subsequent legislation, program
      developments, and changes in the distribution of power. Il-
      lustration, table, index.

688. Silverstone, Roger. Framing Science: The Making of a BBC
      Documentary. London: British Film Institute, 1985. 239p.
         Researching, filming, and editing "A New Green Revolution?"
      in the "Horizon" series, with a commentary and details of the
      intentions, expectations, and response. Appendix, suggestions
      for further reading.

689. Tonight. London: British Film Institute, 1982. 69p.
         Short history of "Tonight," a news-magazine program that
      ran on BBC Television from February 1957 to June 1965. Sup-
      plemented by a lengthy extract from the book Facing the Na-
      tion, by Grace Wyndham Goldie, one of the major influences
      behind the founding of the program, and assessments of the
      program's distinctive qualities and legacy to television journal-
      ism. Illustrations.

690. Tulloch, John, and Manuel Alvarado. Doctor Who: The Un-
      folding Text. New York: St. Martin's Press, 1983. 342p.
         Description, historical account, and critical analysis of BBC
      Television's longest-running series. Illustrations, appendices,
      index.

691. Tumber, Howard. Television and the Riots: A Report for the
      Broadcasting Research Unit of the British Film Institute. Lon-
      don: British Film Institute, 1982. 54p.
         Television coverage of disturbances in a number of inner-
      city areas of Britain in the summer of 1981, attitudes toward
      the image presented, and ways in which it was constructed.
      A major conclusion is that there is no convincing evidence that
      television produced a "copy cat" effect. However, the media
      are criticized for failing to understand and report adequately
      the social situation out of which the disturbances developed.
      Tables, bibliography.

692. Veljanovski, C. G., and W. D. Bishop. Choice by Cable:
      The Economics of a New Era in Television. London: Institute
      of Economic Affairs, 1983. 120p.
         Critical economic analysis of the issues surrounding the
      expansion of cable television systems in the United Kingdom.

Argues that the competitive market should be used to finance
and supply cable services. Opposes exclusive franchises which,
it is asserted, will erect artificial barriers to entry incompatible
with the promotion of competition. Illustration, tables.

693. Wade, Graham. Film, Video and Television: Market Forces,
Fragmentation and Technological Advance. London: Comedia,
1985. 77p.
    Historical overview of each industry in the United Kingdom
and examination of issues of technology, markets, and legislation. Case studies of the Rank Organisation, Palace Group,
BBC Enterprises, Moving Picture Company, Central Independent
Television, and Satellite Television's Sky Channel. Tables,
appendices.

694. Weaver, David H. Videotex Journalism: Teletext, Viewdata,
and the News. Hillsdale, NJ: Lawrence Erlbaum Associates,
1983. 147p.
    Study of actual and likely impact of videotex technology on
journalists, the flow of news and information, and on other
media. Based chiefly on the Ceefax, Oracle, and Prestel systems in the United Kingdom. Illustrations, tables, appendices,
bibliography, name index, subject index.

695. Wenham, Brian (ed.). The Third Age of Broadcasting. London: Faber and Faber, 1982. 139p.
    Broadcast executives' perspectives on the impact of cable,
satellite broadcasting, and video cassettes on the future of
broadcasting in Britain.

696. Wheen, Francis. Television: A History. London: Century,
1985. 256p.
    Based on a 14-hour documentary series by Britain's Granada
Television. Includes television's invention, government's role,
news, entertainment, instructional, and sports programming,
commercials, and future technology. Emphasis on Britain. Illustrations, index.

697. Who's Who On Television: A Fully Illustrated Guide to 1000
Best Known Faces on British Television. Rev. ed. London:
Independent Television Books, in association with Michael
Joseph, 1982. 272p.
    Capsule biographies and photographs, in alphabetical order.
Illustrations.

3. International

698. Drummond, Phillip, and Richard Paterson (eds.). Television
in Transition: Papers from the First International Television
Studies Conference. London: British Film Institute, 1986.
280p.

        Fifteen papers on topics ranging from electronic information
        flows to the politics of television viewing.

699.   Eugster, Ernest. Television Programming Across National
       Boundaries: The EBU and OIRT Experience. Dedham, MA:
       Artech House, 1983. 246p.
        History, operations, problems, and prospects of interna-
       tional television programming. Identification of elements within
       the EBU and OIRT that have contributed to success, examina-
       tion of the kinds of programs exchanged, existing limits to
       freer communications, and the predominant role that govern-
       ments play in the two organizations. Illustrations, tables, ap-
       pendices, bibliography.

700.   Gould, Peter, Jeffrey Johnson, and Graham Chapman. The
       Structure of Television. London: Pion, 1984.
        See entry 620.

701.   Guback, Thomas, and Tapio Varis, with the collaboration of
       José G. Cantor, Heriberto Muraro, Gloria Rojas, and Boonrak
       Booyaketmala. Transnational Communication and Cultural
       Industries. Paris: UNESCO, 1982. 55p.
        Quantitative survey of the flow of mass media materials.
       Transnational film and television businesses, and case studies
       on television and film in Thailand and Argentina. Tables, bib-
       liography.

G.   HISTORY

702.   Barnouw, Erik. Tube of Plenty: The Evolution of American
       Television. Rev. ed. New York: Oxford University Press,
       1982. 552p.
        Condensation and updating of the author's three-volume
       work, A History of Broadcasting in the United States. Pro-
       grams, personalities, challenges, and triumphs through the early
       1980s. Illustrations, chronology, index.

703.   Baughman, James L. Television's Guardians: The FCC and
       the Politics of Programming, 1958-1967. Knoxville: Univer-
       sity of Tennessee Press, 1985. 311p.
        Rejects the notion of industry control of the Federal Com-
       munications Commission and argues that the agency's inability
       to restrain television from its commercial instincts resulted
       largely from congressional and presidential opposition. Illus-
       trations, tables, appendix, bibliography, index.

704.   Castleman, Harry, and Walter J. Podrazik. Watching TV:
       Four Decades of American Television. New York: McGraw-Hill,
       1982. 314p.

Season-by-season account of the programs, personalities, events, and schedules from 1944-45 through 1980-81. Illustrations, index.

705. Cox, Geoffrey. See It Happen: The Making of ITN. London: Bodley Head, 1983. 248p.
    See entry 657.

706. Fischer, Stuart. Kids' TV: The First 25 Years. New York: Facts on File Publications, 1983. 289p.
    See entry 564.

707. Garay, Ronald. Congressional Television: A Legislative History. Westport, CT: Greenwood Press, 1984. 195p.
    Efforts by individual legislators over some 60 years to implement radio and television coverage of congressional hearings, meetings, and chamber deliberations, the resultant coverage, and television's impact on member conduct, legislative procedures, and on the television audience. Bibliographial essay, index.

708. Goldstein, Fred, and Stan Goldstein. Prime-Time Television: A Pictorial History from Milton Berle to "Falcon Crest." New York: Crown, 1983. 384p.
    Season-by-season review from 1948-49 through 1981-82, told in more than 3,000 photographs. The introduction to each season contains a historical overview. Illustrations, index.

709. Groves, Seli, with the Editors of the Associated Press. Soaps: A Pictorial History of America's Daytime Dramas. Chicago: Contemporary Books, 1983. 237p.
    Part one consists of chapters on each of the 14 network soap operas on the air at the time of publication. Part two is a collection of information on soaps and their characters, including motivations for cast changes and plot twists, discussion of some well-known soap opera gimmicks, a look at the life of soap characters, accomplishments of soap stars, Emmy Awards since 1974, and trivia questions and answers. Illustrations, appendix, bibliography, index.

710. Hall, Jim. Mighty Minutes: An Illustrated History of Television's Best Commercials. New York: Harmony Books, 1984. 172p.
    Text and photographs, arranged in eight categories: identifiable characters, women, men, sex, kidvid, humor and innovation, jingles, and sentimentality. Illustrations, index.

711. Hawes, William. American Television Drama: The Experimental Years. University, AL: University of Alabama Press, 1986. 272p.
    Origins and developments at CBS, NBC, and other

companies, from 1928 through 1947. Illustrations, appendices, selected bibliography, index.

712. Hill, Doug, and Jeff Weingrad. Saturday Night: A Backstage History of Saturday Night Live. New York: Beech Tree Books, 1986. 510p.
The birth and life of the NBC late-night program. Illustrations, index.

713. Norman, Bruce. Here's Looking at You: The Story of British Television, 1908-1939. London: British Broadcasting Corporation and The Royal Television Society, 1984. 224p.
See entry 678.

714. Nown, Graham (ed.). Coronation Street: 25 Years, 1960-1985. London: Ward Lock, in association with Granada Television, 1985. 214p.
See entry 679.

715. Rose, Brian G. Television and the Performing Arts: A Handbook and Reference Guide to American Cultural Programming. Westport, CT: Greenwood Press, 1986. 271p.
See entry 545.

716. Sendall, Bernard. Independent Television in Britain. Vol. 1: Origin and Foundation, 1946-62. London: Macmillan, 1982. 418p.
See entry 686.

717. Sendall, Bernard. Independent Television in Britain. Vol. 2: Expansion and Change, 1958-68. London: Macmillan, 1983. 429p.
See entry 687.

718. Settel, Irving. A Pictorial History of Television. 2d ed. New York: Frederick Ungar, 1983. 290p.
Text and photographs tracing the origins of television, its birth, and its decade-by-decade development from the 1940s through the early 1980s. Issues, trends, programs, and personalities. Illustrations, index.

719. Steinberg, Cobbett. TV Facts. Rev. ed. New York: Facts On File Publications, 1985. 478p.
See entry 549.

720. Udelson, Joseph H. The Great Television Race: A History of the American Television Industry, 1925-1941. University, AL: University of Alabama Press, 1982. 197p.
Engineering, programming, and marketing from the first successful demonstration of television to the start of its commercial operation. Illustrations, bibliographical essay, index.

721. Wheen, Francis. Television: A History. London: Century,
      1985. 256p.
          See entry 696.

H. IN SOCIETY

1. General

722. Adams, William C. (ed.). Television Coverage of International
      Affairs. Norwood, NJ: Ablex, 1982. 253p.
          Problems, extent, and focus of coverage by the U.S. com-
      mercial television networks in the Third World, the West, and
      Southeast Asia. Study of the degree to which viewers acquired
      information on an international news story from television.
      Tables, subject index, author index.

723. Altheide, David L. Media Power. Beverly Hills, CA: Sage
      Publications, 1985. 288p.
          Exploration of ways in which the mass media, and especially
      TV, provide formats for perception, expectation, and action.
      Examines the relationships between media formats of time and
      space, the role of TV news in altering the temporal and spa-
      tial character of events, interaction in daily life, and the self-
      conceptions of individuals. Offers a perspective for under-
      standing the mediated social order. Illustrations, tables,
      index.

724. Ball-Rokeach, Sandra J., Milton Rokeach, and Joel W. Grube.
      The Great American Values Test: Influencing Behavior and
      Belief Through Television. New York: Free Press, 1984.
      190p.
          Results of a television program experiment designed to in-
      fluence viewers to adopt or activate egalitarian and pro-
      environmental values, attitudes, and behaviors. Concludes
      that a single, 30-minute exposure to a TV program designed
      to conform to certain theoretical considerations can have a sig-
      nificant effect on the beliefs and behaviors of large numbers
      of people for at least several weeks or months thereafter.

725. Bryant, Jennings, and Dolf Zillmann (eds.). Perspectives
      on Media Effects. Hillsdale, NJ: Lawrence Erlbaum Associates,
      1986. 358p.
          Sixteen scholarly reports. Nine deal exclusively with tele-
      vision and cover the dynamics of the cultivation process, social
      learning of aggression, addiction to TV, educational impact,
      prosocial television, early election projections, personality and
      perceptions of television and its contents, effects on children,
      and theories and measures of attention to TV. Illustrations,
      tables, author index, subject index.

726. Carlson, James M. Prime Time Law Enforcement: Crime Show
      Viewing and Attitudes Toward the Criminal Justice System.
      New York: Praeger, 1985. 220p.
          Examination of the relationships between viewing television
      police-crime shows and the cultivation of attitudes toward the
      criminal justice system, the legal system, and the sociopolitical
      order. Concludes that there is some evidence that TV enter-
      tainment, specifically police-crime shows, promotes social sta-
      bility and control by reinforcing the perceived legitimacy of
      current power arrangements. Tables, appendix, bibliography,
      index.

727. Charren, Peggy, and Martin W. Sandler. Changing Channels:
      Living (Sensibly) with Television. Reading, MA: Addison-
      Wesley, 1983. 272p.
          Strengths, weaknesses, potential, and impact of television.
      Suggestions on making responsible decisions about TV viewing,
      harnessing its resources for education, and community involve-
      ment in cable. Illustrations, appendix, bibliography, index.

728. Cross, Donna Woolfolk. Mediaspeak: How Television Makes
      Up Your Mind. New York: Coward-McCann, 1983. 254p.
          Influence of television in reinforcing the status quo, and
      the part played by advertisers, networks, government,
      writers, and politicians. Bibliography.

729. Donnelly, William J. The Confetti Generation: How the New
      Communications Technology Is Fragmenting America. New York:
      Henry Holt, 1986. 239p.
          Argues that the profusion of electronic media is likely to
      lead to a generation whose members will be disconnected from
      one another because of the explosion of data and images to
      which they will be subjected. Bibliography, index.

730. Dunkley, Christopher. Television Today and Tomorrow: Wall-
      to-Wall Dallas? Harmondsworth, Eng.: Penguin Books, 1985.
      159p.
          See entry 659.

731. Fowles, Jib. Television Viewers vs. Media Snobs: What TV
      Does for People. New York: Stein and Day, 1982. 253p.
          Contends that, despite criticisms by persons labeled by the
      author as "snobs," television generally has a positive value for
      those who view it. Index.

732. Geis, Michael L. The Language of Television Advertising.
      New York: Academic Press, 1982. 257p.
          Analysis of ways in which advertisers use language and how
      consumers can be expected to interpret it. Six chapters on
      advertisements primarily directed at adults and three at chil-
      dren. Illustrations, index of commercials, author index, sub-
      ject index.

733. Greenfield, Patricia Marks. Mind and Media: The Effects of
      Television, Video Games and Computers. Cambridge, MA:
      Harvard University Press, 1984. 210p.
        Strengths and weaknesses of electronic and print media
      and suggestions for using them to promote social growth and
      thinking skills. Emphasis on television. Illustrations, sug-
      gested readings, index.

734. Gunter, Barrie. Dimensions of Television Violence. New York:
      St. Martin's Press, 1985. 282p.
        Report on experiments designed to explore a method of
      assessing TV violence in terms of how viewers perceive and
      evaluate different kinds of violent portrayals in fictional pro-
      gramming. Identifies factors influencing perceptions and the
      kinds of violent content to which special attention should be
      paid. Illustrations, tables, index.

735. Jamieson, Kathleen Hall, and Karlyn Kohrs Campbell. The
      Interplay of Influence: Mass Media and Their Publics in News,
      Advertising, Politics. Belmont, CA: Wadsworth, 1983. 287p.
        Ways in which the media influence their audiences, and vice-
      versa. Strategies available to the media and the problems of,
      and constraints on, the media and those who seek to influence
      their behavior. Emphasis on television. Illustrations, tables,
      appendices, index.

736. Lesher, Stephan. Media Unbound: The Impact of Television
      Journalism on the Public. Boston, MA: Houghton Mifflin,
      1982. 285p.
        Examination of journalism by showing how it is done and
      what it does to us when it is done wrong. Major attention to
      the CBS program "60 Minutes." Bibliography, index.

737. Lichter, S. Robert, Stanley Rothman, and Linda S. Lichter.
      The Media Elite. Bethesda, MD: Adler and Adler, 1986.
      342p.
        The social, psychological, and political milieu of the national
      print and broadcast media, and the relationship between the
      milieu and news coverage of controversial social issues. The
      broadcast media are the three major commercial television net-
      works and public television. The issues are: busing to
      achieve integration, the safety of nuclear power, and the
      oil industry's role in the energy crisis. Illustrations, tables,
      appendix, index.

738. Lodziak, Conrad. The Power of Television: A Critical Ap-
      praisal. London: Frances Pinter, 1986. 217p.
        Assessment of popular and theoretical arguments on the
      crucial power of television. TV's ideological role in contempor-
      ary Western societies and its role in leisure time and social
      fragmentation. Index.

739.   MacDonald, J. Fred.   Television and the Red Menace: The
       Video Road to Vietnam.   New York: Praeger, 1985.   278p.
          Contends that propaganda and misrepresentation in tele-
       vision entertainment and information programs from the 1940s
       through the early 1960s conditioned the American public to
       tolerate an unwanted and unexplained war.   Tables, bibliogra-
       phy, index.

740.   Mattos, Sérgio.   The Impact of the 1964 Revolution on Brazil-
       ian Television.   San Antonio: V. Klingensmith, 1982.   129p.
       See entry 636.

741.   Meyrowitz, Joshua.   No Sense of Place: The Impact of Elec-
       tronic Media on Social Behavior.   New York: Oxford Univer-
       sity Press, 1985.   416p.
          Analysis and examples of ways in which television and other
       media have created new social environments and altered social
       roles.   Case studies on changes in three sets of roles: mascu-
       linity and femininity, childhood and adulthood, and political
       leaders and followers.   Appendix, bibliography, index.

742.   Parenti, Michael.   Inventing Reality: The Politics of the Mass
       Media.   New York: St. Martin's Press, 1986.   258p.
          Attempt to demonstrate how and why the broadcast and print
       media distort important aspects of social and political life.   Ar-
       gues that major distortions are the product not only of deliber-
       ate manipulation, but also of the ideological and economic condi-
       tions under which the media operate.   Focus on national and
       international politico-economic class issues and on the three
       major commercial television networks, The New York Times,
       and The Washington Post.   Index.

743.   Pearl, David, Lorraine Bouthilet, and Joyce Lazar.   Television
       and Behavior: Ten Years of Scientific Progress and Implica-
       tions for the Eighties.   Vol. 2:   Technical Reviews.   Rock-
       ville, MD: National Institute of Mental Health, 1982.   362p.
          Companion volume to the Summary Report (entry 748), con-
       taining reviews of the scientific literature on television's ef-
       fects or influences on behavior.   Cognitive and affective as-
       pects of television, violence and aggression, social beliefs and
       social behavior, television and social relations, television and
       health, and television in American society.   Introductory com-
       ments to each topic.   Illustrations, tables.

744.   Robinson, John P., and Mark R. Levy, with Dennis K. Davis.
       The Main Source: Learning from Television News.   Beverly
       Hills, CA: Sage Publications, 1986.   272p.
          Examination of research into how, what, and where the
       public learns about the news.   Concludes that (1) television
       news should not be considered the public's main source of
       news; (2) heavier exposure to print media is generally associated

with higher levels of news comprehension; (3) interpersonal
discussion of news may be at least as powerful a predictor of
comprehension as exposure to news media; (4) no one news
medium should be viewed as predominant; (5) the news media
can do a more effective job of informing the public. Illustrations, tables, appendices, index.

745. Sigel, Efrem, Erik Barnouw, Anthony Smith, Dan Lacy, Robert
D. Stueart, and Lewis M. Branscomb. Books, Libraries and
Electronics: Essays on the Future of Written Communication.
White Plains, NY: Knowledge Industry Publications, 1982.
139p.
      The impact of video and other electronic technologies on the
printed word, books, authors, publishing, and libraries. Bibliography.

746. Sprafkin, Joyce, Carolyn Swift, and Robert Hess (eds.). Rx
Television: Enhancing the Preventive Impact of TV. New
York: Haworth Press, 1983. 139p.
      Articles describing ways in which television can be used
to teach prosocial behavior, promote health, change attitudes,
and reach viewers with prevention messages. Illustration,
tables.

747. Stewart, David W., and David H. Furse. Effective Television
Advertising: A Study of 1000 Commercials. Lexington, MA:
Lexington Books, 1986. 178p.
      Use of actual commercials to study the effects of various
advertising executional devices on related recall, key message
comprehension, and persuasion as measured by a shift in
brand choice. Tables, appendices, index.

748. Television and Behavior: Ten Years of Scientific Progress and
Implications for the Eighties. Vol. 1: Summary Report. Rock-
ville, MD: National Institute of Mental Health, 1982. 94p.
      Assessment of literature reviews updating and elaborating
on information presented in the 1972 Report of the Surgeon
General's Advisory Committee on Television and Behavior.
Extends the original through consideration of such issues as
cognitive and emotional aspects of television viewing, television
as it relates to socialization and viewers' conceptions of social
reality, television's influences on physical and mental health,
and television as an American institution. Programmatic focus
on entertainment and its influence on all age groups. Appendices.

749. Tumber, Howard. Television and the Riots: A Report for the
Broadcasting Research Unit of the British Film Institute.
London: British Film Institute, 1982. 54p.
      See entry 691.

750. White, Thomas, and Gladys Ganley. The "Death of a Princess"
      Controversy. Cambridge, MA: Program on Information Re-
      sources Policy, Harvard University, 1983. 60p.
         Attempts by Saudi Arabia to prevent the television broad-
      cast of a film about the execution of a Saudi princess for
      adultery, and their political, business, and legal repercus-
      sions. Appendices.

751. Williams, Tannis Macbeth. The Impact of Television: A Natu-
      ral Experiment in Three Communities. Orlando, FL: Academic
      Press, 1986. 446p.
         See entry 641.

752. Zillmann, Dolf, and Jennings Bryant (eds.). Selective Ex-
      posure to Communication. Hillsdale, NJ: Lawrence Erlbaum
      Associates, 1985. 251p.
         Review of past and present theory and research. Among
      the topics: measuring exposure to television, determinants of
      TV viewing preferences, fear of victimization and the appeal of
      crime drama, selective exposure to educational television, cable
      and program choice, and repeated exposure to television pro-
      grams. Illustrations, tables, author index, subject index.

                    2. Children and Youth

753. Barcus, F. Earle. Images of Life on Children's Television:
      Sex Roles, Minorities, and Families. New York: Praeger,
      1983. 219p.
         Study of the portrayals of sex-role behaviors, traditional
      U.S. minorities and persons of identifiable national origin,
      and of family and kinship relations in nearly 50 hours of net-
      work and independent station programs during one week in
      1981. Finds an overwhelming proportion of male characters,
      small number of minority characters, and traditional and stereo-
      typical portrayal of the family. Tables, appendices, bibliogra-
      phy, author index, subject index.

754. Barlow, Geoffrey, and Alison Hill (eds.). Video Violence and
      Children. New York: St. Martin's Press, 1985. 182p.
         Description and analysis of research into the effects on chil-
      dren of their exposure to scenes of violence in videos pro-
      duced primarily for home viewing. Concludes that exposure
      has a harmful effect and that careful censorship and stringent
      controls should be imposed. Illustrations, tables, appendices,
      index.

755. Berry, Gordon L., and Claudia Mitchell-Kernan (eds.). Tele-
      vision and the Socialization of the Minority Child. New York:
      Academic Press, 1982. 289p.
         Television's influence on the social, cognitive, and affective

learning of Afro-American, American Indian, Asian-American, and Hispanic children. Tables, author index, subject index.

756. Bryant, Jennings, and Daniel R. Anderson (eds.). Children's Understanding of Television: Research on Attention and Comprehension. New York: Academic Press, 1983. 370p.
Thirteen chapters examining the assumptions, methodologies, theories, and research findings. Four chapters on attention, five on comprehension, and four on research application or intervention. Illustrations, tables, author index, subject index.

757. Burke, Jacinta, Susanna Agardy, Maria Fricker, and Jim Biles. Children, Television and Food. Melbourne: Australian Broadcasting Tribunal, 1982. 111p.
See entry 631.

758. The Child and Television Drama: The Psychosocial Impact of Cumulative Viewing. New York: Mental Health Materials Center, 1982. 123p.
Observations, ideas, and intuitions by a group of psychiatrists and an examination and appraisal of selected studies. Recommendations and guidelines for parents and recommendations for mental health professionals, public policy makers, and the television industry. Illustrations, bibliography.

759. Cullingford, Cedric. Children and Television. New York: St. Martin's Press, 1984. 239p.
See entry 658.

760. Doerken, Maurine. Classroom Combat: Teaching and Television. Englewood Cliffs, NJ: Educational Technology Publications, 1983. 316p.
Overview of television and how it affects classroom teaching. The impact of TV violence, advertising, and other content, and practical suggestions for using the medium in the classroom, as well as what young people and parents may do at home. Illustrations, tables, bibliography, appendices, index.

761. Dorr, Aimée. Television and Children: A Special Medium for a Special Audience. Beverly Hills, CA: Sage Publications, 1986. 160p.
Television as a conveyor of content and user of children's time. What they watch, what they believe about advertising and programming, the effects that the medium can have, and what television literacy curricula look like. Index.

762. Durkin, Kevin. Television, Sex Roles and Children: A Developmental Social Psychological Account. Milton Keynes, Eng.: Open University Press, 1985. 148p.
Description and evaluation of the main findings of recent

research on television and sex role acquisition, the gaps and
limitations in present inquiry, and a framework for future research. Author index, subject index.

763. Howe, Michael J. A. (ed.). Learning from Television: Psychological and Educational Research. London: Academic Press,
1983. 226p.
    Summaries of research on the effects of television on view-
ers, particularly children and young people. Influences of
programs designed to achieve educational goals and of everyday
viewing. Responsibilities of children's television from a producer's viewpoint and the construction and evaluation of a
curriculum aimed at making children more intelligent consumers
of the programs they see. Illustrations, tables, subject index.

764. Huesmann, L. Rowell, and Leonard D. Eron (eds.). Television
and the Aggressive Child: A Cross National Comparison.
Hillsdale, NJ: Lawrence Erlbaum Associates, 1986. 326p.
    See entry 622.

765. Johnnson-Smaragdi, Ulla. TV Use and Social Interaction in
Adolescence: A Longitudinal Study. Stockholm, Sweden:
Almqvist and Wiksell, 1983. 239p.
    See entry 645.

766. Johnston, Jerome, and James S. Ettema. Positive Images:
Breaking Stereotypes with Children's Television. Beverly Hills,
CA: Sage Publications, 1982. 263p.
    The evolution, development, and effects of the television
series "Freestyle," which was designed to reduce the influence
of sex and ethnic group stereotyping on children's career interests. Illustrations, tables, appendices, bibliography.

767. Kelley, Michael R. A Parents' Guide To Television: Making
The Most Of It. New York: John Wiley and Sons, 1983.
129p.
    The content, methods, and influences of television, and
ways in which the medium can be used to improve young people's
abilities in communication, creative imagination, and critical and
evaluative thinking. Suggested readings, appendices.

768. Liebert, Robert M., Joyce N. Sprafkin, and Emily S. Davidson.
The Early Window: Effects of Television on Children and Youth.
2d ed. Elmsford, NY: Pergamon Press, 1982. 257p.
    Theory and research on television and children's attitudes,
development, and behavior, and exploration of the social, political, and economic factors that surround them. Examines TV
as a business, television violence, the Surgeon General's Report and its aftermath, advertising, race and sex on TV, and
television's potential to benefit children and society. Illustrations, tables, appendices, name index, subject index.

769. Meyer, Manfred (ed.). Children and the Formal Features of Television: Approaches and Findings of Experimental and Formative Research. New York: K. G. Saur, 1983. 333p.
    Experimental treatment of television's formal features and the effects on children's attention, comprehension, and social behavior. New approaches to their cognitive and emotional interaction with what is offered to them on the screen, and the nature and complexity of the viewing process itself. Rationale, goals, methods, and methodological aspects of formative research. Illustrations, table.

770. Milavsky, J. Ronald, Ronald C. Kessler, Horst H. Stipp, and William S. Rubens. Television and Aggression: A Panel Study. New York: Academic Press, 1982. 505p.
    Study of some 3,200 elementary schoolchildren and teenage boys, designed to relate patterns of normal television viewing behavior to changes in aggression over periods between a few months and three years. Does not find evidence that TV violence is causally implicated in the development of aggressive behavior patterns among children and adolescents over the time period studied. Tables, bibliography, index.

771. Murray, John P., and Gavriel Salomon (eds.). The Future of Children's Television: Results of the Markle Foundation/Boys Town Conference. Boys Town, NE: Boys Town, 1984. 174p.
    Summary of the 1982 conference, and papers on research evidence on the impact of television on children, the potential of television as an educational tool, and the costs and strategies for obtaining a program schedule to enhance the emotional and intellectual development of children. Illustrations, tables.

772. Palmer, Patricia. The Lively Audience: A Study of Children Around the TV Set. Sydney: Allen and Unwin, 1986. 166p.
    See entry 633.

773. Postman, Neil. The Disappearance of Childhood. New York: Delacorte Press, 1982. 177p.
    Origins of the idea of childhood, and ways in which television has made childhood as a social structure difficult to sustain and irrelevant. Bibliography, index.

774. Schwarz, Meg (ed.). TV and Teens: Experts Look at the Issues. Reading, MA: Addison-Wesley, 1982. 222p.
    Essays on the characteristics and needs of adolescents, what teenagers learn from television, and creative programming ideas to meet their requirements. Topics include entertainment and informational programming, role models, the world of work, sex and sexuality, radio, and advertising. Case studies on alcohol, drug abuse, and teenage suicide. Illustrations, index.

775. Voort, T. H. A. van der. Television Violence: A Child's-Eye

View. Amsterdam: North-Holland, 1986. 440p.
  Explores ways in which children aged nine to 12 perceive
and experience violent television drama. Illustrations, tables,
appendices, author index, subject index.

776. Ward, Scott, Tom Robertson, and Ray Brown (eds.). Commer-
     cial Television and European Children: An International Re-
     search Digest. Aldershot, Eng.: Gower, 1986. 243p.
     See entry 647.

777. Wilkins, Joan Anderson. Breaking the TV Habit. New York:
     Charles Scribner's Sons, 1982. 178p.
       The dangers of watching television and guidelines to aid
     parents in limiting the amount of time their children view.
     Illustrations, bibliography, index.

778. Winn, Marie. The Plug-In Drug: Television, Children, and
     the Family. Rev. ed. New York: Penguin Books, 1985.
     288p.
       The influence of watching television and the use of the
     medium as a time-killer on child development, child rearing,
     and family life. New chapter on television and the school.
     Illustrations, index.

                   3. Education and Instruction

779. Arnall, Gail. Instructional Television Fixed Services: An
     Analysis of ITFS Operations. Washington, DC: Corporation
     for Public Broadcasting, 1984. 82p.
       Distribution, licensees, programming, audiences, and fi-
     nances of ITFS systems. Case studies of six systems operated
     by different types of licensee. Illustrations, tables.

780. Blume, Wilbur T., and Paul Schneller (eds.). Toward Inter-
     national Tele-Education. Boulder, CO: Westview Press, 1984.
     256p.
       Description of global and domestic educational needs and
     evaluation of current plans and programs. Resources, capa-
     cities for implementation, previous efforts, and technological
     developments. Prospects and educational, economic, legal, and
     political issues. Illustrations, tables, index.

781. Doerken, Maurine. Classroom Combat: Teaching and Tele-
     vision. Englewood Cliffs, NJ: Educational Technology Publica-
     tions, 1983. 316p.
     See entry 760.

782. Dorr, Aimée. Television and Children: A Special Medium for
     a Special Audience. Beverly Hills, CA: Sage Publications,
     1986. 160p.
     See entry 761.

783. Hawkridge, David. New Information Technology in Education. London: Croom Helm, 1983. 238p.

Survey of technology, its applications, problems associated with its use, formal and informal learning environments, and predictions for the year 2000. Covers videocassette and videodisc, teletext and videotex, cable television, network TV, microcomputers, and calculators. Illustrations, index.

784. Hays, Kim (ed.). TV, Science, and Kids: Teaching Our Children to Question. Reading, MA: Addison-Wesley, 1984. 210p.

Essays on science teaching in school and on television, the economic and political dangers of scientific illiteracy, and suggestions for using television to help children feel more comfortable with, and knowledgeable about, science. Illustrations, appendices, index.

785. Hilliard, Robert L. (ed.). Television and Adult Education. Cambridge, MA: Schenkman Books, 1985. 215p.

See entry 621.

786. Howe, Michael J. A. (ed.). Learning from Television: Psychological and Educational Research. London: Academic Press, 1983. 226p.

See entry 763.

787. Hudspeth, DeLayne R., and Ronald G. Brey. Instructional Telecommunications: Principles and Applications. New York: Praeger, 1986. 241p.

Guidelines and procedures for planning, creating, and administering telecourse instruction. Illustrations, table, glossary, appendices, index.

788. Lusted, David, and Phillip Drummond (eds.). TV and Schooling. London: British Film Institute, 1985. 124p.

See entry 674.

789. Masterman, Len. Teaching the Media. London: Comedia, 1985. 341p.

How to teach, with emphasis on the development of a conceptual framework characterized by key principles, concepts, and areas of continuity across a range of media experiences. Emphasis on television. Illustrations, appendices, select annotated bibliography.

790. Ploghoft, Milton E., and James A. Anderson. Teaching Critical Television Viewing Skills: An Integrated Approach. Springfield, IL: Charles C. Thomas, 1982. 193p.

Directions on the integration of viewing skills into the regular curriculum using commercial messages, entertainment content, and television news. Illustrations, index, index of names.

791. Sinofsky, Esther R. Off-Air Videotaping in Education: Copy-
      right Issues, Decisions, Implications. New York: R. R. Bowker,
      1984. 163p.
         Historical overview of copyright, the Copyright Act of
      1976, perspectives of copyright proprietors and educators,
      and the "fair use" doctrine and its interpretations by the
      courts. Guidelines and suggested solutions to the off-air
      taping dilemma. Table, appendices, bibliography, relevant
      court cases.

                        4. Government and Politics

792. Adams, William C. (ed.). Television Coverage of the 1980
      Presidential Campaign. Norwood, NJ: Ablex, 1983. 197p.
         Network coverage of the primaries, party conventions, de-
      bates, and election night, their treatment of energy issues,
      and use of opinion polls. Comparison of coverage by CBS
      and UPI and factors to estimate the impact of TV content.
      Illustrations, tables, name index, subject index.

793. Blume, Keith. The Presidential Election Show: Campaign '84
      and Beyond on the Nightly News. South Hadley, MA: Bergin
      and Garvey, 1985. 340p.
         Description and commentary on television's coverage of the
      campaign in particular, public-policy issues in general, and
      the impact on American democracy. Follows coverage from
      Labor Day to Election Day on the weeknight newscasts of ABC,
      CBS, and NBC, and PBS' "The MacNeil/Lehrer NewsHour."
      Illustrations, appendix, selected bibliography, index.

794. Blumler, Jay G. (ed.). Communicating to Voters: Television
      in the First European Parliamentary Elections. Beverly Hills,
      CA: Sage Publications, 1983. 389p.
         See entry 643.

795. Diamond, Edwin, and Stephen Bates. The Spot: The Rise of
      Political Advertising on Television. Cambridge, MA: MIT
      Press, 1984. 416p.
         Evolution of political advertising in presidential elections
      from 1952 to 1980, with analysis of persuasive techniques and
      visual styles, how spots work, and the effects of television
      campaigns. Argues that spots may be turning campaigns into
      a kind of spectator sport. Index.

796. Garay, Ronald. Congressional Television: A Legislative His-
      tory. Westport, CT: Greenwood Press, 1984. 195p.
         See entry 707.

797. Gunter, Barrie, Michael Svennerig, and Mallory Wober. Tele-
      vision Coverage of the 1983 General Election: Audiences,

Appreciation and Public Opinion. Aldershot, Eng.: Gower,
1986. 136p.
See entry 661.

798. Kaid, Lynda Lee, Dan Nimmo, and Keith R. Sanders (eds.).
New Perspectives on Political Advertising. Carbondale, IL:
Southern Illinois University Press, 1986. 388p.
Explores the effects of TV advertising on political candi-
dates and the audience.

799. Kern, Montague. Television and Middle East Diplomacy: President Carter's Fall 1977 Peace Initiative. Washington, DC:
Center for Contemporary Arab Studies, Georgetown University,
1983. 51p.
Analysis of television coverage between September 15 and
October 5, 1977 of negotiations on reconvening a Middle East
conference in Geneva under the aegis of the United States and
the U.S.S.R. Considers Carter's goals and coverage of Israel, the Arabs, and the administration. Concludes that the
Carter administration failed to change the pattern of coverage
in order to gain public support for its diplomacy through the
electronic media. Illustrations.

800. Lang, Gladys Engel, and Kurt Lang. The Battle for Public
Opinion: The President, the Press, and the Polls During
Watergate. New York: Columbia University Press, 1983.
353p.
The role of the electronic and print media in placing Water-
gate on the public agenda and in fashioning public opinion.
Includes chapters on the gavel-to-gavel TV broadcasts of the
Ervin committee hearings and the impeachment deliberations
of the House Judiciary Committee and on television coverage
of the transition to the Ford presidency. Appendix, index.

801. Lang, Gladys Engel, and Kurt Lang. Politics and Television
Re-Viewed. Beverly Hills, CA: Sage Publications, 1984.
223p.
Ways in which live TV coverage has shaped public images
of politics and political personalities and thus has influenced
the nature and course of political life. Includes several chapters from the authors' Politics and Television (1968). New
chapters on Watergate and the first Ford-Carter debate in
1976. Tables.

802. Larson, James F. Television's Window on the World: International Affairs Coverage on the U.S. Networks. Norwood, NJ:
Ablex, 1984. 195p.
Growth of television as an international news medium and
content of international affairs coverage on weeknight news
broadcasts of ABC, CBS, and NBC from 1972 through 1981.
Influences that shape television's view of the world and

consequences of coverage, particularly on the foreign policy
process. Illustrations, tables, appendices, author index,
subject index.

803. Linsky, Martin (ed.). Television and the Presidential Elec-
      tions: Self-Interest and the Public Interest. Lexington, MA:
      Lexington Books, 1983. 139p.
          Summary of presentations and discussions at a 1981 confer-
      ence of academics and network representatives. Focus on day-
      to-day questions confronting the networks and the politicians
      in their relationships with one another. Includes considera-
      tion of the restraints on television in the presidential process,
      the landscape of an election, network-candidate interaction,
      problems politicians face in dealing with networks, and regula-
      tory issues. Illustrations, bibliography.

804. Ranney, Austin. Channels of Power: The Impact of Tele-
      vision on American Politics. New York: Basic Books, 1983.
      207p.
          Concludes that, for most Americans, political reality con-
      sists mostly of what they see on television. Accordingly, the
      medium has had a powerful impact on American political cul-
      ture, political office-holders and candidates, and on the chal-
      lenge of governing in the television age. Index.

805. Robinson, Michael J., and Margaret A. Sheehan. Over the
      Wire and on TV: CBS and UPI in Campaign '80. New York:
      Russell Sage Foundation, 1983. 332p.
          Comparison of the verbal messages of presidential campaign
      coverage on the Monday through Friday early evening news-
      cast and the wire service from January 1 through December
      31, 1980. Concludes that wires and networks usually stay in-
      side the limits of "objective reporting" and the boundaries of
      balance and fairness, and that they confine themselves to the
      "horse race" metaphor in well over half the stories. Hard
      political coverage on CBS was more personal, mediating, ana-
      lytical, "political," critical, and thematic. The implications
      and consequences of the findings for politicians, press secre-
      taries, and the public. Illustrations, tables, index.

806. Tannenbaum, Percy H., and Leslie J. Kostrich. Turned-On
      TV/Turned-Off Voters: Policy Options for Election Projections.
      Beverly Hills, CA: Sage Publications, 1983. 240p.
          Examination of research on election night broadcast projec-
      tions and their effects on the presidential vote, turnout, and
      local elections. Consideration of alternatives to early returns,
      exit polls, and broadcast dissemination, and strategies for
      dealing with the projection problem. Tables, appendix.

5. Religion

807. Hoover, Stewart M. The Electronic Giant: A Critique of the
Telecommunications Revolution from a Christian Perspective.
Elgin, IL: Brethren Press, 1982. 171p.
   Evaluation of the role and influence of television and new
technologies and an agenda for the formulation of a Christian
perspective on their effects on ministry in contemporary society. Illustrations, index.

808. Horsfield, Peter G. Religious Television: The American Experience. New York: Longman, 1984. 197p.
   Historical overview of the development of religious television in America, analysis of the factors contributing to its
structure, and the issues it raises. Survey of research on
the nature of changes in the structure of TV religion, the
size and characteristics of its audience, attitudinal and cultural
effects, and the local church and its relationship to televised
religion. A look at the future and a strategy for the religious
use of television. Illustrations, tables, bibliography, index.

809. Oberdorfer, Donald N. Electronic Christianity: Myth or Ministry. Taylor Falls, MN: John L. Brekke and Sons, 1982.
159p.
   Interpreting television and employing it in the life of the
church. Historical relationship between the church and electronic media, media theory and theological implications, communication models and their potential application, and opportunities
presented by emerging technologies. Illustrations, bibliography.

6. Sports

810. Patton, Phil. Razzle-Dazzle: The Curious Marriage of Television and Professional Football. Garden City, NY: Dial
Press, 1984. 230p.
   Argues that the theatricality of football's presentation on
the television screen has been echoed in its evolution on the
field.

811. Powers, Ron. Supertube: The Rise of Television Sports.
New York: Coward-McCann, 1984. 288p.
   History of television's treatment of sports in America and
the growth of TV sports into a multi-billion-dollar industry.
The transformation of sports by television and vice-versa, the
people behind it, and its impact on sports figures and specta-
tors. Bibliography, index.

812. Rader, Benjamin G. In Its Own Image: How Television Has
Transformed Sports. New York: Free Press, 1984. 228p.
   The impact of television on the ethos of athletic competition,

sports rules, organizations, and management, and on the attitudes and behavior of players, owners, and fans. Bibliography, index.

I. LAW, REGULATION, AND POLICY

1. Law and Regulation

813. Barker, Martin (ed.). The Video Nasties: Freedom and Cen-
      sorship in the Media. London: Pluto Press, 1984. 131p.
          See entry 653.

814. Baughman, James L. Television's Guardians: The FCC and
      the Politics of Programming, 1958-1967. Knoxville: Univer-
      sity of Tennessee Press, 1985. 311p.
          See entry 703.

815. Etter, Terry (ed.). License Renewal Kit for Television Sta-
      tions. Washington, DC: National Association of Broadcasters,
      1986.
          Details of required documentation, analysis of renewal form
      questions, pre- and post-filing announcements, and the FCC's
      inspection process. Appendices.

816. Firestone, Charles M. (ed.). International Satellite Television:
      Resource Manual for the Third Biennial Communications Law
      Symposium. Los Angeles: UCLA Communications Law Pro-
      gram, 1983. 377p.
          Articles, charts, and documents on historical and technical
      perspectives of global television, market prospects, the world's
      telecommunications regulatory framework, and mechanisms for
      resolving international disputes. Illustrations, tables, bibli-
      ography, glossary.

817. Glenn, Robin Day. Legal Issues Affecting Licensing of TV
      Programs in the European Economic Community from the Per-
      spective of the U.S. Exporter. Washington, DC: Interna-
      tional Law Institute, Georgetown University Law Center, 1983.
      49p.
          See entry 644.

818. Miller, Jerome K. Using Copyrighted Videocassettes in Class-
      rooms and Libraries. Champaign, IL: Copyright Information
      Services, 1984. 91p.
          Rights of proprietors, educators, and librarians, and an
      examination of copyright contracts. Appendix, table of cases,
      index.

819. New York University School of Law. Law and the Television

of the '80's. New York: Oceana Publications, 1983. 264p.
Seven papers presented at a 1980 conference. Topics are
legal problems, copyright and the new communications technologies, the role of antitrust, two-way TV and privacy, cable
television franchising and local regulation, public broadcasting,
and proposed federal legislation.

820. Sinofsky, Esther R. Off-Air Videotaping in Education: Copy-
right Issues, Decisions, Implications. New York: R. R.
Bowker, 1984. 163p.
See entry 791.

2. Policy

821. Besen, Stanley M., Thomas G. Krattenmaker, A. Richard Metzger, Jr., and John R. Woodbury. Misregulating Television:
Network Dominance and the FCC. Chicago: University of
Chicago Press, 1984. 202p.
Explores the premises that network dominance threatens
important public policy goals and that such dominance may be
tempered or prevented by regulating the networks' commercial
practices. Tables, index.

822. Cultures in Collision: The Interaction of Canadian and U.S.
Television Broadcast Policies. A Canadian-U.S. Conference
on Communications Policies. New York: Praeger, 1984.
210p.
See entry 637.

823. McQuail, Denis, and Karen Siune (eds.). New Media Politics:
Comparative Perspectives in Western Europe. Beverly Hills,
CA: Sage Publications, 1986. 216p.
See entry 625.

824. Rowland, Willard D., Jr. The Politics of TV Violence: Policy
Uses of Communication Research. Beverly Hills, CA: Sage
Publications, 1983. 320p.
Interaction among the federal political process of communication policy-making, the broadcast industry, the public or
citizens' interest groups, and the communication researchers'
community. The role of the last in influencing the conditions
of the interaction.

825. Schement, Jorge Reina, Felix Gutierrez, and Marvin A. Sirbu,
Jr. (eds.). Telecommunications Policy Handbook. New York:
Praeger, 1982. 318p.
Twenty-one papers first delivered at the Seventh and Eighth
Telecommunications Policy Research Conferences. Converging
technologies, public broadcasting, pricing of communication ser-
vices, understanding change, influencing policy, and redefining

information.   Includes chapters on communication satellites for
rural development, subscription television and multipoint distribution service, Operation Prime Time, special-interest citizen groups and the networks, and communications and information relationships between the United States and Canada.   Illustrations, tables, index.

J.   PROGRAMS AND CONTENT

1.   Children's

826.   Doney, Ruane L.   Guide to Innovative Children's Programs for
       Television.   Washington, DC: National Association of Broad-
       casters, 1984.   35p.
          See entry 537.

827.   Fischer, Stuart.   Kids' TV: The First 25 Years.   New York:
       Facts on File Publications, 1983.   289p.
          See entry 564.

828.   Kids' Stuff: A Resource Book for Children's Television Pro-
       gramming.   Washington, DC: National Association of Broad-
       casters, 1983.
          See entry 540.

829.   Woolery, George W.   Children's Television: The First Thirty-
       Five Years, 1946-1981.   Part I: Animated Cartoon Series.
       Metuchen, NJ: Scarecrow Press, 1983.   386p.
          See entry 572.

830.   Woolery, George W.   Children's Television: The First Thirty-
       Five Years, 1946-1981.   Part II: Live, Film, and Tape Series.
       Metuchen, NJ: Scarecrow Press, 1985.   788p.
          See entry 573.

2.   Entertainment

831.   Allen, Robert C.   Speaking of Soap Operas.   Chapel Hill, NC:
       University of North Carolina Press, 1985.   245p.
          Examination of the American soap opera as narrative form,
       cultural product, advertising vehicle, and source of aesthetic
       pleasure.   Appendices, bibliography, index.

832.   Andrews, Bart.   The "I Love Lucy" Book.   Garden City, NY:
       Doubleday, 1985.   423p.
          Revision of Lucy and Ricky and Fred and Ethel (E. P. Dut-
       ton, 1976).   Behind-the-scenes look at the still-popular tele-
       vision series, its characters, and the ingredients of its success.

Season-by-season log with title, synopsis, and supporting
cast of all 179 episodes. Illustrations, index.

833. Ang, Ien. Watching Dallas: Soap Opera and the Melodramatic
      Imagination. Translated by Della Couling. London: Methuen,
      1985. 148p.
      Determinants and structurings of pleasure in the prime-time
      television serial, and implications for mass culture and feminism.
      Index.

834. Blythe, Cheryl, and Susan Sackett. Say Goodnight, Gracie! :
      The Story of Burns and Allen. New York: E. P. Dutton,
      1986. 304p.
      See entry 58.

835. Buckman, Peter. All For Love: A Study in Soap Opera.
      Salem, NH: Salem House, 1985. 226p.
      See entry 618.

836. Cassata, Mary, and Thomas Skill. Life on Daytime Television:
      Tuning-In American Serial Drama. Norwood, NJ: Ablex, 1983.
      214p.
      Analysis of the people, problems, environment, and interac-
      tions in daytime serial drama, with introductory essays on the
      genre by a social scientist and a humanist. Illustrations,
      tables, bibliography, author index, subject index.

837. Christensen, Mark, and Cameron Stauth. The Sweeps: Behind
      the Scenes in Network TV. New York: William Morrow, 1984.
      416p.
      The programs and the stakes involved in the 1983-84 sea-
      son from NBC's perspective, with emphasis on "Cheers." The
      two sections deal with the challenges of getting into prime-time
      TV and staying there. Illustrations, index.

838. Crescenti, Peter, and Bob Columbe. The Official Honeymooners
      Treasury: To the Moon and Back with Ralph, Norton, Alice
      and Trixie. New York: Putnam, 1985. 317p.
      Script excerpts and trivia questions and answers from each
      of the 39 episodes of "The Honeymooners." Reminiscences by
      the writers, actors, and others involved with the program.
      Illustrations, appendices.

839. Dynasty: The Authorized Biography of the Carringtons. Gar-
      den City, NY: Doubleday, 1984. 158p.
      See entry 63.

840. Feuer, Jane, Paul Kerr, and Tise Vahimagi (eds.). MTV
      "Quality Television." London: British Film Institute, 1984.
      308p.
      Seven essays exploring the history of MTM Enterprises, its

most celebrated series ("The Mary Tyler Moore Show," "Lou
Grant," and "Hill Street Blues"), and its style. List of MTM
programs with credits, synopses, and critical commentary. Illustrations.

841. Gerrold, David. <u>The World of Star Trek</u>. Rev. ed. New York:
      Bluejay Books, 1984. 209p.
          The "Star Trek" myth and how it happened. Gene Rodden-
      berry's dream of a TV series about an interstellar starship,
      how the cast and crew made the dream a reality, and the
      reality that the program's fans created. Illustrations.

842. Gitlin, Todd. <u>Inside Prime Time</u>. New York: Pantheon Books,
      1983. 369p.
          Behind-the-scenes exploration of how prime-time TV shows
      get on the air, remain there, and are shaped by the political
      and cultural climate of the times. Network calculations on
      reaching the maximum audience, their reliance on a small, re-
      volving world of major suppliers and agents, and the role of
      politics in their decisions on prime-time series. The last, and
      longest, chapter traces the history of "Hill Street Blues." In-
      dex.

843. Grote, David. <u>The End of Comedy: The Sit-Com and the
      Comedic Tradition</u>. Hamden, CT: Archon Books, 1983. 206p.
          The revolution in comedy brought about by the television
      situation-comedy, which the author suggests is like no other
      form of literature and shares almost nothing with what has al-
      ways been known as comedy. Characteristics and audiences of
      the sit-com, and contrasts with traditional comedy. Appendix,
      bibliography, index.

844. Groves, Seli, with the Editors of the Associated Press. <u>Soaps:
      A Pictorial History of America's Daytime Dramas</u>. Chicago: Con-
      temporary Books, 1983. 237p.
          See entry 709.

845. Hill, Doug, and Jeff Weingrad. <u>Saturday Night: A Backstage
      History of Saturday Night Live</u>. New York: Beech Tree
      Books, 1986. 510p.
          See entry 712.

846. Hobson, Dorothy. <u>"Crossroads": The Drama of a Soap Opera</u>.
      London: Methuen, 1982. 176p.
          See entry 665.

847. Intintoli, Michael James. <u>Taking Soaps Seriously: The World
      of Guiding Light</u>. New York: Praeger, 1984. 261p.
          The production process of "The Guiding Light" and descrip-
      tion and analysis of ways in which it shapes performances.
      The relationship of performances and the practices that generate

them to the larger society in terms of organizational relationships, market competition, the hierarchical and collective nature
of the work process, and interaction with the audience. Illustrations, tables, index.

848. Kalter, Suzy. The Complete Book of Dallas: Behind the
Scenes at the World's Favorite Television Program. New York:
Harry N. Abrams, 1986. 239p.
    Dramatic elements and their employment in "Dallas." Char-
acter traits of love, strength, greed, envy, gluttony, pride,
lust, wrath, and sloth. Synopses of episodes for 1977-78
through 1985-86 and details of the making of an episode. Illustrations.

849. Kalter, Suzy. The Complete Book of M*A*S*H. New York:
Harry N. Abrams, 1984. 240p.
    Summaries of the series' 251 episodes, organized by year of
broadcast and accompanied by color and black-and-white photographs. Observations by the program's creative staff and
stars. Illustrations, appendices.

850. Kelly, Richard Michael. The Andy Griffith Show. Rev. ed.
Winston-Salem, NC: John F. Blair, 1984. 286p.
    Development of the show from its conception to conclusion.
Its artistic qualities, updates on the careers of cast members,
and scripts. List and summary of all 249 episodes, arranged
according to the date of their original presentation. Illustrations, index.

851. LaGuardia, Robert. Soap World. New York: Arbor House,
1983. 408p.
    History of daytime serials. Background, plot summary,
cast and creative staff of 13 television serials on the air at
the time of publication and of seven that had disappeared from
the schedule, including the long-running "Love of Life" (1951-
1980) and the short-lived "Texas" (1980-82). Illustrations,
appendices, bibliography, index.

852. McCarty, John, and Brian Kelleher. Alfred Hitchcock Presents: An Illustrated Guide to the Ten-Year Television Career
of the Master of Suspense. New York: St. Martin's Press,
1985. 338p.
    The origins of the series "Alfred Hitchcock Presents" and
"The Alfred Hitchcock Hour," contributions of their acting and
creative personnel, and problems with censors and advertisers.
Complete chronology of the 359 episodes that constituted the
series' 10-year run, with pertinent credits and synopses. Illustrations, appendix, bibliography, index.

853. MacDonald, J. Fred. Television and the Red Menace: The
Video Road to Vietnam. New York: Praeger, 1985. 278p.
    See entry 739.

854. Nevins, Francis M., Jr., and Martin Harry Greenberg (eds.).
      Hitchcock in Prime Time. New York: Avon Books, 1985.
      356p.
      Twenty tales of suspense that were adapted for "Alfred
      Hitchcock Presents" or "The Alfred Hitchcock Hour." Each
      selection is followed by a listing of the original cast, episode
      scriptwriter and director, and a commentary on the production.

855. Nown, Graham (ed.). Coronation Street: 25 Years, 1960-1985.
      London: Ward Lock, in association with Granada Television,
      1985. 214p.
      See entry 679.

856. Perry, George. Life of Python. Boston, MA: Little, Brown,
      1983. 192p.
      See entry 681.

857. Reiss, David S. M*A*S*H: The Exclusive, Inside Story of
      TV's Most Popular Show. Updated. Indianapolis: Bobbs-
      Merrill, 1983. 168p.
      History, the players and producers, capsule summary of
      all 251 episodes, fan mail, and a chronology of awards and
      nominations. Illustrations.

858. Rose, Brian G. Television and the Performing Arts: A Hand-
      book and Reference Guide to American Cultural Programming.
      Westport, CT: Greenwood Press, 1986. 271p.
      See entry 545.

859. Sackett, Susan, and Cheryl Blythe. You Can Be a Game Show
      Contestant and Win. New York: Dell, 1982. 165p.
      See entry 547.

860. Schemering, Christopher. The Soap Opera Encyclopedia. New
      York: Ballantine Books, 1985. 358p.
      See entry 555.

861. Self, David. Television Drama: An Introduction. London:
      Macmillan, 1984. 173p.
      See entry 685.

862. Sutton, Shaun. The Largest Theatre in the World: Thirty
      Years of Television Drama. London: British Broadcasting
      Corporation, 1982. 160p.
      The role of the writer, producer, and director, and the re-
      sponsibilities of television as a dramatic medium. Illustrations,
      index.

863. Television Looks at Aging. New York: Television Information
      Office, 1985. 103p.
      Network and local entertainment and news programs and

program segments dealing with older Americans, organized by
topic. Includes housing, economics, health, society's attitudes, gray power, and adapting to aging. Each entry gives
program or segment title, summary of content, and network
or station. Illustrations.

864. Thomas, David, and Ian Irvine. Bilko: The Fort Baxter
Story. London: Vermilion/Hutchinson, 1985. 111p.
Reminiscences of Bilko and gambling, love, in Hollywood
and on Broadway, his relationship with Colonel Hall, and a
portrait of Doberman. An A to Z of people, places, and
events from the series, and title and summary of each episode.
Illustrations.

865. Trimble, Bjo. On the Good Ship Enterprise: My 15 Years
with Star Trek. Norfolk, VA: Donning, 1983. 286p.
Anecdotes and stories about "Star Trek" by the "fan liai-
son" for both the television and motion picture versions. Illustrations.

866. Tulloch, John, and Manuel Alvarado. Doctor Who: The Unfolding Text. New York: St. Martin's Press, 1983. 342p.
See entry 690.

867. Van Wormer, Laura. Dallas: The Complete Ewing Family Saga,
Including Southfork Ranch, Ewing Oil, and the Barnes-Ewing
Feud, 1860-1985. Garden City, NY: Doubleday, 1985. 214p.
Text and photographs of the people, places, and events of
the television serial. Illustrations.

868. Weissman, Ginny, and Coyne Steven Sanders. The Dick Van
Dyke Show: Anatomy of a Classic. New York: St. Martin's
Press, 1983. 146p.
Evolution of the program from its pilot, the selection of the
cast, and the process of writing, rehearsing, improvising, and
polishing. Synopses of all 158 episodes, and a complete script
of one ("That's My Boy??"). Awards won by the show, its
cast during the five-year run, and an update on their activities as of the date of publication. Illustrations, index.

869. White, Thomas, and Gladys Ganley. The "Death of a Princess"
Controversy. Cambridge, MA: Program on Information Re-
sources Policy, Harvard University, 1983. 60p.
See entry 750.

870. Whitley, Dianna, and Ray Manzella. Soap Stars: America's
31 Favorite Daytime Actors Speak for Themselves. Garden
City, NY: Doubleday/Dolphin, 1985. 187p.
See entry 599.

871. Zicree, Marc Scott. The Twilight Zone Companion. New York:

Bantam Books, 1982. 447p.
Synopses of the 156 episodes of "The Twilight Zone" that
aired on CBS-TV from 1959 to 1964, listing of cast and credits
for each, commentary, recollections by series creative personnel, and a profile of Rod Serling. Illustrations, index.

3. Information

872. Adams, William C. (ed.). Television Coverage of International
      Affairs. Norwood, NJ: Ablex, 1982. 253p.
      See entry 722.

873. Adams, William C. (ed.). Television Coverage of the 1980
      Presidential Campaign. Norwood, NJ: Ablex, 1983. 197p.
      See entry 792.

874. Barrett, Marvin (ed.). Broadcast Journalism 1979-1981: The
      Eighth Alfred I. du Pont/Columbia University Survey. New
      York: Everest House, 1982. 256p.
      Developments in television journalism and TV coverage of
      major events in the period. The credibility problem, launch
      of CNN, televised religion, politics, and public broadcasting.
      Eight essays on subjects ranging from new technology and the
      news to investigative reporting. Lists of du Pont/Columbia
      University award winners for 1979-80 and 1980-81. Index.

875. Benjamin, Burton. The CBS Benjamin Report: CBS Reports
      "The Uncounted Enemy: A Vietnam Deception": An Examina-
      tion. Washington, DC: Media Institute, 1984.
      Examination of charges in a TV Guide cover article on how
      the CBS documentary was prepared, written by a senior news
      producer at the network and ordered released by a federal
      judge. Includes a transcript of the documentary.

876. Blume, Keith. The Presidential Election Show: Campaign '84
      and Beyond on the Nightly News. South Hadley, MA: Bergin
      and Garvey, 1985. 340p.
      See entry 793.

877. CNN vs. The Networks: Is More News Better News? Washing-
      ton, DC: Media Institute, 1983. 42p.
      Content analysis of domestic business and economic news
      stories in the early-evening television newscasts of ABC, CBS,
      NBC, and CNN's "Primenews." Finds that CNN's coverage was
      more balanced and less sensational than that of the other net-
      works; that CNN's coverage had less depth, relative to the
      time available; and that the news priorities of CNN and the
      other networks did not differ significantly. Illustrations,
      tables, appendix.

878. Fury, Kathleen. <u>Dear 60 Minutes</u>. New York: Simon and
Schuster, 1984. 236p.
Collection of viewers' letters to CBS' "60 Minutes" correspondents and Andy Rooney, who recall their celebrity
guests and favorite letters. Topics include pollution, gun control, doctors, taxes, and the family pet.

879. Hallin, Daniel C. <u>The "Uncensored War": The Media and
Vietnam</u>. New York: Oxford University Press, 1986. 285p.
The first part is an analysis of coverage by <u>The New York
Times</u> from 1961 through mid-1965; the second part deals with
a sample of network evening news from August 1965 through
the cease-fire in January 1973. Concludes that television was
particularly patriotic in its early coverage but changed as the
political climate shifted at home and among American soldiers
in the field. Tables, bibliography, appendices, index.

880. Harrison, Martin. <u>Television News: Whose Bias? A Case-
book Analysis of Strikes, Television and Media Studies</u>.
Hermitage, Eng.: Policy Journals, 1985. 400p.
See entry 662.

881. Hazlett, Thomas W. <u>TV Coverage of the Oil Crises: How Well
Was the Public Served? Vol. 3: An Economist's Perspective,
1973-74/1978-79</u>. Washington, DC: Media Institute, 1982. 51p.
Economic analysis of the accuracy, relevance, and balance
of the portrayal of the crises on network television evening
newscasts.

882. Hetherington, Alastair. <u>News, Newspapers and Television</u>.
London: Macmillan, 1985. 329p.
See entry 664.

883. Hewitt, Don. <u>Minute by Minute</u>.... New York: Random
House, 1985. 223p.
On-screen and behind-the-scenes at "60 Minutes," by the
program's creator and executive producer. Quotes and partial
transcripts from memorable interviews. Illustrations.

884. Karnow, Stanley. <u>Vietnam: A History</u>. New York: Viking
Press, 1983. 752p.
Parallels the 1983 PBS documentary series "Vietnam: A
Television History," on which the author served as chief cor-
respondent. Illustrations, index.

885. Kern, Montague. <u>Television and Middle East Diplomacy: President Carter's Fall 1977 Peace Initiative</u>. Washington, DC:
Center for Contemporary Arab Studies, Georgetown University,
1983. 51p.
See entry 799.

886. Kowet, Don. A Matter of Honor: General William C. Westmore-
      land Versus CBS. New York: Macmillan, 1984. 317p.
      The making of the CBS documentary "The Uncounted Enemy:
      A Vietnam Deception," in which General Westmoreland, the
      former commander of U.S. forces in Vietnam, was accused of
      engineering a conspiracy to suppress the numerical size of the
      enemy. The furor that followed the broadcast in January 1982,
      the filing by General Westmoreland of a $120 million libel suit,
      the TV Guide investigation, and CBS' internal inquiry. Index.

887. Kurtis, Bill. Bill Kurtis on Assignment. Chicago: Rand Mc-
      Nally, 1983. 192p.
      See entry 597.

888. Larson, James F. Television's Window on the World: Interna-
      tional Affairs Coverage on the U.S. Networks. Norwood, NJ:
      Ablex, 1984. 195p.
      See entry 802.

889. Lashner, Marilyn A. The Chilling Effect in TV News: Intimi-
      dation by the Nixon White House. New York: Praeger, 1984.
      297p.
      Study of political commentary on U.S. commercial television
      networks and in newspapers to determine whether the govern-
      mentally regulated medium of broadcasting can be expected to
      engage in vigorous debate and criticism of government with the
      same integrity as the printed press. Concludes that TV news
      commentators allowed themselves to be manipulated by White
      House pressure and that, as anti-media pressure mounted, they
      avoided criticism and controversy and concentrated instead on
      less sensitive areas. Illustrations, tables, appendices, glos-
      sary, bibliography, index.

890. Lawler, Philip F. The Alternative Influence: The Impact of
      Investigative Reporting Groups on America's Media. Washing-
      ton, DC: Media Institute; Lanham, MD: University Press of
      America, 1984. 92p.
      Profile of nine groups, their methods, and their contribu-
      tions to investigative reporting by the television networks,
      newspapers, and magazines.

891. Lesher, Stephan. Media Unbound: The Impact of Television
      Journalism on the Public. Boston, MA: Houghton Mifflin,
      1982. 285p.
      See entry 736.

892. Lichter, S. Robert, Stanley Rothman, and Linda S. Lichter.
      The Media Elite. Bethesda, MD: Adler and Adler, 1986.
      342p.
      See entry 737.

893. McCrum, Robert, William Cran, and Robert MacNeil. The Story of English. New York: Elisabeth Sifton Books/Viking Press, 1986. 384p.
     Companion volume to the PBS television series recording the evolution of spoken and written English. Illustrations, index.

894. MacDonald, J. Fred. Television and the Red Menace: The Video Road to Vietnam. New York: Praeger, 1985. 278p.
     See entry 739.

895. Madsen, Axel. 60 Minutes: The Power and The Politics of America's Most Popular TV News Show. New York: Dodd, Mead, 1984. 255p.
     The program's ethics, morals, and techniques; ways in which it uses its power; and the politics behind the selection and editing of its stories. Bibliography, index.

896. Matusow, Barbara. The Evening Stars: The Making of the Network News Anchor. Boston, MA: Houghton Mifflin, 1983. 302p.
     Evolving importance of network evening news and the influence of the anchor. Network news strategies and the role of, among others, David Brinkley, Walter Cronkite, Chet Huntley, Dan Rather, Harry Reasoner, and Barbara Walters. Illustrations, bibliography, index.

897. Nimmo, Dan, and James E. Combs. Nightly Horrors: Crisis Coverage by Television Network News. Knoxville: University of Tennessee Press, 1985. 216p.
     Study of how ABC, CBS, and NBC reported six major crises on their nightly news programs: the Jim Jones-People's Temple murders and mass suicides, the Three Mile Island nuclear accident, the crash of American Airlines flight 191, the eruption of Mount St. Helens, the Iranian hostage crisis, and the Tylenol poisonings. Concludes that the networks define crises in distinctly different ways. Tables, index.

898. Robinson, John P., and Mark R. Levy, with Dennis K. Davis. The Main Source: Learning from Television News. Beverly Hills, CA: Sage Publications, 1986. 272p.
     See entry 744.

899. Robinson, Michael J., and Margaret A. Sheehan. Over the Wire and on TV: CBS and UPI in Campaign '80. New York: Russell Sage Foundation, 1983. 332p.
     See entry 805.

900. Swerdlow, Joel L. Beyond Debate: A Paper on Televised Presidential Debates. New York: Twentieth-Century Fund, 1984. 89p.
     Reviews recent history of debates and examines and makes recommendations on format, participation, and sponsorship.

901. Tannenbaum, Percy H., and Leslie J. Kostrich. Turned-On
      TV/Turned-Off Voters: Policy Options for Election Projections.
      Beverly Hills, CA: Sage Publications, 1983. 240p.
      See entry 806.

902. Teague, Bob. Live and Off-Color: News Biz. New York:
      A and W, 1982. 239p.
      An inside look at the workings of local television news by
      a WNBC-TV reporter and anchor. Ratings and their influence,
      personality clashes, programming controversies, the trend
      toward "infotainment," and proposals for achieving the poten-
      tial of TV news. Illustrations, index.

903. Television Looks At Aging. New York: Television Information
      Office, 1985. 103p.
      See entry 863.

904. Theberge, Leonard J. (ed.). TV Coverage of the Oil Crises:
      How Well Was the Public Served? Vol. 1: A Qualitative Analy-
      sis, 1973-74/1978-79. Washington, DC: Media Institute, 1982.
      59p.
      Analysis of the substance of 1,462 stories broadcast on the
      early evening newscasts of the three major commercial television
      networks. Examination of the general dimensions of the cover-
      age and the networks' portrayals of the solutions, causes,
      and effects of the crises. Illustrations.

905. Theberge, Leonard J. (ed.). TV Coverage of the Oil Crises:
      How Well Was the Public Served? Vol. 2: A Quantitative
      Analysis, 1973-74/1978-79. Washington, DC: Media Institute,
      1982. 62p.
      Content similarities and differences among the networks
      during each crisis and between the two crises. Illustrations.

906. Voices and Values: Television Stations in the Community.
      New York: Television Information Office, 1984. 130p.
      Examples of public service work of 308 commercial television
      stations in newscasts, public affairs programs, public service
      announcements, editorials, and off-air activities. Organized
      in nine categories: the family, education, health, social prob-
      lems, the economy, minority groups, local government and poli-
      tics, the consumer and the environment, and good neighbors.
      Each entry includes title, station call letters and location, and
      format. Illustrations, station index.

907. Westin, Av. Newswatch: How TV Decides the News. New
      York: Simon and Schuster, 1982. 274p.
      Insider's account of life in the television newsroom: the
      people, procedures, and pressures. The achievements and
      shortcomings of TV news and its challenges and responsbilities.
      Illustrations, index.

4. Portrayals

908. Anwar, Muhammad, and Anthony Shang. Television in a Multi-
     racial Society: A Research Report. London: Commission for
     Racial Equality, 1982. 84p.
     See entry 652.

909. Barcus, F. Earle. Images of Life on Children's Television:
     Sex Roles, Minorities, and Families. New York: Praeger, 1983.
     219p.
     See entry 753.

910. Davis, Richard H., and James A. Davis. TV's Image of the
     Elderly: A Practical Guide for Change. Lexington, MA:
     D. C. Heath, 1985. 265p.
          Examination of television's treatment of aging and the elder-
     ly, and suggestions for gaining access to the medium and pro-
     ducing programs to convey information and ideas of concern
     to the aging. Tables, appendices, glossary, index.

911. DeGooyer, Janice, and Farfalla Borah. What's Wrong With This
     Picture? A Look at Working Women on Television. Washington,
     DC: National Commission on Working Women, 1982. 22p.
          The portrayal of working women in Nielsen's top-25 network
     prime-time programs in the period 1972-1981. Among the con-
     clusions: women on television are younger than in real life,
     tend to be white, are more likely to work in a professional oc-
     cupation, and are more likely to appear in situation comedies
     than in action/crime programs. Examination of cable and satel-
     lites, their current programming for and about working women,
     and possibilities for the future.

912. Diamond, Edwin. Sign-Off: The Last Days of Television.
     Cambridge, MA: MIT Press, 1982. 273p.
          Analysis of ways in which television presents major American
     institutions and reflects American culture and society. Among
     the topics covered: sex on television, the "electronic church,"
     labor, the Iranian hostage crisis, Three Mile Island, and argu-
     ments about television's alleged omnipotence and liberalism. In-
     dex.

913. Fighting TV Stereotypes: An ACT Handbook. Newtonville,
     MA: Action for Children's Television, 1983. 22p.
          Perspectives on ways in which television programs can pro-
     vide more positive role models and fewer negative stereotypes.
     Illustrations.

914. Glasgow University Media Group. Really Bad News. New
     York: Writers and Readers, 1982. 170p.
          See entry 660.

915. Jackson, Anthony W. Black Families and the Medium of Television. Ann Arbor, MI: Bush Program in Child Development
and Social Policy, University of Michigan, 1982. 108p.
Collection of papers presented at a 1980 conference on the
TV image of blacks, and especially black families. Covers the
role of television in image creation, the influence of ratings
and the creative process, the role of government and advocacy
groups, and suggested solutions to the problems identified.

916. Johnston, Jerome, and James S. Ettema. Positive Images:
Breaking Stereotypes with Children's Television. Beverly Hills,
CA: Sage Publications, 1982. 263p.
See entry 766.

917. Kalisch, Philip A., Beatrice J. Kalisch, and Margaret Scobey.
Images of Nurses on Television. New York: Springer, 1983.
214p.
Describes and analyzes the development of the televised
image of nurses and nursing from the 1950s through the early
1980s. Concludes that there is little resemblance between contemporary nursing practice and its largely fictional depiction
on television. Bibliography, appendix, index.

918. Lichter, Linda S., and S. Robert Lichter. Prime Time Crime:
Criminals and Law Enforcers in TV Entertainment. Washington, DC: Media Institute, 1983. 64p.
The extent and nature of crime and law enforcement in 263
prime-time programs aired on ABC, CBS, and NBC in the 1980-
81 season. Concludes that: crime pervades television entertainment; TV crime is far more violent than real crime; TV
criminals tend to come from the "establishment"; and most crime
is punished, but policemen are rarely the heroes. Tables, appendices.

919. MacDonald, J. Fred. Blacks and White TV: Afro-Americans
in Television since 1948. Chicago: Nelson-Hall, 1983. 288p.
Argues that, despite significant achievements, television
has failed to match its potential to reverse centuries of ridicule,
inaccurate portrayals, and inequitable utilization of talented
Afro-Americans. Illustrations, bibliography, index of television programs, index.

920. McLoone, Martin, and John MacMahon (eds.). Television and
Irish Society: 21 Years of Irish Television. Dublin: Radio
Telefís Éireann, 1984. 151p.
See entry 648.

921. Meehan, Diana M. Ladies of the Evening: Women Characters
of Prime-Time Television. Metuchen, NJ: Scarecrow Press,
1983. 190p.
The portrayals of women in 33 network series from 1950 to

1980. Concludes that they represent arrant distortions of
American womanhood. Illustrations, bibliography, appendices,
general index, index of characters.

922. Parks, Rita. The Western Hero in Film and Television: Mass
Media Mythology. Ann Arbor, MI: UMI Research Press, 1982.
190p.
The creation and evolution of the Western hero from historical figure to mass media myth, and the movement of the
hero between film and television. Appendices, bibliography,
index.

923. Shaheen, Jack G. The TV Arab. Bowling Green, OH: Bowling
Green State University Popular Press, 1984. 146p.
The portrayal of Arabs in children's, private eye and police,
comedy, and documentary programs. Contends that the medium
tends to perpetuate four basic myths about Arabs: that they
are all fabulously wealthy, are barbaric and uncultured, are
sex maniacs with a penchant for white slavery, and that they
revel in acts of terrorism. Offers suggestions for dispelling
the stereotypes. Index.

924. Signorielli, Nancy (comp. and ed.). Role Portrayal and Stereotyping on Television: An Annotated Bibliography of Studies
Relating to Women, Minorities, Aging, Sexual Behavior, Health
and Handicaps. Westport, CT: Greenwood Press, 1985. 214p.
See entry 531.

925. Steenland, Sally. The Picture Improves: A Look at the 1984
Television Season. Washington, DC: National Commission on
Working Women, 1984. 12p.
The image of women in network prime-time television programs premiering in 1984, and comparisons with 1983. Finds
greater visibility of minority and older women and of working
mothers and that women's roles have become more diverse and
their characters expanded.

926. Stewart, Donald E. The Television Family: A Content Analysis
of the Portrayal of Family Life in Prime Time Television.
Melbourne: Institute of Family Studies, 1983. 66p.
See entry 635.

5. Scripts

927. Kuralt, Charles. On the Road with Charles Kuralt. New York:
G. P. Putnam's Sons, 1985. 316p.
Scripts of 92 "On the Road" stories on people, places, and
events. Illustrations.

K. PUBLIC AND COMMUNITY

928. Carey, John, Thomas Gherardi, Harold Kappes, and Mitchell
      Moss. Modularization and Packaging of Public Television Pro-
      grams. Washington, DC: Corporation for Public Broadcasting,
      1983. 102p.
        Opportunities for public television to harness new distribu-
      tion methods, such as cable, videocassettes, and interactive
      video, to reach new audiences or the same audiences with a
      targeted programming approach. Illustrations, tables, ap-
      pendices.

929. Eastman, Susan Tyler, and Robert A. Klein (eds.). Strategies
      in Broadcast and Cable Promotion: Commercial Television,
      Radio, Cable, Pay-Television, Public Television. Belmont, CA:
      Wadsworth, 1982. 355p.
        See entry 351.

930. Frank, Ronald E., and Marshall G. Greenberg. Audiences for
      Public Television. Beverly Hills, CA: Sage Publications, 1982.
      230p.
        See entry 581.

931. Karnow, Stanley. Vietnam: A History. New York: Viking
      Press, 1983. 752p.
        See entry 884.

932. LeRoy, David, and Judith M. LeRoy. The Impact of the Cable
      Television Industry on Public Television. Washington, DC:
      Corporation for Public Broadcasting, 1983. 82p.
        Analysis and discussion using data from the national Niel-
      sen ratings, Electronic Media Tracking Service, and a national
      mail survey by the Benton and Bowles advertising agency.
      Among the conclusions: public television will not be deserted
      by cable subscribers, but they will view fewer minutes and are
      less likely to become public TV members. Tables, appendices.

933. Lichter, S. Robert, Stanley Rothman, and Linda S. Lichter.
      The Media Elite. Bethesda, MD: Adler and Adler, 1986.
      342p.
        See entry 737.

934. McCrum, Robert, William Cran, and Robert MacNeil. The Story
      of English. New York: Elisabeth Sifton Books/Viking Press,
      1986. 384p.
        See entry 893.

935. The Making of The Jewel in the Crown. New York: St. Mar-
      tin's Press, 1983. 134p.
        Text and photographs of the production of the PBS series

based on Paul Scott's Raj Quartet. Episode outlines, a personal view of the last days of the Raj, memoirs of Scott, and capsule biographies of the cast and production team. Illustrations.

936. Mendel, Robin, Natan Katzman, and Solomon Katzman. Public Television Programming Content by Category: Fiscal Year 1982. Washington, DC: Corporation for Public Broadcasting, 1984. 88p.
Based on the programming schedules of 284 stations, classified by budget, region of the country, broadcaster class, and population served. Data are reported as follows: instructional television series, "Sesame Street" and "The Electric Company," general and news/public affairs programs, special or target audience programs, local programming, and PBS and prime-time programming. Illustrations, tables, appendices.

937. Reed, Robert M. The American Telecommunications Market: Commercial/Public TV, Cable, STV, MDS, LPTV, Home Video. Syosset, NY: National Video Clearinghouse, 1982. 202p. + appendices.
See entry 544.

938. Tourigny, Patrick. Community Television Handbook for Northern and Underserved Communities. Ottawa: Canadian Radio-television and Telecommunications Commission, 1983. 35p.
See entry 640.

939. White, Thomas, and Gladys Ganley. The "Death of a Princess" Controversy. Cambridge, MA: Program on Information Resources Policy, Harvard University, 1983. 60p.
See entry 750.

L. PUBLICATION

940. Byron, Christopher M. The Fanciest Dive: What Happened When the Media Empire of Time/Life Leaped Without Looking into the Age of High-Tech. New York: W. W. Norton, 1986. 280p.
Account of the circumstances leading to the birth and quick death of TV-Cable Week magazine, by its senior editor.

M. TECHNIQUE AND TECHNOLOGY

1. Advertising, Marketing, and Promotion

941. Baldwin, Huntley. Creating Effective TV Commercials. Chicago:

Crain Books, 1982. 245p.
Copywriter's perspective on the process of developing advertising ideas and translating them into commercials. Illustrations, index.

942. Conrad, Jon J. The TV Commercial: How It Is Made. New
York: Van Nostrand Reinhold, 1983. 160p.
Preproduction and film and videotape production and post-
production. Types of commercials and the role of the adver-
tising agency in their creation, production, and placement.
Illustrations, glossary, index.

943. De Sarlo, Carmine R. TV Commercial Film Editing: Professional Motion Picture Pre- and Post-Production Including Animation,
Rotoscoping, and Video Tape. Jefferson, NC: McFarland,
1985. 243p.
Step-by-step procedures and explanations, using three
imaginary spots. Index.

944. Hall, Jim. Mighty Minutes: An Illustrated History of Television's Best Commercials. New York: Harmony Books, 1984.
172p.
See entry 710.

945. Logan, Tom. Acting in the Million Dollar Minute: The Art and
Business of Performing in TV Commercials. Washington, DC:
Communications Press, 1984. 176p.
The "art" includes basic principles, terminology and procedures, commercial dialogue, and camera staging. "Business"
covers getting started, obtaining an agent, unions and agency
contracts, the commercial interview, and pay and working conditions. Illustrations, appendices.

946. Poltrack, David. Television Marketing: Network, Local, and
Cable. New York: McGraw-Hill, 1983. 395p.
Overview of the television advertising process. The role
of networks, stations, and cable systems, buying time, commercial production, campaign planning, ratings, measuring effective-
ness, and advertising regulation. Illustrations, tables, index.

947. White, Hooper. How to Produce Effective TV Commercials. 2d
ed. Lincolnwood, IL: NTC Business Books, 1986. 305p.
Twelve essential steps, from preparing the idea through the
addition of the opticals. Chapters on casting, selection of film
or videotape, on-set and on-location production, music, live
action, animation, and the use of computers and other special
effects. Illustrations, glossaries, appendices, index.

948. Wiese, Michael. The Independent Film and Videomakers Guide.
4th ed. Westport, CT: Michael Wiese Film Productions, 1984.
386p.

Tips on financing, producing, distributing, and promoting film and video product. Illustrations, appendix, bibliography, filmography.

2. Engineering

949. Benson, K. Blair (ed.). Television Engineering Handbook. New York: McGraw-Hill, 1986.
  Technical information for engineers engaged in design and development, as well as in maintenance and operation. Includes fundamental concepts of television imagery and transmission, signal generation and processing, transmission, reception, picture reproduction, and reference data. Illustrations, tables, index.

950. Ingram, Dave. Video Electronics Technology. Blue Ridge Summit, PA: TAB Books, 1983. 250p.
  Details and working explanations of black-and-white and color TV, MDS, satellite receiver, and video recording and playback systems. Illustrations, tables, index.

951. Kiver, Milton, and Milton Kaufman. Television Electronics: Theory and Service. 8th ed. New York: Van Nostrand Reinhold, 1983. 974p.
  Designed to prepare persons in electronics technology for careers in television. Includes cable television, videotape and video recorders, satellites, and video games. Chapters conclude with examination questions and problems. Illustrations, glossary, index.

952. Prentiss, Stan. Television: From Analog to Digital. Blue Ridge Summit, PA: TAB Books, 1985. 343p.
  State-of-the-art transmitters, receivers, transmission lines, and analog/digital troubleshooting techniques. Written for professional engineers and technicians. Illustrations, tables, glossary, index.

953. White, Gordon. Video Techniques. London: Butterworth, 1982. 299p.
  Principles of television engineering and their application to equipment, production, transmission, and reception. Illustrations, index.

3. Management

954. Bortz, Paul I., Mark C. Wyche, and James M. Trautman. Great Expectations: A Television Manager's Guide to the Future. Washington, DC: National Association of Broadcasters, 1986. 140p.

Review of major change factors in television broadcasting
since 1980, projections of anticipated changes over the next
several years, and strategies for meeting them. Factors include audience demographics, competing technologies, viewing
trends, advertising volume, prices and composition, the program marketplace, audience measurement techniques, technological changes, and legislation and regulation. Illustrations,
tables, appendices.

4. News

955. Lewis, Carolyn Diana. Reporting For Television. New York:
      Columbia University Press, 1984. 184p.
         Practical manual for students and for new reporters and
      producers at local television stations. Combines the basics of
      field reporting with some theories and practices in the report-
      ing process. Illustrations, glossary, index.

956. Sadashige, Ernie. ENG One: A Practical Guide to Electronic
      News Gathering. Gibbsboro, NJ: Highlights, 1985. 173p.
         Problems and solutions. Sources, formats, field work,
      videography, newscast production, and finding a job. Illustra-
      tions, index.

957. Shook, Frederick. The Process of Electronic News Gathering.
      Englewood, CO: Morton, 1982. 180p.
         Methods of news gathering and reporting, and shooting and
      editing with ENG. Development of videotape recording, and the
      ethics of ENG reporting. Illustrations, appendices, index.

958. Yoakam, Richard D., and Charles F. Cremer. ENG: Televi-
      sion News and the New Technology. New York: Random
      House, 1985. 354p.
         Writing, reporting, editing, producing, and delivering the
      news in the ENG era. The technology and its impact, and
      ENG and the law. Illustrations, appendices, glossary, bibli-
      ography, index.

5. Performance

959. Baygan, Lee. Makeup for Theatre, Film, and Television: A
      Step-by-Step Photographic Guide. New York: Drama Book,
      1982. 183p.
         Corrective, straight, middle age, aging, and three-dimensional
      makeup. Beards and mustaches, wigs and falls, scars, and ori-
      ental makeup. Each procedure is accompanied by a series of
      photographs. Illustrations, glossary.

960. Blythin, Evan, and Larry A. Samovar. Communicating

Effectively on Television. Belmont, CA: Wadsworth, 1985.
220p.
  Information and advice for persons whose occupation may
require them to appear on television, such as educators, lawyers, doctors, and politicians. Covers the nature of televised
communication, the gathering and organization of material, personnel and equipment in the TV studio, visual and sound presentation techniques, and the TV interview. Illustrations,
recommended readings, index.

961. Logan, Tom. Acting in the Million Dollar Minute: The Art
and Business of Performing in TV Commercials. Washington,
DC: Communications Press, 1984. 176p.
  See entry 945.

6. Production and Direction

(a) General

962. Armer, Alan A. Directing Television and Film. Belmont, CA:
Wadsworth, 1986. 337p.
  Theoretical approach to directing, in three parts. Part
one examines the characteristics and work of the director, elements of entertainment, and principles of visual composition.
The second part focuses on directing fiction and includes chapters on the script, characterization, staging, and techniques
for building suspense. The final part discusses five nonfiction
TV genres: interviews, demonstrations, news programs, commercials, and music programs. Illustrations, glossary, index.

963. Breyer, Richard, and Peter Moller. Making Television Programs: A Professional Approach. New York: Longman, 1984.
188p.
  The process of planning and producing programs for commercial, institutional, public, and pay-per-program television. The
importance of team work and the role of producers, directors,
writers, and designers. Illustrations, bibliography.

964. Broughton, Irv (ed.). Producers on Producing: The Making
of Film and Television. Jefferson, NC: McFarland, 1986.
308p.
  Interviews with 22 producers from a variety of program
genres on their philosophies, problems, and day-to-day workings. Interviewees include Fred Rogers, Mark Goodson, David
Wolper, Earl Hamner, Jr., Pat Weaver, and Al Masini. Illustrations, index.

965. Burrows, Thomas D., and Donald N. Wood. Television Production: Disciplines and Techniques. 3rd ed. Dubuque, IA:
Wm. C. Brown, 1986. 444p.

Teaching text covering audio, lighting, cameras, switcher, videotape recorder, sets and graphics, talent, single-camera and studio production, and directing techniques. Illustrations, appendices, glossary, bibliography, index.

966. Chambers, Everett. Producing TV Movies. New York: Prentice Hall Press, 1986. 229p.
       Steps in getting a movie on a network. Development, preproduction, production, and post-production. Reflections on the state of television. Appendix, index.

967. Compesi, Ronald J., and Ronald E. Sherriffs. Small Format Television Production: The Technique of Single-Camera Television Field Production. Boston, MA: Allyn and Bacon, 1985. 465p.
       Camera and recording equipment and their use, lighting, graphics, sound, editing, and production planning and projects. Illustrations, appendices, glossary, bibliography, index.

968. Conrad, Jon J. The TV Commercial: How It Is Made. New York: Van Nostrand Reinhold, 1983. 160p.
       See entry 942.

969. Drucker, Malka, and Elizabeth James. Series TV: How a Television Show Is Made. New York: Clarion Books, 1983. 110p.
       Young person's guide to the creation and production of an episode of a television series. Illustrations, index.

970. Elliott, Geoff. Video Production in Education and Training. London: Croom Helm, 1984. 150p.
       Production planning, script development, single- and multicamera production, camera and presentation techniques, editing, post-production, interactive video, and program evaluation. Illustrations, glossary, index.

971. Fuller, Barry J., Steve Kanaba, and Janyce Brisch-Kanaba. Single-Camera Video Production: Techniques, Equipment, and Resources for Producing Quality Video Programming. Englewood Cliffs, NJ: Prentice-Hall, 1982. 252p.
       Basic information on black-and-white and color studio and field production for the educational, industrial, or independent producer. Advice on entering the business and making it profitable. Illustrations, glossary, index.

972. Glasser, Jeffrey, Stephen Gach, and Pamela Levine. Progressive Video Programming: A Strategy for Making Informational Video on Location. Los Angeles, CA: Videowares, 1984. 326p.
       A 20-step plan, from concept through marketing and distribution. Illustrations, appendix, index.

973. Iezzi, Frank. Understanding Television Production. Englewood Cliffs, NJ: Prentice-Hall, 1984. 158p.
     Introduction to production through consideration of the
functions of the person responsible for audio, lighting, floor,
and camera, and those of the switcher and director. Illustrations, glossary, bibliography, index.

974. Inside BBC Television: A Year Behind the Camera. Exeter,
Eng.: Webb and Bower, 1983. 224p.
     See entry 670.

975. Kowet, Don. A Matter of Honor: General William C. Westmoreland Versus CBS. New York: Macmillan, 1984. 317p.
     See entry 886.

976. LeBaron, John, and Philip Miller. Portable Video: A Production Guide for Young People. Englewood Cliffs, NJ: Prentice-
Hall, 1982. 176p.
     Introduction to equipment and its operation, production
skills and ideas, planning and scripting TV programs, and the
creation and use of graphics and special effects. Illustrations,
tables, bibliography, glossary, index.

977. Levinson, Richard, and William Link. Off Camera: Conversations with the Makers of Prime-Time Television. New York:
New American Library, 1986. 279p.
     Techniques, motives, and opinions of writers, actors, pro-
ducers, and directors, and of their support structure of
agents, suppliers, and the network. Includes drama and
comedy series, long-form programming, and interviews with,
among others, Steven Bochco, Angela Lansbury, Aaron Spelling,
and Brandon Tartikoff. Index.

978. Lukas, Christopher. Directing for Film and Television: A
Guide to the Craft. Garden City, NY: Anchor Press/Double-
day, 1985. 193p.
     The work of the director, from the script or idea stage
through to the final print. Reading and analyzing a prospective
script, making budgetary decisions, casting, technical and artistic preparations, aesthetics, shooting, post-production, and
dealing with film laboratories. Illustrations, glossary, bibliography, index.

979. McNulty, Sally. Television. Vero Beach, FL: Rourke Enterprises, 1984.
     Child's introduction to the people, equipment, and pro-
cesses of the broadcast of "The Moonbird Story." Illustrations.

980. McQuillin, Lon. Computers in Video Production. White Plains,
NY: Knowledge Industry Publications, 1986. 188p.
     What computers are, how they work, and the functions that

they can perform in production. Selection of computers, per-
ipherals, and software. Illustrations, appendices, glossary,
index.

981. McQuillin, Lon. The Video Production Guide. Indianapolis,
      IN: Howard W. Sams, 1983. 382p.
         A look at the production process from pre-production
      through post-production and distribution. Single- and multi-
      camera work and studio and remote production. Written for
      the novice as well as the more advanced student. Illustrations,
      appendices, glossary, index.

982. The Making of The Jewel in the Crown. New York: St. Mar-
      tin's Press, 1983. 134p.
         See entry 935.

983. Mathias, Harry, and Richard Patterson. Electronic Cinema-
      tography: Achieving Photographic Control over the Video
      Image. Belmont, CA: Wadsworth, 1985. 251p.
         Technology and creative skills for motion picture production
      on video and opportunities for higher quality video through
      high-definition television. Production, recording, and post-
      production considerations. Illustrations, glossary, index.

984. Medoff, Norman J., and Tom Tanquary. Portable Video: ENG
      and EFP. White Plains, NY: Knowledge Industry Publications,
      1986. 189p.
         Operation and maintenance of equipment, shooting tech-
      niques, scriptwriting, pre-production, and editing. Illustra-
      tions, tables, appendix, glossary, bibliography, index.

985. Millerson, Gerald. Effective TV Production. 2d ed. Boston,
      MA: Focal Press, 1983. 192p.
         Practical approach to production. Audio, video, lighting,
      staging, make-up, wardrobe, scripting, planning, and rehearsal.
      Single- and multi-camera techniques, and uses of graphics,
      film, and videotape. Illustrations, appendix, glossary, bib-
      liography.

986. Millerson, Gerald. The Technique of Television Production.
      11th ed. Boston, MA: Focal Press, 1985. 448p.
         How and why to carry out the various production tasks.
      Illustrations, glossary, bibliography, index.

987. Millerson, Gerald. Video Camera Techniques. Boston, MA:
      Focal Press, 1983. 160p.
         Essentials of handling a camera in the studio, street, and
      wherever video is used. Illustrations, further readings, glos-
      sary.

988. Millington, Bob, and Robin Nelson. Boys from the Blackstuff:

Making a TV Drama. London: Comedia, 1986. 192p.
See entry 676.

989. Moran, Albert. Making a TV Series: The "Bellamy" Project.
Woollahra, New South Wales: Currency Press, 1982. 175p.
See entry 632.

990. Newcomb, Horace, and Robert S. Alley. The Producer's
Medium: Conversations with Creators of American TV. New
York: Oxford University Press, 1983. 262p.
Commentary and interviews with 11 producers of prime-time
commercial fictional television, exploring their personal style,
observations on creative control, and assessment of their social
responsibility and the effects of their work. The producers
are Quinn Martin, David Victor, John Mantley, Richard Levinson, William Link, Earl Hamner, Norman Lear, James L. Brooks,
Allan Burns, Grant Tinker, and Garry Marshall. Illustrations,
index.

991. Oringel, Robert S. Television Operations Handbook. Boston,
MA: Focal Press, 1984. 182p.
Equipment and its use in program production. Lights and
lenses, the camera, switcher, audio, equipment interconnection,
videotape recorder, field production, editing, and post-production.
A chapter on mounting the studio cable television program. Illustrations, glossary, index.

992. Robinson, Richard. The Video Primer: Equipment, Production
and Concepts. 3rd ed. New York: Putnam, 1983. 382p.
Equipment, its practical applications and its potential. Illustrations, appendices, index.

993. Rosen, Frederic W. Shooting Video. Boston, MA: Focal
Press, 1984. 186p.
Video equipment, camera operations, lighting, shooting, and
working with subjects in video portraits. Tips on making money
covering events such as weddings, sports, reunions, and audi-
tions. Illustrations.

994. Shanks, Bob. The Primal Screen: How to Write, Sell, and
Produce Movies for Television. New York: W. W. Norton,
1986. 414p.
Tips and guidelines using the author's "Drop-Out Father"
as example. Illustrations, appendix, index.

995. Silverstone, Roger. Framing Science: The Making of a BBC
Documentary. London: British Film Institute, 1985. 239p.
See entry 688.

996. Stokes, Judith, and the Editors at Knowledge Industry Publications, Inc. Microcomputers in TV Studios. White Plains,
NY: Knowledge Industry Publications, 1986. 125p.

Profiles of microcomputer use in in-house corporate studios, production facilities, academic institutions, cable access centers, broadcast studios, and elsewhere. Entries include type of facility, population served, micros and software packages owned, and contact person. Illustrations, tables, glossary, suggested reading, index.

997. White, Hooper. How to Produce Effective TV Commercials. 2d ed. Lincolnwood, IL: NTC Business Books, 1986. 305p.
       See entry 947.

998. Wiegand, Ingrid. Professional Video Production. White Plains, NY: Knowledge Industry Publications, 1985. 215p.
       Guide to program development and script preparation, the studio, shooting in the studio and in the field, editing, post-production effects, and budgets. Illustrations, technical appendix, glossary, selected bibliography, index.

999. Wiese, Michael. The Independent Film and Videomakers Guide. 4th ed. Westport, CT: Michael Wiese Film Productions, 1984. 386p.
       See entry 948.

1000. Wurtzel, Alan. Television Production. 2d ed. New York: McGraw-Hill, 1983. 632p.
       Studio, ENG, and remote equipment and techniques. Lighting, audio, video recording and editing, special effects, graphics, film, set, and staging design, scripts, and talent. Illustrations, glossary, additional readings, index.

1001. Zettl, Herbert. Television Production Handbook. 4th ed. Belmont, CA: Wadsworth, 1984. 614p.
       Principles and techniques. The camera, lighting, audio, editing, design, talent, producing and directing, and remotes. Illustrations, glossary, index.

1002. Zettl, Herbert. Television Production Workbook. 4th ed. Belmont, CA: Wadsworth, 1985. 213p.
       Tests and exercises on the contents of the fourth edition of the author's Television Production Handbook (entry 1001). May be used with or without the handbook and is designed so that the basics of production may be learned without the use of actual equipment. Illustrations.

(b) Budgets

1003. Wiese, Michael. Film and Video Budgets. Westport, CT: Michael Wiese Film Productions, 1984. 347p.
       Supplement to The Independent Film and Videomakers Guide (entry 948). Principles, line items, sample budgets, money-saving ideas, computerized budgets, and procedures for monitoring expenses. Illustrations, appendix, bibliography.

(c) Editing

1004. Anderson, Gary H. Video Editing and Post-Production: A
Professional Guide. White Plains, NY: Knowledge Industry
Publications, 1984. 166p.
Introduction to the techniques, equipment, and procedures
of offline and online editing. Illustrations, tables, appendices,
glossary, bibliography, index.

1005. Browne, Steven E. The Video Tape Post-Production Primer:
A Professional "Overview" of Electronic Editing. Burbank, CA:
Wilton Place Communications, 1982. 218p.
Videotape, tape formats, preparation for and carrying out
edits, on-line and off-line editing, and editing film-on-tape.
Glossary.

1006. De Sarlo, Carmine R. TV Commercial Film Editing: Professional Motion Picture Pre- and Post-Production Including Animation, Rotoscoping, and Video Tape. Jefferson, NC: Mc-
Farland, 1985. 243p.
See entry 943.

1007. Shetter, Michael D. Videotape Editing: Communicating with
Pictures and Sound. Elk Grove Village, IL: Swiderski Elec-
tronics, 1982. 164p.
Techniques of videotape editing, and esthetics of the
editing process. Emphasis on the use of computers in editing.
Illustrations, glossary, index.

(d) Graphics

1008. Ayers, Ralph. Graphics for Television. Englewood Cliffs,
NJ: Prentice-Hall, 1984. 155p.
Basic details of the television medium, and steps in cre-
ating pleasing pictures and backgrounds, supporting graphics
and illustrations, appropriate titles, and the use of color.
Illustrations, glossary, index.

1009. Blank, Ben, and Mario Garcia. Professional Video Graphic
Design. New York: Prentice Hall Press, 1986. 157p.
Designing for the screen, typography, photograph design,
art and illustration, design and use of maps, graphics of
major anticipated news events, production tips, and computer-
generated graphics. Illustrations.

(e) Lighting

1010. Millerson, Gerald. The Technique of Lighting for Television
and Motion Pictures. 2d ed. Boston, MA: Focal Press,
1982. 391p.
Creative analysis approach to studio and film lighting. Basic

principles and tools of lighting; portraiture, still-life, persuasive, and scene lighting. Illustrations, bibliography, index.

1011. Millerson, Gerald. TV Lighting Methods. 2d ed. Boston,
       MA: Focal Press, 1982. 152p.
       Equipment and techniques for lighting people and objects
       in the studio and on location. Illustrations, bibliography,
       glossary.

(f) Staging

1012. Millerson, Gerald. Basic TV Staging. 2d ed. Boston, MA:
       Focal Press, 1982. 173p.
       Mechanics and methods of staging, set construction and
       erection, costs and cost-cutting, dressing and lighting the
       set, floor treatment, and shooting suggestions. Illustrations,
       annotated reading list, glossary.

7. Writing

1013. Baldwin, Huntley. Creating Effective TV Commercials. Chi-
       cago: Crain Books, 1982. 245p.
       See entry 941.

1014. Blum, Richard A. Television Writing: From Concept to Con-
       tract. Rev. ed. Boston, MA: Focal Press, 1984. 282p.
       Techniques and formats used by professionals to sell their
       ideas in the marketplace. Original program proposals and
       series presentations, theory and practice of writing pilot
       stories and movies-of-the-week treatments, specific formats
       involved in writing scripts for TV film and videotape, and
       the pragmatics of marketing the property. Illustrations, ap-
       pendices, annotated bibliography, index.

1015. Brady, Ben. The Keys to Writing for Television and Film.
       4th ed. Dubuque, IA: Kendall/Hunt, 1982. 297p.
       Steps in writing a dramatic script for television and film,
       using a reconstruction of the writing of Richard Alan Simmons'
       Emmy-winning TV play, "The Price of Tomatoes." Appendix,
       glossary, index.

1016. Edgar, David, Trevor Griffiths, David Hare, Julian Mitchell,
       Peter Prince, Howard Schuman, and Hugh Whitemore. Ah!
       Mischief: The Writer and Television. London: Faber and
       Faber, 1982. 110p.
       Reflections on the satisfactions and frustrations of work-
       ing as writers in television.

1017. Goodman, Evelyn. Writing Television and Motion Picture
       Scripts That Sell. Chicago: Contemporary Books, 1982. 219p.

Step-by-step guide to writing the teleplay or screenplay.
Includes a full-length teleplay in its original typewritten format to explain the mechanics of constructing a professional
script. Illustrations, index.

1018. Gronbeck, Bruce E. Writing Television Criticism. Chicago:
Science Research Associates, 1984. 44p.
Nature and types of criticism, journalistic and academic
criticism and writing styles, and a sample of academic criticism. Illustrations, suggested readings.

1019. Poole, Mike, and John Wyver. Powerplays: Trevor Griffiths
in Television. London: British Film Institute, 1984. 203p.
The relationship of the writer (Trevor Griffiths) to the
medium (television), and ways in which the elements of the
relationship produce the meanings within finished texts. Illustrations, bibliography.

1020. Rouverol, Jean. Writing for the Soaps. Cincinnati, OH:
Writer's Digest Books, 1984. 220p.
The evolution of the soap opera, conversion of a story
line into a script, influences on story lines, and the interaction of the writing, casting, and production staffs. Illustrations, appendices, bibliography, glossary, index.

1021. Shanks, Bob. The Primal Screen: How to Write, Sell, and
Produce Movies for Television. New York: W. W. Norton,
1986. 414p.
See entry 994.

PART IV: CABLE

A. REFERENCES

1. Bibliography

1022. Kellough, Patrick Henry. Cable Television and Censorship: A Bibliography. Monticello, IL: Vance Bibliographies, 1985. 5p.

Forty-seven listings, from journal articles, law cases, and books, on problems associated with the censorship of cable television and the First Amendment.

2. Dictionary

1023. Delson, Donn, and Edwin Michalove. Delson's Dictionary of Cable, Video and Satellite Terms. Thousand Oaks, CA: Bradson Press, 1983. 63p.

Definitions of the most commonly used words and phrases in the cable, satellite programming, and home video industries. Illustrations.

3. Directories and Guides

1024. Broadcasting/Cablecasting Yearbook. Washington, DC: Broadcasting Publications, annual.

See entry 21.

1025. The Home Video and Cable Yearbook, 1982-83. New York: Facts on File Publications, 1982. 263p.

Facts and figures on cable television, pay cable services, advertising on cable, interactive cable, satellites, subscription television, multipoint distribution services, and low-power television. Also, VCRs and videodisc players and software, home video games, personal computers, and videotext. Details of mergers, acquisitions, and joint ventures from January 1981 through June 1982, financial summaries of selected home video companies, and industry developments in Europe and Japan. Illustrations, tables, index.

1026. Howard, Herbert H. Ownership Trends in Cable Television:
       1985. Washington, DC: National Association of Broadcasters,
       1985. 13p.
           List of the 50 largest multiple-system operators based on
       basic subscribership, analysis of the 50 largest MSOs by own-
       ership types, and the status of franchises in the top 25 ADI
       core cities. Tables.

1027. The Interactive Cable TV Handbook. 3rd ed. Bethesda, MD:
       Phillips, 1983. 222p.
           Profile of the interactive cable TV business. Subscriber
       and institutional networks, experimental systems, hardware
       and software suppliers, technical and information services,
       and communications law terms. Glossary, appendices, index.

1028. International Television Almanac. New York: Quigley, annual.
       See entry 539.

1029. Kenney, Brigitte L. (ed.). Cable for Information Delivery:
       A Guide for Librarians, Educators and Cable Professionals.
       White Plains, NY: Knowledge Industry Publications, 1984.
       172p.
           Current state and potential of non-entertainment uses of
       cable television. Cable technology, regulation, satellite-
       cable networks, data communications, and proposals for a
       library-cable partnership. Illustrations, tables, appendices,
       index.

1030. Reed, Robert M. The American Telecommunications Market:
       Commercial/Public TV, Cable, STV, MDS, LPTV, Home Video.
       Syosset, NY: National Video Clearinghouse, 1982. 202p. +
       appendices.
       See entry 544.

1031. Sterling, Christopher H. Electronic Media: A Guide to Trends
       in Broadcasting and Newer Technologies, 1920-1983. New
       York: Praeger, 1984. 337p.
       See entry 37.

1032. Television and Cable Factbook. 2 vols. Washington, DC:
       Television Digest, annual.
       See entry 550.

1033. Terrace, Vincent. Encyclopedia of Television. Vol. 2:
       Series, Pilots and Specials, 1974-1984. New York: New York
       Zoetrope, 1985. 458p.
       See entry 557.

4. Surveys

1034. Baldwin, Thomas F., and D. Stevens McVoy. Cable

Communication. Englewood Cliffs, NJ: Prentice-Hall, 1983.
416p.
     Survey of cable communication, in five parts: technology,
services, public policy, organization and operations, and the
future. Illustrations, appendices, index.

1035. Hollowell, Mary Louise (ed.). The Cable/Broadband Communi-
       cations Book. Vol. 3: 1982-1983. White Plains, NY: Knowl-
       edge Industry Publications, 1983. 167p.
            Focuses on cable, with chapters on technology, franchising,
       programming, advertising, emerging issues, and cable's role
       in electronic mail. Other chapters treat direct-broadcast satel-
       lite and national telecommunications policy. Glossary.

1036. Jesuale, Nancy (ed.), with Ralph Lee Smith. CTIC Cable-
       books. Vol. 1: The Community Medium. Arlington, VA:
       Cable Television Information Center, 1982. 182p.
            Technology; economics; services; and local government,
       educational, and health uses of cable television systems. Il-
       lustrations, tables, appendices, glossary, bibliography.

1037. Roman, James W. Cable Mania: The Cable Television Source-
       book. Englewood Cliffs, NJ: Prentice-Hall, 1983. 278p.
            History, regulation, technology, programming, franchising,
       foreign systems, and employment opportunities. Corporations,
       broadcasters, and publishers active in cable television, and
       minority ownership and services. Primer for public access
       production. Illustrations, appendices, glossary, bibliography,
       index.

1038. Weinstein, Stephen B. Getting the Picture: A Guide to CATV
       and the New Electronic Media. New York: Institute of Elec-
       trical and Electronics Engineers, 1986. 258p.
            Growth of cable and its technology, programming, ancillary
       services, and regulation. Competition to cable, including sub-
       scription television, multipoint distribution service, private
       cable (SMATV), direct satellite broadcasting, videocassette
       recorders, and the telephone network. Illustrations, tables,
       appendices, glossary, index.

                          5. Who's Who

1039. Scheuer, Steven H. (ed.). Who's Who in Television and
       Cable. New York: Facts On File Publications, 1983. 579p.
            See entry 579.

B. AUDIO

1040. Listening to the Future: Cable Audio in the 80s. Washington,

DC: National Public Radio, 1982. 69p.
Report of a study on the potential of cable audio. Description of the cable industry, range of cable audio carried and planned, technical considerations in the distribution of audio programs by cable, financial analysis and predictive models, and an illustrative model of a service for the print-handicapped. Illustrations, tables.

C. BUSINESS

1041.   Besen, Stanley M., and Leland L. Johnson. An Economic Analysis of Mandatory Leased Channel Access for Cable Television. Santa Monica, CA: Rand Corporation, 1982. 91p.
Analysis of access arrangements between cable operators and service packagers, effects of government regulation on access, and effects of mandated leased access on subscriber prices and range of services offered. Problems of implementing a leased access arrangement, and the effects of competitive technologies. Illustrations, tables.

1042.   Brotman, Stuart N., and Larry S. Levine. The Opportunities of Channel Leasing: Strategic Considerations for Broadcasters. Washington, DC: National Association of Broadcasters, 1982. 11p.
Details of ways in which broadcasters can take advantage of channel leasing, with emphasis on leasing arrangements between broadcasters and cable television operators.

1043.   Cable Television in a New Era. New York: Practising Law Institute, 1983. 421p.
Financial aspects, regulation, copyright, rulemaking and legislation, acquisition and sale of CATV systems, franchises, and antitrust.

1044.   Hamburg, Morton I. All About Cable: Legal and Business Aspects of Cable and Pay Television. Rev. ed. New York: Law Journal Seminars-Press, 1984.
Federal, state, and local regulation of cable television. Pay cable and pay TV operation, regulation, and business considerations, and problems facing the cable TV industry. Fourteen appendices include federal cable rules and regulations, franchising workbook, franchise contracts and grants, program and network affiliation agreements, and the Cable Telecommunications Act of 1983. Looseleaf. Table of cases, index.

1045.   Howard, Herbert H. Ownership Trends in Cable Television: 1985. Washington, DC: National Association of Broadcasters, 1985. 13p.
See entry 1026.

1046.   Nadel, Mark, and Eli Noam (eds.).   The Economics of Cable
        Television (CATV): An Anthology.   New York: Graduate
        School of Business, Columbia University, 1983.   195p.
           Costs, revenues, audience and financial projections.   Il-
        lustrations, tables.

1047.   Webb, G. Kent.   The Economics of Cable Television.   Lexington,
        MA: Lexington Books, 1983.   197p.
           Identification of the market, regulatory forces that have
        shaped the cable television industry, and investigation of the
        issues of price, design, and regulation.   Use of an econometric
        and engineering analysis of the market and technology to de-
        sign a computer model simulating the economic behavior of a
        cable system, and a description of the results.   Illustrations,
        tables, appendices, bibliography, index.

D.   CAREERS

1048.   Berlyn, David W.   Exploring Careers in Cable/TV.   New York:
        Rosen, 1985.   127p.
           See entry 592.

1049.   Bone, Jan.   Opportunities in Cable Television.   Lincolnwood,
        IL: National Textbook, 1984.   152p.
           Guidebook for persons seeking a career in cable TV.   Pre-
        ferred personal qualities and educational preparation, and de-
        scription of franchises, finance, construction, sales and
        marketing, advertising, programming, and technical positions.
        Job-hunting tips and overview of cable's development and sys-
        tem operation.   Illustrations, appendices, glossary.

1050.   Careers In Cable.   Washington, DC: National Cable Tele-
        vision Association, 1983.   30p.
           Opportunities in franchising, construction, and operation,
        with qualifications and representative salaries.   Appendices,
        bibliography, glossary.

1051.   Cohen, Daniel, and Susan Cohen.   How to Get Started in
        Video.   New York: Franklin Watts, 1986.   112p.
           See entry 594.

1052.   Denny, Jon S.   Careers in Cable TV.   New York: Barnes
        and Noble Books, 1983.   278p.
           Opportunities in local systems, cable networks, and sup-
        porting services.   Hints from professionals and steps to land-
        ing the first job.   Glossary, appendix, index.

1053.   Directory of Cable Education and Training Programs.   Wash-
        ington, DC: National Cable Television Association, 1984.   84p.

Cable technology and management programs offered by community colleges and universities; local, state, and federal
agencies; and multiple system operators. Course descrip-
tion(s), eligibility, application dates, fees, financial assistance,
and accreditation status.

1054. Reed, Maxine K., and Robert M. Reed. Career Opportuni-
ties in Television, Cable, and Video. 2d ed. New York:
Facts on File Publications, 1986. 266p.
See entry 598.

1055. Sapan, Joshua. Making It in Cable TV: Career Opportunities in Today's Fastest Growing Media Industry. New York:
Putnam, 1984. 128p.
History of cable TV, corporate structures, departments
and jobs in each, salary ranges, required skills, and hints
on job-searching. Appendices, glossary, index.

1056. Weinstein, Bob. Breaking into Communications. New York:
Arco, 1984. 116p.
See entry 91.

1057. Zacharis, John C., Frances Forde Plude, and Andrew S.
Rancer. Exploring Careers in Communications and Telecom-
munications. New York: Rosen, 1985. 161p.
See entry 92.

E. COMPARATIVE AND FOREIGN

1. Comparative

1058. Flaherty, David H. Protecting Privacy in Two-Way Electronic
Services. White Plains, NY: Knowledge Industry Publications, 1985. 173p.
Challenges to the protection of personal privacy in the
context of two-way cable technology, and U.S., Canadian, and
international initiatives to deal with them. Appendices, index.

1059. Murphy, Brian. The World Wired Up: Unscrambling the New
Communications Puzzle. London: Comedia, 1983. 155p.
Computer communications systems, with emphasis on satellite broadcasting, cable television, and "informatics." Organizations and companies involved and their activities in the
United States, Canada, Europe, Japan, the Third World, and
the United Kingdom. Illustrations, glossary, bibliography.

1060. Negrine, Ralph M. (ed.). Cable Television and the Future of
Broadcasting. New York: St. Martin's Press, 1985. 223p.
Survey of cable television developments in the United States,

Canada, the Low Countries, Great Britain, France, West
Germany, Australia, and Japan. Cable's promise and its likely
impact on existing broadcast services. Illustration, tables,
glossary, index.

2. Foreign

1061.   Hollins, Timothy. Beyond Broadcasting: Into the Cable Age.
        London: British Film Institute, 1984. 385p.
           See entry 666.

1062.   Hughes, Patrick, Gary Wersky, Neil McCartney, and John
        Ainsley. Hunt on Cable TV: Chaos or Coherence? London:
        Campaign for Press and Broadcasting Freedom, 1982. 76p.
           See entry 669.

1063.   Report on Cable Systems. London: Her Majesty's Stationery
        Office, 1982. 54p.
           See entry 683.

1064.   Veljanovski, C. G., and W. D. Bishop. Choice by Cable:
        The Economics of a New Era in Television. London: Institute
        of Economic Affairs, 1983. 120p.
           See entry 692.

1065.   Woodrow, R. Brian, and Kenneth B. Woodside (eds.). The
        Introduction of Pay-TV in Canada: Issues and Implications.
        Montreal: Institute for Research on Public Policy, 1982. 240p.
           See entry 642.

F. HISTORY

1066.   The First 50 Years of Broadcasting: The Running Story of
        the Fifth Estate. Washington, DC: Broadcasting Publications,
        1982. 297p.
           See entry 186.

1067.   Rasmussen, Bill. Sports Junkies Rejoice! : The Birth of
        ESPN. Hartsdale, NY: QV, 1983. 255p.
           Events leading to the launch of the Entertainment and
        Sports Programming Network, recounted by its president and
        chairman of the board. Illustrations, glossary, appendix.

G. IN SOCIETY

1068.   Cable Television: An Assessment of Critical Issues in

Washington, DC. Washington, DC: Institute for District Affairs of the University of the District of Columbia and The
DC Cable Coalition, 1984. 174p.
    Eighteen papers presented at a series of public seminars
in 1984. Impact of the introduction of cable TV to the District
of Columbia on politics, economics, quality of life, education,
and culture. Illustration, tables.

1069. Hollander, Richard. Video Democracy: The Vote-from-Home
Revolution. Mt. Airy, MD: Lomond Publications, 1985. 161p.
    Futuristic look at ways in which two-way cable may affect
our society. Argues for establishment of a commission to as-
sess the potential uses of interactive cable for voting and related processes. Bibliography, index.

1070. LeRoy, David, and Judith M. LeRoy. The Impact of the Cable
Television Industry on Public Television. Washington, DC:
Corporation for Public Broadcasting, 1983. 82p.
    See entry 932.

1071. Pepper, Robert. Competition In Local Distribution: The
Cable Television Industry. Cambridge, MA: Program on Information Resources Policy, Harvard University, 1983. 63p.
    The implications arising from cable's potential entry into
local telecommunications distribution.

1072. Webster, James G. The Impact of Cable and Pay Cable Television on Local Station Audiences. Washington, DC: National
Association of Broadcasters, 1982. 108p.
    See entry 582.

H. LAW, REGULATION, AND POLICY

1073. Brenner, Daniel L., and Monroe E. Price. Cable Television
and Other Nonbroadcast Video: Law and Policy. New York:
Clark Boardman, 1986. 750p.
    Includes microwave transmission, SMATV, ownership, fran-
chising, SMATV, ownership, franchising, the 1984 Policy Act,
and the regulation of program content. Index.

1074. Cable Television in a New Era. New York: Practising Law
Institute, 1983. 421p.
    See entry 1043.

1075. Cable Television: Retrospective and Prospective. New York:
Practising Law Institute, 1985. 884p.
    Cable technology; finance; copyright and signal piracy;
labor relations; FCC, state, and local regulation; free speech;
antitrust developments; then-pending federal legislation. Illustrations, tables, appendices.

1076. Chronology of Telecommunications and Cable Television Regulation in the United States. Cambridge, MA: Program on Information Resources Policy, Harvard University, 1984. 57p.
See entry 251.

1077. Dolan, Edward V. TV or CATV? A Struggle for Power.
Port Washington, NY: Associated Faculty Press, 1984. 125p.
Influences on the content of broadcast and cable television and perspectives on the present and future control of cable. Bibliography, appendix, index.

1078. Ferris, Charles D., Frank W. Lloyd, and Thomas J. Casey. Cable Television Law: A Video Communications Practice Guide. 3 vols. New York: Matthew Bender, 1986.
The first volume treats broadcast and cable television regulation. Volume two deals with cable access and privacy issues, regulation of other video technologies, common legal problems of cable and other technologies, and international developments in cable TV. The third volume contains appendices and includes statutes, regulations, forms, directories, glossary, and bibliography.

1079. Flaherty, David H. Protecting Privacy in Two-Way Electronic Services. White Plains, NY: Knowledge Industry Publications, 1985. 173p.
See entry 1058.

1080. Hamburg, Morton I. All About Cable: Legal and Business Aspects of Cable and Pay Television. Rev. ed. New York: Law Journal Seminars-Press, 1984.
See entry 1044.

1081. Jesuale, Nancy (ed.), with Richard M. Neustadt and Nicholas P. Miller. CTIC Cablebooks. Vol. 2: A Guide for Local Policy. Arlington, VA: Cable Television Information Center, 1982. 131p.
Policy options and regulatory procedures for local governments. The franchising process, cable TV ordinances, rate regulation, franchise enforcement and administration, franchise negotiation, antitrust, and consumer issues. Illustrations, appendices.

1082. Neustadt, Richard M. The Birth of Electronic Publishing: Legal and Economic Issues in Telephone, Cable and Over-the-Air Teletext and Videotext. White Plains, NY: Knowledge Industry Publications, 1982. 146p.
Explanation of relevant current laws and rules governing broadcasting, cable, and telephone, and their effect on electronic publishing. Suggestions for new policies, and methods by which regulators and legislators can implement them. Illustrations, tables, appendix, index.

1083. The New Era in CATV: The Cable Franchise Policy and Com-
      munications Act of 1984. New York: Practising Law Institute,
      1985. 289p.
          Policy objectives and the Act's provisions on FCC and
      state/municipal roles. Relationships between the cable opera-
      tor and systems users or programmers, potential competitors,
      subscribers, and employees.

1084. Orton, Barry (ed.). Cable Television and the Cities: Local
      Regulation and Municipal Uses. Madison, WI: University of
      Wisconsin Extension, 1982. 83p.
          Proceedings from a 1980 conference for municipal officials.
      Includes franchising, assessment of local communications needs,
      planning and utilization, evaluation of franchise applicants,
      and regulation.

1085. Pool, Ithiel de Sola. Technologies of Freedom. Cambridge,
      MA: Belknap Press of Harvard University Press, 1983. 299p.
      See entry 296.

1086. A Practical Guide to the Cable Communications Policy Act of
      1984. New York: Practising Law Institute, 1985. 445p.
          Franchising and fees, standards and procedures for fran-
      chise renewal, rate regulation, theft of service, First Amend-
      ment considerations, consumer relations and privacy, and im-
      plementation and enforcement of the Act. Appendices.

1087. Rice, Jean (ed.). Cable TV Renewals and Refranchising.
      Washington, DC: Communications Press, 1983. 212p.
          Overview of the renewal and refranchising process and
      perspectives of franchisor and franchisee. Review of key
      factors in the process, including programming and technology,
      legal considerations, leased access channels, community ac-
      cess, and rural service. Appendix, glossary, bibliography.

1088. Shapiro, George H., Philip B. Kurland, and James P. Mer-
      curio. "Cablespeech": The Case for First Amendment Pro-
      tection. New York: Law and Business/Harcourt Brace Jo-
      vanovich, 1983. 258p.
          Argues that many demands placed on cable television by
      government are outside the bounds set by the First Amend-
      ment. Supporting arguments include regulations of "offensive"
      programming, the Fairness Doctrine, political advertising rules,
      mandatory access requirements, "must carry" rules, subscrip-
      tion rates, and limits on the number of cable systems. Table
      of authorities, index.

1089. Television Piracy. New York: Practising Law Institute, 1985.
      123p.
          Provisions of the Cable Communications Policy Act of 1984
      on the unauthorized reception of cable services and other

communications, and comparison with Section 605 of the Communications Act of 1934 and state anti-piracy laws. Injunc-
tive relief, money damages, and other remedies available under the 1984 Act, and effective settlement agreements.

1090. Thorpe, Kenneth E. Cable Television, Market Power and
       Regulation. Santa Monica, CA: Rand Corporation, 1985.
       88p.
          The present structure of cable television regulation, fed-
       eral policy goals, implications for those goals of the evolving
       pricing structure in the cable industry, and the impact of
       competing technologies on cable. Illustrations, tables, ap-
       pendices, bibliography.

I. PROGRAMS AND CONTENT

1091. Beck, Kirsten. Cultivating the Wasteland: Can Cable Put
       the Vision Back in TV? New York: American Council for
       the Arts, 1983. 249p.
          Cable television technology, business and regulation, and
       fine arts programming. The potential of cable for cultural
       programming and advice to cultural groups on access. Tech-
       nical, legal, and business considerations in program production
       and distribution. Illustrations, bibliography.

1092. DeGooyer, Janice, and Farfalla Borah. What's Wrong With
       This Picture? A Look at Working Women on Television. Wash-
       ington, DC: National Commission on Working Women, 1982.
       22p.
          See entry 911.

1093. Jones, Maxine Holmes. See, Hear, Interact: Beginning De-
       velopments in Two-Way Television. Metuchen, NJ: Scarecrow
       Press, 1985. 155p.
          Description of prototype systems in education, social and
       community services, telemedicine, citizen participation, and
       in-service information. Glossary, annotated bibliography,
       appendices, index.

1094. Rasmussen, Bill. Sports Junkies Rejoice!: The Birth of
       ESPN. Hartsdale, NY: QV, 1983. 255p.
          See entry 1067.

1095. Shaffer, Wm. Drew, and Richard Wheelwright (eds.). Creating
       Original Programming for Cable TV. White Plains, NY: Knowl-
       edge Industry Publications, 1983. 161p.
          Nine chapters by cable and cable-related professionals on
       programming sources, production and distribution possibilities,
       legal considerations, and opportunities for the sale of

advertising. Discussion of the need for responsible self-
regulation by the cable industry and independent producers.
Glossary.

1096. Shakeout: The Year in Cable Programming. Washington, DC:
       Television Digest, 1983. 123p.
       Selection of articles published in Television Digest from
       May 1982 through October 1983. Includes pay-per-view, DBS,
       and signal scrambling.

1097. Terrace, Vincent. Encyclopedia of Television. Vol. 2:
       Series, Pilots and Specials, 1974-1984. New York: New York
       Zoetrope, 1985. 458p.
       See entry 557.

J. PUBLICATION

1098. Byron, Christopher M. The Fanciest Dive: What Happened
       When the Media Empire of Time/Life Leaped Without Looking
       into the Age of High-Tech. New York: W. W. Norton, 1986.
       280p.
       See entry 940.

K. TECHNIQUE AND TECHNOLOGY

       1. Advertising, Marketing, and Promotion

1099. Eastman, Susan Tyler, and Robert A. Klein (eds.). Strategies
       in Broadcast and Cable Promotion: Commercial Television,
       Radio, Cable, Pay-Television, Public Television. Belmont, CA:
       Wadsworth, 1982. 355p.
       See entry 351.

1100. Heighton, Elizabeth J., and Don R. Cunningham. Advertising
       in the Broadcast and Cable Media. 2d ed. Belmont, CA:
       Wadsworth, 1984. 368p.
       See entry 353.

1101. Jones, Kensinger, Thomas F. Baldwin, and Martin P. Block.
       Cable Advertising: New Ways to New Business. Englewood
       Cliffs, NJ: Prentice-Hall, 1986. 148p.
       Advantages, how it works, sponsorship opportunities, ad-
       vertising basics, and commercial flexibility. Buying, schedul-
       ing, and evaluating. Illustrations, appendices, glossary.

1102. Kaatz, Ronald B. Cable Advertiser's Handbook. 2d ed.
       Lincolnwood, IL: Crain Books, 1985. 262p.

The beginnings and current status of new media and their
impact on traditional media. Planning, creating, and producing
cable advertising, measuring the results, and a buying checklist. Illustrations, tables, glossary, index.

1103. Poltrack, David. Television Marketing: Network, Local, and
       Cable. New York: McGraw-Hill, 1983. 395p.
       See entry 946.

1104. Strauss, Lawrence. Electronic Marketing: Emerging TV and
       Computer Channels for Interactive Home Shopping. White
       Plains, NY: Knowledge Industry Publications, 1983. 141p.
       Development, participants, services, and prospects for
       direct marketing using the new electronic media. Illustrations,
       tables, appendix, glossary, bibliography, index.

1105. Warner, Charles. Broadcast and Cable Selling. Belmont, CA:
       Wadsworth, 1986. 452p.
       See entry 355.

2.   Engineering

1106. Bretz, Rudy, with Michael Schmidbauer. Media for Inter-
       active Communication. Beverly Hills, CA: Sage Publications,
       1983. 264p.
       Issues and problems in interactive system design. Audio
       and video systems in operation, including teletext and video-
       tex. Illustrations, glossary, index.

1107. Grant, William. Cable Television. Reston, VA: Reston,
       1983. 362p.
       Introduction to terminology, equipment, and system de-
       signs, with explanations of the principles and basic character-
       istics of coaxial cable RF transmission systems. Illustrations,
       tables, glossary, index.

1108. Harrell, Bobby. The Cable Television Technical Handbook.
       Dedham, MA: Artech House, 1985. 312p.
       Fundamentals of the basic cable television system, written
       for telecommunications installers, technicians, and engineers.
       Illustrations, tables, appendix, glossary.

3.   Management

1109. McCavitt, William E., and Peter K. Pringle. Electronic Media
       Management. Boston, MA: Focal Press, 1986. 325p.
       See entry 376.

1100. Marcus, Norman. Broadcast and Cable Management.

Englewood Cliffs, NJ: Prentice-Hall, 1986.   308p.
See entry 377.

4. News

1111.   Garvey, Daniel E., and William L. Rivers.   Newswriting for
the Electronic Media: Principles, Examples, Applications.
Belmont, CA: Wadsworth, 1982.   250p.
See entry 388.

1112.   Smeyak, G. Paul.   Broadcast News Writing.   2d ed.   Columbus, OH: Grid, 1983.   297p.
See entry 395.

5. Production

1113.   Community Cable for and by Children: An ACT Handbook.
Newtonville, MA: Action for Children's Television, 1983.   21p.
Guide to the production of programs by and with the as-
sistance of young people.   Illustrations.

1114.   Floyd, Steve, and Beth Floyd, with David Hon, Patrick Mc-
Entee, Kenneth G. O'Bryan, and Michael Schwarz.   Handbook
of Interactive Video.   White Plains, NY: Knowledge Industry
Publications, 1982.   168p.
Components of an interactive video system, and the planning, design, production, and evaluation of programs.   Illustrations, tables, appendices, bibliography, index.

1115.   Oringel, Robert S.   Television Operations Handbook.   Boston,
MA: Focal Press, 1984.   182p.
See entry 991.

6. Programming

1116.   Eastman, Susan Tyler, Sydney W. Head, and Lewis Klein.
Broadcast/Cable Programming: Strategies and Practices.
2d ed.   Belmont, CA: Wadsworth, 1985.   529p.
See entry 410.

PART V: NEW TECHNOLOGIES

A. GENERAL

1117. Barr, Trevor. The Electronic Estate: New Communications
Media and Australia. Ringwood, Victoria: Penguin Books,
1985. 271p.
See entry 630.

1118. Bortz, Paul I., and Harold Mendelsohn. Radio Today--and
Tomorrow. Washington, DC: National Association of Broad-
casters, 1982. 75p.
See entry 432.

1119. Carey, John. Telecommunications Technologies and Public
Broadcasting. Washington, DC: Corporation for Public
Broadcasting, 1986. 113p.
See entry 346.

1120. Carey, John, Thomas Gherardi, Harold Kappes, and Mitchell
Moss. Modularization and Packaging of Public Television Programs. Washington, DC: Corporation for Public Broadcasting,
1983. 102p.
See entry 928.

1121. D'Agostino, Peter (ed.). Transmission. New York: Tanam
Press, 1985. 326p.
See entry 603.

1122. DeSonne, Marcia L. Radio New Technology and You. Washington, DC: National Association of Broadcasters, 1982. 24p.
See entry 434.

1123. Donnelly, William J. The Confetti Generation: How the New
Communications Technology Is Fragmenting America. New
York: Henry Holt, 1986. 239p.
See entry 729.

1124. Gibbons, Arnold. Information, Ideology and Communication:
The New Nations' Perspectives on an Intellectual Revolution.

Lanham, MD: University Press of America, 1985.   219p.
See entry 142.

1125.   Gross, Lynne Schafer.   The New Television Technologies.
2d ed.   Dubuque, IA: Wm. C. Brown, 1986.   240p.
Overview and details of traditional distribution processes.
Description, history, and issues surrounding satellites, com-
puters, cable television, subscription TV, low-power TV,
MMDS, SMATV, direct broadcast satellite, videocassettes,
videodiscs, teletext, videotex, and reception technologies.
Concluding chapter on implications and interrelationships.
Illustrations, glossary, index.

1126.   Hawkridge, David.   New Information Technology in Education.
London: Croom Helm, 1983.   238p.
See entry 783.

1127.   Hoover, Stewart M.   The Electronic Giant: A Critique of the
Telecommunications Revolution from a Christian Perspective.
Elgin, IL: Brethren Press, 1982.   171p.
See entry 807.

1128.   Howkins, John.   New Technologies, New Policies?   A Report
from the Broadcasting Research Unit.   London: British Film
Institute, 1982.   74p.
See entry 157.

1129.   Lyman, Peter.   Canada's Video Revolution: Pay-TV, Home
Video and Beyond.   Toronto: James Lorimer, 1983.   173p.
See entry 638.

1130.   McCavitt, William E.   Television Technology: Alternative
Communication Systems.   Lanham, MD: University Press of
America, 1983.   142p.
Non-broadcast uses of video.   Cable TV and corporate,
social service, educational, and home entertainment applications.   Computer technology in business, education, and the
home; teletext; videotex.   Illustrations, glossary, appendices,
bibliography, index.

1131.   McGee, William L., Joseph H. Caton, and Lucy E. Garrick.
Changes, Challenges and Opportunities in the New Electronic
Media.   San Francisco: BMC Publications, 1982.
Evolution, operation, and impact of the new media, and their
prospects.   Looseleaf format in five chapters: pay television;
low-power television; direct-to-home satellite broadcasting; videotex, teletext, and cable text; home video cassettes, discs,
games, and personal computers.   Each chapter contains a bibliography and name/subject index.   Appendix.

1132.   McLean, Mick (ed.).   The Information Explosion: The New

Electronic Media in Japan and Europe. Westport, CT: Greenwood Press, 1985. 130p.
  See entry 624.

1133. McQuail, Denis, and Karen Siune (eds.). New Media Politics:
       Comparative Perspectives in Western Europe. Beverly Hills,
       CA: Sage Publications, 1986. 216p.
         See entry 625.

1134. Moorfoot, Rex. Television in the Eighties: The Total Equa-
       tion. London: British Broadcasting Corporation, 1982. 128p.
         New systems for distributing TV programs and comparisons
       with television broadcasting. New sources of programs and
       services and the challenges they pose to traditional broad-
       casting for audiences, programs, talent, and money. Illustra-
       tions, index.

1135. Murphy, Brian. The World Wired Up: Unscrambling the New
       Communications Puzzle. London: Comedia, 1983. 155p.
         See entry 1059.

1136. New Program Opportunities in the Electronic Media. New
       York: Practising Law Institute, 1983. 615p.
         Methods of program distribution, production and distribu-
       tion agreements and strategy, deal-making, and structures for
       presenting sports programming. Labor and antitrust con-
       siderations in programming ventures. Illustrations, appendices.

1137. The New Technologies: Changes and Challenges in Public
       Relations--A Sourcebook of General Information. Washington,
       DC: Media Institute, 1983. 60p.
         Description of cable television, conventional and direct
       broadcast satellites, teleconferencing, low power television,
       videotex, and teletext. Selected bibliographies, cable services,
       DBS operators, teleconferencing service suppliers, and busi-
       ness, financial, and economic news programs on radio, tele-
       vision, and cable.

1138. Patten, David A. Newspapers and New Media. White Plains,
       NY: Knowledge Industry Publications, 1986. 137p.
         Challenges to and opportunities for newspapers growing
       out of the new media, including cable television, cellular
       radio, teletext, videotex, multichannel microwave, low-power
       television, and direct-broadcast satellites. Evaluation of new
       media ventures, newspaper-cable programming, advertising
       and other profitability prospects, and community television.
       Illustration, bibliography, index.

1139. Reed, Robert M. The American Telecommunications Market:
       Commercial/Public TV, Cable, STV, MDS, LPTV, Home Video.
       Syosset, NY: National Video Clearinghouse, 1982. 202p. +

appendices.
See entry 544.

1140. A Report from the Working Party on the New Technologies.
London: Broadcasting Research Unit, 1983. 346p.
See entry 682.

1141. Schement, Jorge Reina, Felix Gutierrez, and Marvin A. Sirbu,
Jr. (eds.). Telecommunications Policy Handbook. New York:
Praeger, 1982. 318p.
See entry 825.

1142. Singleton, Loy A. Telecommunications in the Information Age:
A Nontechnical Primer on the New Technologies. Cambridge,
MA: Ballinger, 1983. 239p.
Development, operation, applications, and predictions for
the future of 17 new technologies. Cable television, low-
power television, subscription television, multipoint distribution service, communication satellites, direct broadcast satellites, satellite master-antenna television, and high-definition
television. Also, videotex, teletext, videocassette recorders,
videodisc, personal computers, new business communication
networks, teleconferencing, telecommuting, and portable telecommunications. Illustrations, glossary, suggestions for
further reading, index.

1143. Stover, William James. Information Technology in the Third
World: Can I.T. Lead to Humane National Development?
Boulder, CO: Westview Press, 1984. 183p.
See entry 145.

1144. Syfret, Toby. Television Today and Television Tomorrow:
A Guide to New Electronic Media and Trends in Commercial
Television in Western Europe. London: J. Walter Thompson,
1983. 95p.
See entry 628.

1145. The Video Age: Television Technology and Applications in the
1980s. White Plains, NY: Knowledge Industry Publications,
1982. 264p.
Collection of chapters selected from books and studies published by Knowledge Industry, describing and analyzing the
television explosion. The scope of the video industry, emergence of cable TV, videodiscs, videotex, non-broadcast and
corporate television, and an overview of video in hospitals
and health care institutions. Original essay on the future of
television technology. Illustrations, tables.

1146. Weinstein, Stephen B. Getting the Picture: A Guide to CATV
and the New Electronic Media. New York: Institute of Electrical and Electronics Engineers, 1986. 258p.
See entry 1038.

1147.   Wenham, Brian (ed.). The Third Age of Broadcasting. Lon-
        don: Faber and Faber, 1982. 139p.
        See entry 695.

1148.   Williams, Frederick. The Communications Revolution. Bever-
        ly Hills, CA: Sage Publications, 1982. 291p.
        See entry 196.

B.   CELLULAR RADIO

1149.   Ozanich, Gary W. Cellular Radio: A Business Assessment
        for Broadcasters. Washington, DC: National Association of
        Broadcasters, 1982. 25p.
            Operation, regulation, economic potential and risks in
        markets of all sizes. Illustrations, appendices.

1150.   Shosteck, Herschel. Update Cellular Radio: Its Economic
        Feasibility for Smaller Markets. Washington, DC: National
        Association of Broadcasters, 1983. 18p.
            Advantages and disadvantages of investment in smaller
        cellular radio markets, and clarification of cost components of
        cellular service. Demand for cellular mobile telephone ser-
        vice. Illustrations, appendix.

C.   ELECTRONIC PUBLISHING AND INSTRUCTION

1151.   Alber, Antone F. Videotex/Teletext: Principles and Prac-
        tices. New York: McGraw-Hill, 1985. 498p.
            Components of the videotex system, economics, information
        base, planning, managing, and marketing. Consideration of
        regulation and policy issues. Illustrations, appendices, index.

1152.   Aldrich, Michael. Videotex: Key to the Wired City. London:
        Quiller Press, 1982. 115p.
        See entry 650.

1153.   Bretz, Rudy, with Michael Schmidbauer. Media for Inter-
        active Communication. Beverly Hills, CA: Sage Publications,
        1983. 264p.
        See entry 1106.

1154.   Electronic Information Publishing: Old Issues in a New In-
        dustry. New York: Practising Law Institute, 1984. 635p.
            Profile of the industry, development and distribution of
        product, copyright, and other legal considerations. Illustra-
        tions, tables, appendices.

1155.   Hooper, Richard. Prestel, Escher, Bach: Changes Within
        Changes. Cambridge, MA: Program on Information Resources
        Policy, Harvard University, 1984. 13p.
        See entry 668.

1156.   Information Systems Report. Washington, DC: American
        Newspaper Publishers Association, 1983. 72p.
        See entry 623.

1157.   Look, Hugh Evison (ed.).   Electronic Publishing: A Snap-
        shot of the Early 1980s. Oxford, Eng.:   Learned Information,
        1983. 200p.
        See entry 673.

1158.   Martin, James. Viewdata and the Information Society. Engle-
        wood Cliffs, NJ: Prentice-Hall, 1982. 293p.
        Technology, applications, impact, problems, and prospects.
        Explanation of different systems and guidelines for their
        implementation. Illustrations, glossary, index.

1159.   Mosco, Vincent. Pushbutton Fantasies: Critical Perspectives
        on Videotex and Information Technology. Norwood, NJ:
        Ablex, 1982. 195p.
        Growth of communication technologies, their applications,
        and domestic and international effects. Illustrations, tables,
        bibliography, index.

1160.   Neustadt, Richard M. The Birth of Electronic Publishing:
        Legal and Economic Issues in Telephone, Cable and Over-the-
        Air Teletext and Videotext. White Plains, NY: Knowledge
        Industry Publications, 1982. 146p.
        See entry 1082.

1161.   Nugent, Gwen, P. J. Peters, and Lee Rockwell. Instructional
        Development for Videotex: Flowcharts and Scripting. San
        Diego: Electronic Text Consortium, San Diego State Univer
        sity, 1984. 24p.
        Procedures for developing videotex instruction and specific
        steps of flowcharting and scripting. Extracted from Designing
        and Producing Videotex Instruction: A Producer's Handbook,
        prepared by the Nebraska Interactive Cable Project (1983).
        Illustrations, bibliography.

1162.   Sigel, Efrem. The Future of Videotext: Worldwide Prospects
        for Home/Office Electronic Information Services. White Plains,
        NY: Knowledge Industry Publications, 1983. 197p.
        See entry 627.

1163.   Spigai, Fran, and Peter Sommer. Guide to Electronic Publish-
        ing: Opportunities in Online and Viewdata Services. White
        Plains, NY: Knowledge Industry Publications, 1982. 163p.

Technology, services, costs, and business potential, aimed
primarily at print publishers. Illustrations, tables, glossary,
bibliography, index.

1164. Tydeman, John, Hubert Lipinski, Richard P. Adler, Michael
       Nyhan, and Laurence Zwimpfer. Teletext and Videotex in the
       United States: Market Potential, Technology, Public Policy
       Issues. New York: McGraw-Hill, 1982. 314p.
         Study assessing the impact of teletext and videotex over
       the next 10 to 20 years. The state of the two technologies
       around the world and the market potential in the United
       States. Likely technological developments from the perspec-
       tives of the user, influences on society, and the implications
       for public policy. Illustrations, tables, appendices, bibli-
       ography, index.

1165. Veith, Richard H. Television's Teletext. New York: North-
       Holland, 1983. 180p.
         See entry 629.

1166. The Videotex Marketplace. Bethesda, MD: Phillips, 1984.
       204p.
         Guide to the North American videotex industry, with de-
       tails of equipment suppliers, online and broadcast services,
       access networks, standards groups, and business and tech-
       nical services. Also, associations and educational institutions,
       communications attorneys, the regulatory environment, and
       forecasts for the industry. Illustrations, glossary, general
       index, advertisers' index.

1167. A Videotex/Teletext Bibliography. Bethesda, MD: Phillips,
       annual.
         See entry 553.

1168. Weaver, David H. Videotex Journalism: Teletext, Viewdata,
       and the News. Hillsdale, NJ: Lawrence Erlbaum Associates,
       1983. 147p.
         See entry 694.

D. HIGH-DEFINITION TELEVISION

1169. Johnson, Tim. Strategies for Higher-Definition Television.
       London: Ovum, 1983. 410p.
         Main concepts of higher-definition television, outline of how
       the technology is expected to develop, and recommended ac-
       tions that organizations can take to prepare the ground. Tech-
       nology, markets, and applications. Illustrations, tables, ap-
       pendices.

E. LOW-POWER TELEVISION

1170. Biel, Jacquelyn. Low Power Television: Development and
       Current Status of the LPTV Industry. Washington, DC:
       National Association of Broadcasters, 1985. 71p.
       History, ownership, programming, equipment, finances,
       regulation, and economic outlook. Illustrations, tables,
       appendices.

1171. Carey, John. An Assessment of Low-Power Television for
       the Nonprofit Community. Washington, DC: Corporation
       for Public Broadcasting, 1983. 43p.
       Guide for nonprofit groups seeking to operate an LPTV
       station and for those who plan to provide programming. Part
       one covers the history of LPTV, regulation, and transmission,
       channel selection, and studio designs. Part two provides a
       market analysis, with emphasis on nonprofit operations in
       small markets, and includes a review of competitive technolo-
       gies and station and programming models and their potential
       revenues. Illustrations, tables, appendix.

1172. Nadel, Mark, and Eli Noam (eds.). The Economics of Low
       Power Television (LPTV): An Anthology. New York: Gradu-
       ate School of Business, Columbia University, 1983. 87p.
       Costs, penetration, and growth projections, and the eco-
       nomics of station operation. Illustrations, tables.

F. MULTIPOINT DISTRIBUTION SERVICE

1173. Frank, Peter. Multichannel MDS: New Allocations, New Sys-
       tems and New Market Opportunities. Washington, DC: Na-
       tional Association of Broadcasters, 1984. 30p.
       Operation and economics of MMDS systems and their de-
       velopment by broadcasters. Illustrations, tables, appendices.

1174. Frank, Peter, and John Shackleford. Business Opportunities
       For Broadcasters in MDS Pay Television. Washington, DC:
       National Association of Broadcasters, 1982. 29p.
       Regulation and technology, competitive analysis of both
       cable and STV, and development and planning of an MDS
       operation. Tables, appendices.

1175. Nadel, Mark, and Eli Noam (eds.). The Economics of Multi-
       point Distribution Service (MDS): An Anthology. New York:
       Graduate School of Business, Columbia University, 1983. 71p.
       Breakeven analysis for single and multichannel MDS, pro-
       jected revenues, system costs, staffing levels, penetration
       projections, and programming expenditures. Illustrations,
       tables.

G. RADIO SUBCARRIERS

1176. Byers, Susan, and W. Lawrence Patrick. Making Money With
       Subcarriers. Bethesda, MD: Phillips, 1983. 85p.
       Economic opportunities for AM and FM broadcasters through
       use of their subcarriers. Technical and business considera-
       tions and potential services and customers. Illustrations, ap-
       pendices, tables.

1177. Shooshan, Harry M., III, and Charles L. Jackson. Radio
       Subcarrier Services: How To Make Dollars and Sense Out of
       New Business Opportunities. Washington, DC; National
       Association of Broadcasters, 1983. 30p.
       Legal and technical considerations, actual and potential
       subcarrier markets, pricing, costs, and revenues. Illustra-
       tions, appendices.

1178. Waters, Dennis P. FM Subcarriers and Broadcast Data Trans-
       mission. Washington, DC: National Association of Broad-
       casters, 1984. 11p.
       Business opportunities using subcarriers. SCA data tech-
       nology, economics, and market segments. Illustrations.

H. SATELLITE MASTER ANTENNA TELEVISION

1179. Howard, Herbert H., and Sidney L. Carroll. SMATV: A
       Changing Environment for Private Cable. Washington, DC:
       National Association of Broadcasters, 1984. 27p.
       History and technical operations of satellite master an-
       tenna television. Establishing an SMATV system, growth, po-
       tential, and programming update. Other emerging telecommuni-
       cations delivery systems, economic comparison with SMATV,
       financial options, and market strategies. Illustrations, ap-
       pendices.

1180. Howard, Herbert H., and Sidney L. Carroll. SMATV: Stra-
       tegic Opportunities in Private Cable. Washington, DC: Na-
       tional Association of Broadcasters, 1982. 98p.
       History of SMATV and its emergence as a broadcast op-
       tion. Financial simulation formula for installation design and
       recommendations on assessing, developing, and maintaining a
       successful operation. Illustrations, tables, appendices, bib-
       liography.

1181. Nadel, Mark, and Eli Noam (eds.). The Economics of Satel-
       lite Master Antenna Television (SMATV): An Anthology.
       New York: Graduate School of Business, Columbia University,
       1983. 50p.

Penetration projections, programming, economic feasibility
factors, costs, and a financial model. Illustrations, tables.

I. SATELLITES

1182. Aldershoff-Gaemers, Lidy. New Media Developments: Satellite TV. Hilversum, Netherlands: Intomart, 1984. 152p.
See entry 617.

1183. Alper, Joel, and Joseph N. Pelton (eds.). The Intelsat
Global Satellite System. New York: American Institute of
Aeronautics and Astronautics, 1984. 425p.
History, organization, operations, services, and role.
Illustrations, tables, appendix, author index.

1184. Baylin, Frank, with Amy Toner. Satellites Today: The Complete Guide to Satellite Television. Boulder, CO; ConSol
Network and Aerowave Corporation, 1984. 160p.
History, technology, programming, legal considerations,
and a look to the future. Illustration, tables, appendices.

1185. Clifford, Martin. The Complete Guide to Satellite TV. Blue
Ridge Summit, PA: TAB Books, 1984. 250p.
Development, equipment, and operation of satellite broadcasting, and guidelines for installing a satellite TV receiving
system. Illustrations, appendix, glossary, index.

1186. Cook, Rick, and Frank Vaughan. All About Home Satellite
Television. Blue Ridge Summit, PA: TAB Books, 1983.
326p.
History, operation, and applications of satellite television.
Guide to programming; guidelines for purchasing, installing,
and using an earth station; direct broadcast satellites; legal
and social implications. Illustrations, appendices, index.

1187. Countdown II: Jockeying at the DBS Starting Gate. Washington, DC: Television Digest, 1983. 105p.
Chronological developments in DBS from April 5, 1982
through May 23, 1983, taken from the pages of the weekly
newsletter Satellite Week. Index.

1188. The DBS Summit Conference. Washington, DC: Television
Digest, 1983. 102p.
See entry 619.

1189. Delson, Donn, and Edwin Michalove. Delson's Dictionary of
Cable, Video and Satellite Terms. Thousand Oaks, CA:
Bradson Press, 1983. 63p.
See entry 1023.

1190. DeSonne, Marcia L. Earth Station Planning and Construction.
       Washington, DC: National Association of Broadcasters, 1984.
       15p.
          Market environment, influences on earth station performance,
       and guidelines for broadcasters on equipment, installation, and
       construction.

1191. Easton, Anthony T. The Home Satellite TV Book: How To
       Put the World in Your Backyard. New York: Playboy Press,
       1982. 381p.
          History, operation, and program services of satellite tele-
       vision, and guidelines for the installation and use of satellite
       TV in the home, in business, and by nonprofit organizations.
       More than 150 pages of appendices include a glossary and
       bibliography, FCC and copyright requirements, manufacturers
       and suppliers of satellite and CATV equipment, and directions
       for locating satellites and aligning the antenna. Illustrations,
       tables.

1192. Firestone, Charles M. (ed.). International Satellite Television:
       Resource Manual for the Third Biennial Communications Law
       Symposium. Los Angeles: UCLA Communications Law Pro-
       gram, 1983. 377p.
          See entry 816.

1193. Goldberg, Joel. Satellite Television Reception: A Personal
       User's Guide. Englewood Cliffs, NJ: Prentice-Hall, 1984.
       103p.
          Television receive only (TVRO) systems, satellite opera-
       tion, location, and programs, requirements for a receiving
       system, and antenna location and installation. Requires basic
       knowledge of electronics. Illustrations, glossary, appendices,
       index.

1194. Harrington, Thomas P., and Bob Cooper, Jr. The Hidden
       Signals on Satellite TV: The Secret Signals on Satellite TV.
       Columbus, OH: Universal Electronics, 1984. 180p.
          Explanations of transmission signals, networks, audio sub-
       carriers, and teletext, mainly for home dish owners. Illustra-
       tions, index.

1195. Hudson, Heather (ed.). New Directions in Satellite Communi-
       cations: Challenges for North and South. Dedham, MA:
       Artech House, 1985. 315p.
          Papers presented at a 1984 conference at the University of
       Texas, most dealing with applications of satellite technology.
       New directions in technology and service, satellites and the
       developing world, international implications, and telecommuni-
       cations requirements in developing countries.

1196. International Institute of Communications. The Use of Satellite

Communication for Information Transfer. Paris: UNESCO,
1982. 125p.
Participants, requirements, and resources for transferring
information for development purposes. Implications of satellite use, elements of network planning and implementation,
national and international policy issues, and applicable international law and regulation. Illustration, table, appendices,
index.

1197. International Satellite Directory. Corte Madera, CA: SFP
Designs, annual.
See entry 28.

1198. Jansky, Donald M., and Michel C. Jeruchim. Communication
Satellites in the Geostationary Orbit. Dedham, MA: Artech
House, 1983. 519p.
Development, utilization, and management of the geostationary orbit, and domestic and international regulation and
policy on its use. Illustrations, tables, appendices, bibliography, index.

1199. Long, Mark, and Jeffrey Keating. The World of Satellite
Television. Summertown, TN: Book, 1983. 224p.
Buying, installing, operating, and maintaining a home
earth station, satellite services, and a preview of direct
broadcast satellites. Illustrations, tables, bibliography, index.

1200. Martinez, Larry. Communication Satellites: Power Politics
in Space. Dedham, MA: Artech House, 1985. 186p.
The political issues surrounding satellite communications,
the reasons for the politicization, the states and international
organizations involved, and the effect on relations between
countries. Tables, appendix, glossary, bibliography.

1201. Matte, Nicolas Mateesco. Aerospace Law: Telecommunications
Satellites. Toronto: Butterworth, 1982. 354p.
See entry 313.

1202. Murray, Catherine A. Managing Diversity: Federal-Provincial
Collaboration and the Committee on Extension of Services to
Northern and Remote Communities. Kingston, Ontario: Insti-
tute of Intergovernmental Relations, Queen's University,
1983. 179p.
See entry 639.

1203. Nadel, Mark, and Eli Noam (eds.). The Economics of Direct
Broadcast Satellites (DBS): An Anthology. New York:
Graduate School of Business, Columbia University, 1983.
160p.
History, pricing tactics, system costs, demand, growth
projections, financial model, and potential competition. Illustrations, tables.

1204. Oderman, Mark. Current Trends in the Direct Broadcast
       Satellite Industry. Bethesda, MD: Phillips, 1984. 24p.
           Issues in the DBS debate in the United States and then-
       current DBS plans of more than a dozen companies.

1205. Ploman, Edward W. Space, Earth and Communication. West-
       port, CT: Quorum Books, 1984. 237p.
           The advent of satellite communications in the context of
       the space age and the information age. Uses and users of
       satellites, policy and law, the struggle for "satellite power"
       and the problems of dealing with the technology, and implica-
       tions for international relations. Index.

1206. Powell, Jon T. International Broadcasting by Satellite: Is-
       sues of Regulation, Barriers to Communication. Westport, CT:
       Quorum Books, 1985. 300p.
           See entry 314.

1207. Pratt, Timothy, and Charles W. Postian. Satellite Communica-
       tions. New York: John Wiley and Sons, 1986. 472p.
           Fundamentals and applications for engineers. Orbital as-
       pects, satellite link design, modulation and multiplexing tech-
       niques, multiple access, earth station technology, and Intelsat
       and Immarsat. Illustrations, tables.

1208. Prentiss, Stan. Satellite Communications. Blue Ridge Summit,
       PA: TAB Books, 1983. 280p.
           Satellites in orbit and under construction, their signals,
       and fixed and direct broadcast services. TVRO receivers,
       design, interference and mounting constraints, security and
       scrambling devices, and satellites in CATV. Illustrations,
       table, index.

1209. Rainger, Peter, David N. Gregory, Robert V. Harvey, and
       Antony Jennings. Satellite Broadcasting. Chichester, Eng.:
       John Wiley and Sons, 1985. 326p.
           Mechanics, technology, regulation, and economics of di-
       rect satellite broadcasting. Illustrations, tables, appendices,
       index.

1210. Regulation of Transnational Communications: 1984 Michigan
       Yearbook of International Legal Studies. New York: Clark
       Boardman, 1984. 411p.
           See entry 315.

1211. The Satellite Directory. Coral Springs, FL: B. Klein Publi-
       cations, annual.
           See entry 35.

1212. Schnapf, Abraham. Communication Satellites: Overview and
       Options for Broadcasters. Washington, DC: National Associa-
       tion of Broadcasters, 1982. 37p.

Evolution of satellites, and U.S. domestic systems and their impact on broadcasting. Reasons for broadcasting via satellite and guidelines for entering the business, including preliminary business assessment, implementation, and satellite leasing. Tables, appendices.

1213. The Scramble to Scramble: A Satellite Television Dilemma. Washington, DC: Television Digest, 1986. 200p.
Developments in the scrambling of satellite signals. Traces the history, examines the present, and speculates about the future of scrambling.

1214. Sutphin, S. E. Understanding Satellite Television Reception. Englewood Cliffs, NJ: Prentice-Hall, 1986. 111p.
Written for the homeowner who has, or plans to buy, a personal earth station. Technology and components, the birth and current status of the satellite TV industry, and a photo section containing a sampling of what is available from equipment manufacturers. Illustrations, glossary, appendices, index.

1215. Taylor, Leslie (ed.). Expanding the Orbital Arc. Washington, DC: International Law Institute, Georgetown University Law Center, 1984. 145p.
See entry 332.

1216. Traister, Robert J. Build a Personal Earth Station for Worldwide Satellite TV Reception. 2d ed. Blue Ridge Summit, PA: TAB Books, 1985. 370p.
The nature of satellite broadcasting, earth station equipment and assembly, and site selection. Illustrations, tables, appendices, glossary, index.

J. SUBSCRIPTION TELEVISION

1217. Nadel, Mark, and Eli Noam (eds.). The Economics of Subscription Television (STV): An Anthology. New York: Graduate School of Business, Columbia University, 1983. 112p.
Costs, past and projected revenues, growth and penetration prospects, and an economic model. Illustrations, tables.

PART VI: HOME VIDEO

1218. Apar, Bruce, and Henry B. Cohen. The Home Video Book.
New York: Amphoto Books, 1982. 144p.
Guide to the operation, use, and maintenance of the TV
set, videocassette recorder, and video camera. Chapter on
video games, home computers, and videodisc players. Illustrations, glossary, index.

1219. Barlow, Geoffrey, and Alison Hill (eds.). Video Violence
and Children. New York: St. Martin's Press, 1985. 182p.
See entry 754.

1220. Blumenthal, Howard J. The Media Room: Creating Your Own
Home Entertainment and Information Center. New York: Penguin Books, 1983. 184p.
Designing and equipping media rooms for flexibility and expansion. The workings of different components; assembling;
checklist for buying TV sets, videodisc players, videocassette recorders, video cameras, video games, personal computers, and word processors. Illustrations, glossary, appendix, index.

1221. Butterfield, David C., and Patrick M. Irvin. Home Video
and Broadcast Television: Impacts and Opportunities. Washington, DC: National Association of Broadcasters, 1984. 20p.
The home video industry and consumer use of home video
equipment. Likely effects of home video's growth, and
strategies whereby television broadcasters may capitalize on
them. Illustrations.

1222. Caiati, Carl. Video Production--The Professional Way. Blue
Ridge Summit, PA: TAB Books, 1985. 247p.
Equipment, techniques, and procedures for VCR shooting,
taping, and editing. Lighting, electronic effects, animation,
titling, audio dubbing, and film-to-tape transfer. Illustrations, tables, glossary, index.

1223. Cohen, Henry B., with Bruce Apar. The Home Video Survival
Guide. New York: Amphoto Books, 1983. 192p.
Planning a home video system and purchasing, installing,

and operating the equipment. Illustrations, appendices, glossary, index.

1224. Cook, Rick, and Frank Vaughan. All About Home Satellite
Television. Blue Ridge Summit, PA: TAB Books, 1983.
326p.
See entry 1186.

1225. Countdown II: Jockeying at the DBS Starting Gate. Washington, DC: Television Digest, 1983. 105p.   .
See entry 1187.

1226. David, Ed. The Intelligent Idiot's Guide To Getting The Most
Out Of Home Video Equipment. Phildelphia, PA: Running
Press, 1982. 219p.
Advice on the purchase, installation, and operation of
videocassette recorders, off-air recording, cable TV, and the
care and use of cassettes and cameras. Names, addresses,
and telephone numbers of manufacturers and of equipment,
blank tape, and program distributors. Illustrations, index.

1227. The DBS Summit Conference. Washington, DC: Television
Digest, 1983. 102p.
See entry 619.

1228. Delson, Donn, and Edwin Michalove. Delson's Dictionary of
Cable, Video and Satellite Terms. Thousand Oaks, CA:
Bradson Press, 1983. 63p.
See entry 1023.

1229. Easton, Anthony T. The Home Satellite TV Book: How To
Put the World in Your Backyard. New York: Playboy Press,
1982. 381p.
See entry 1191.

1230. Goldberg, Joel. Satellite Television Reception: A Personal
User's Guide. Englewood Cliffs, NJ: Prentice-Hall, 1984.
103p.
See entry 1193.

1231. Graham, Margaret B. W. RCA and the VideoDisc: The Business of Research. New York: Cambridge University Press,
1986. 258p.
See entry 585.

1232. Harrington, Thomas P., and Bob Cooper, Jr. The Hidden
Signals on Satellite TV: The Secret Signals on Satellite TV.
Columbus, OH: Universal Electronics, 1984. 180p.
See entry 1194.

1233. The Home Video and Cable Yearbook, 1982-83. New York:

Facts on File Publications, 1982.   263p.
See entry 1025.

1234. Kybett, Harry, and Peter L. Dexnis. Complete Handbook of
Home Video Systems. Reston, VA: Reston, 1982. 277p.
Operation and use of a color camera, videocassette machine,
and videodisc, with the emphasis on the camera. Illustrations,
index.

1235. Lanzendorf, Peter. The Video Taping Handbook: The Newest
Systems, Cameras and Techniques. New York: Harmony
Books, 1983. 240p.
Resources and procedures for scripting, shooting, and
editing home video productions. Illustrations, index.

1236. Lenk, John D. Complete Guide to Laser/Videodisc Player
Troubleshooting and Repair. Englewood Cliffs, NJ: Prentice-
Hall, 1985. 314p.
Basic approach to servicing all types of players. Operation
of laser video and capacitance electronic disc, test equipment,
tools, installation and maintenance, and circuits. Illustrations,
index.

1237. Lenk, John D. Complete Guide to Videocassette Recorder
Operation and Servicing. Englewood Cliffs, NJ: Prentice-
Hall, 1983. 365p.
Simplified practical approach for electronic technicians. Required equipment and tools; circuits; mechanical operation;
procedures for adjustment, cleaning, lubrication and maintenance; troubleshooting techniques. Illustrations, index.

1238. Long, Mark, and Jeffrey Keating. The World of Satellite
Television. Summertown, TN: Book, 1983. 224p.
See entry 1199.

1239. Lyman, Peter. Canada's Video Revolution: Pay-TV, Home
Video and Beyond. Toronto: James Lorimer, 1983. 173p.
See entry 638.

1240. McCavitt, William E. Television Technology: Alternative
Communication Systems. Lanham, MD: University Press of
America, 1983. 142p.
See entry 1130.

1241. McGee, William L., Joseph H. Caton, and Lucy E. Garrick.
Changes, Challenges and Opportunities in the New Electronic
Media. San Francisco: BMC Publications, 1982.
See entry 1131.

1242. McNitt, Jim. The Home Video Sourcebook. New York: Col-
lier Books, 1982. 176p.

Advice on shopping for videocassette recorders, videodisc
players, projection TV, video cameras, and home satellite
receivers. Guide to programming available on tapes and discs.
Illustrations, glossary.

1243. Mattingly, E. Grayson. Expert Techniques for Home Video
Production. Blue Ridge Summit, PA: TAB Books, 1983.
170p.
Planning and producing a variety of content, with tips on
multi-camera systems, sound, lighting, and electronic editing.
Illustrations, recommended reading, glossary, index.

1244. Nadel, Mark, and Eli Noam (eds.). The Economics of Direct
Broadcast Satellites (DBS): An Anthology. New York:
Graduate School of Business, Columbia University, 1983.
160p.
See entry 1203.

1245. Nadel, Mark, and Eli Noam (eds.). The Economics of Physical
Distribution--Video Cassettes/Discs and Movie Theater: An
Anthology. New York: Graduate School of Business, Columbia University, 1983. 58p.
The demand for, use, costs, sales, and growth projections
for videocassette recorders. Sales, costs, and projected
revenues of videodisc players. Estimated growth of cassettes
and discs. Tables.

1246. Oderman, Mark. Current Trends in the Direct Broadcast
Satellite Industry. Bethesda, MD: Phillips, 1984. 24p.
See entry 1204.

1247. Pasternak, Bill. Video Cassette Recorders: Buying, Using
and Maintaining. Blue Ridge Summit, PA: TAB Books, 1983.
143p.
Evolution of video recording; the recording process; Beta-
max and VHS systems; tips on purchasing recorders, cameras,
and software; steps in making a video movie. Illustrations,
appendices, index.

1248. Powell, Jon T. International Broadcasting by Satellite: Is-
sues of Regulation, Barriers to Communication. Westport, CT:
Quorum Books, 1985. 300p.
See entry 314.

1249. Prentiss, Stan. Satellite Communications. Blue Ridge Summit,
PA: TAB Books, 1983. 280p.
See entry 1208.

1250. Rainger, Peter, David N. Gregory, Robert V. Harvey, and
Antony Jennings. Satellite Broadcasting. Chichester, Eng.:
John Wiley and Sons, 1985. 326p.
See entry 1209.

1251.   Reed, Robert M.   The American Telecommunications Market:
        Commercial/Public TV, Cable, STV, MDS, LPTV, Home Video.
        Syosset, NY: National Video Clearinghouse, 1982.   202p. +
        appendices.
        See entry 544.

1252.   Singleton, Loy A.   Telecommunications in the Information Age:
        A Nontechnical Primer on the New Technologies.   Cambridge,
        MA: Ballinger, 1983.   239p.
        See entry 1142.

1253.   Sutphin, S. E.   Understanding Satellite Television Reception.
        Englewood Cliffs, NJ: Prentice-Hall, 1986.   111p.
        See entry 1214.

1254.   Traister, Robert J.   Build a Personal Earth Station for World-
        wide Satellite TV Reception.   2d ed.   Blue Ridge Summit,
        PA: TAB Books, 1985.   370p.
        See entry 1216.

1255.   Traister, Robert J.   Make Your Own Professional Home Video
        Recordings.   Blue Ridge Summit, PA: TAB Books, 1982.
        304p.
           Cameras, recorders, videodiscs, and tips on lighting and
        special effects.   Illustrations, index.

1256.   Utz, Peter.   The Complete Home Video Book: A Source Book
        of Information Essential to the Video Enthusiast.   Englewood
        Cliffs, NJ: Prentice-Hall, 1983.   562p.
           Hints on buying, installing, operating, and maintaining
        equipment.   Producing and recording, use of lighting, graphics,
        editing, planning, and scripting.   Illustrations, appendices,
        index.

1257.   Utz, Peter.   Do-It-Yourself Video: A Beginner's Guide to
        Home Video.   Englewood Cliffs, NJ: Prentice-Hall, 1984.
        300p.
           What to do and how to do it.   Cameras and techniques,
        videocassette recorders, recording audio, lighting, graphics,
        copying and editing a videotape, planning and scripting, main-
        tenance, and hints on reading specifications and buying equip-
        ment.   Illustrations, tables, appendices, index.

1258.   Utz, Peter.   Video User's Handbook.   2d ed.   Englewood
        Cliffs, NJ: Prentice-Hall, 1982.   500p.
           Purchasing, operating, and maintaining TV cameras, video-
        tape recorders, and monitor/receivers.   Editing, sound, light-
        ing, graphics, special effects, and creative production tech-
        niques.   Illustrations, appendices, bibliography, index.

1259.   The VCR Explosion.   Washington, DC: Television Digest,
        1983.   121p.

Articles on technological, economic, legal, and other VCR developments originally published in Television Digest from June 7, 1982 through June 13, 1983. Index.

1260. Video Cassettes: Production, Distribution, and Programming for the VCR Marketplace. New York: Practising Law Institute, 1985. 500p.
Legal considerations, including off-air recording in education, duplication licensing, distribution in the international marketplace, union agreements, and copyright and piracy. Also, music agreements for original production, licensing the product to distributors, and the impact of VCR on broadcast television. Tables.

1261. Williams, Gene B., and Tommy Kay. Chilton's Guide to VCR Repair and Maintenance. Radnor, PA: Chilton, 1985. 164p.
Step-by-step diagnosis and repair instructions for the non-professional. VHS and Beta electronics and operation, safety precautions, required tools, troubleshooting guide, and when to seek professional help. Illustrations, appendix, glossary, index.

PART VII: PERIODICALS

A. BROADCASTING

1262. AIM Report. Washington, DC: Accuracy in Media. Twice monthly.
Accuracy in Media newsletter, concerned with issues of accuracy in both print and broadcast news.

1263. Better Broadcasts News. Madison, WI: The American Council for Better Broadcasts. Bimonthly.
Official newsletter of the ACBB, whose goal is improvement in the quality of both radio and television.

1264. BM/E - Broadcast Management Engineering. New York: Broadband Information Services. Monthly.
Management and engineering topics geared toward the broadcast and cable manager.

1265. Broadcast Engineering. Overland Park, KS: Intertec. Monthly.
News articles and features on broadcast technology.

1266. Broadcast Investor. Carmel, CA: Paul Kagan Associates. Twice monthly.
Deals with investments in both radio and television facilities.

1267. Broadcasting. Washington, DC: Broadcasting Publications. Weekly.
A variety of information on the many aspects of radio and television.

1268. Communication Booknotes. Washington, DC: Center for Telecommunication Studies, George Washington University. Bimonthly.
Annotated bibliographies of new publications in film, telecommunications, mass media, broadcasting, and information services.

194

1269. Communications and the Law. Westport, CT: Meckler.
       Quarterly.
       Legal issues related to the broadcast industry.

1270. Media Industry Reporter. New York: MIN. Weekly.
       News of media and marketing.

1271. The News Media and the Law. Washington, DC: Reporters
       Committee for Freedom of the Press. Quarterly.
       Summaries of legislative and judicial actions that have an
       impact on the press.

1272. Perry's Broadcasting and the Law. Oak Ridge, TN: Perry
       Publications. Twice monthly.
       Recent broadcast actions by the FCC and judicial systems.

1273. Public Broadcasting Report. Washington, DC: Television
       Digest. Fortnightly.
       Public radio and television newsletter.

1274. Religious Broadcasting. Parsippany, NJ: National Religious
       Broadcasters. Monthly.
       Official publication of the NRB.

1275. Television/Radio Age. New York: Television Editorial Cor-
       poration. Fortnightly.
       Deals with economic issues of the broadcast industry.

1276. Television/Radio Age International Newsletter. New York:
       TV/Radio Age. Biweekly.
       Focuses on television programming and technological de-
       velopments.

B. RADIO

1277. Airwaves. San Francisco: Audio Independents. Bimonthly.
       Independent radio production topics.

1278. Inside Radio. Cherry Hill, NJ: Inside Radio. Weekly.
       Newsletter on issues pertinent to the radio industry.

1279. NAB Today/Radio. Washington, DC: National Association of
       Broadcasters. Weekly.
       Official newsletter of the NAB, with news of interest to
       radio broadcasters.

1280. Radio News. Bethesda, MD: Phillips. Fortnightly.
       Newsletter for the radio industry.

1281. Radio Only. Cherry Hill, NJ: Inside Radio. Monthly.
       Radio broadcasting news and features.

C. TELEVISION

1282. ETV Newsletter. Danbury, CT: C. S. Tepfer. Fortnightly.
       Educational and instructional television topics.

1283. LPTV. Prairie Village, KS: Globecom. Bimonthly.
       News and feature articles of interest to the low-power
       television industry.

1284. NAB Today/Television. Washington, DC: National Associa-
       tion of Broadcasters. Weekly.
       NAB newsletter for television broadcasters.

1285. Post. New York: Post Pro. Monthly.
       Feature and news articles for persons in station and cor-
       porate post-production.

1286. Re: ACT. Newtonville, MA: Action for Children's Tele-
       vision. Semiannually.
       The news magazine of ACT.

1287. Television Broadcast Communications. Prairie Village, KS:
       Globecom. Monthly.
       International broadcast technology. Formerly Broadcast
       Communications.

1288. TV Technology. Falls Church, VA: Industrial Marketing
       Advisory Services. Twice monthly.
       News and feature articles on the technological aspects of
       television.

D. CABLE

1289. Cable Television Business. Englewood, CO: Cardiff. Twice
       monthly.
       Cable television industry news and features. Formerly
       TVC.

1290. Cable TV Investor. Carmel, CA: Paul Kagan Associates.
       Twice monthly.
       Cable television finance. Formerly Cablecast.

1291. CableAge. New York: Television Editorial Corporation. Fort-
       nightly.
       The business of cable television.

1292. CableVision. Denver: Titsch Communications. Weekly.
       Cable television news and related feature articles.

1293. CATACable. Oklahoma City: Community Antenna Television
       Association. Monthly.
       Official newsletter of the CATA.

E. NEW TECHNOLOGIES

1294. DBS News. Bethesda, MD: Phillips. Monthly.
       Coverage of direct broadcast satellites and related news.

1295. International Videotex Teletext News. Washington, DC: Ar-
       len Communications. Monthly.
       Developments in videotex and teletext.

F. HOME VIDEO

1296. Video Week. Washington, DC: Television Digest. Weekly.
       Newsletter dealing with the sales and distribution of video
       cassettes, videodiscs, and related media.

AUTHOR INDEX

Adams, Douglas 448, 485
Adams, William C. 722, 792, 872, 873
Adler, Renata 300
Adler, Richard P. 1164
Agardy, Susanna 631, 757
Agarwal, Bina 121, 340
Ainsley, John 669, 1062
Aitken, Hugh G. J. 465
Alber, Antone F. 1151
Albert, James A. 268
Aldershoff-Gaemers, Lidy 617, 1182
Aldrich, Michael 650, 1152
Allen, Robert C. 831
Allen, Yolanda 123, 181
Alley, Robert S. 990
Alper, Joel 1183
Alten, Stanley R. 359
Altheide, David L. 723
Alvarado, Manuel 651, 690, 866
Anderson, Daniel R. 756
Anderson, Gary H. 1004
Anderson, James A. 790
Andrews, Bart 334, 576, 832
Ang, Ien 833
Antébi, Elizabeth 182
Anwar, Muhammad 652, 908
Apar, Bruce 1218, 1223
Armer, Alan A. 962
Armstrong, Mark 124, 125, 247, 248, 317
Arnall, Gail 779
Arno, Andrew 99, 198
Arterton, F. Christopher 217
Aubrey, Crispin 146
Ayers, Ralph 1008

Bachman, John W. 244
Bacon, James 55
Baehr, Helen 449
Bagdikian, Ben H. 78
Bakr, Yahya Abu 138
Baldwin, Huntley 941, 1013
Baldwin, Thomas F. 1034, 1101
Ball-Rokeach, Sandra J. 724
Balle, Francis 116
Bannerman, R. LeRoy 56
Barcus, F. Earle 753, 909
Barker, Martin 653, 813
Barlow, Geoffrey 754, 1219
Barnouw, Erik 702, 745
Barr, Trevor 630, 1117
Barrett, Marvin 874
Barron, Jerome A. 257
Bates, A. W. 212
Bates, Anthony W. 213
Bates, Stephen 795
Baughman, James L. 703, 814
Baygan, Lee 959
Baylin, Frank 1184
Beck, Kirsten 1091
Bellaire, Arthur 583
Benjamin, Burton 875
Bennett, Tony 152, 202, 600
Bennett, W. Lance 219
Benoit, Philip 521
Bensinger, Charles 535
Bensman, Marvin R. 249
Benson, K. Blair 949
Bentley, J. Geoffrey 80
Bergendorff, Fred L. 349
Berlyn, David W. 592, 1048
Berry, Gordon L. 755
Besen, Stanley M. 308, 309, 318, 821, 1041
Beville, Hugh Malcolm, Jr. 51

Bhasin, Kamla 121, 340
Biagi, Shirley 383
Biel, Jacquelyn 1170
Bilby, Kenneth 57
Biles, Jim 631, 757
Bishop, W. D. 692, 1064
Bittner, John R. 44, 250
Blakeney, Michael 125, 248
Blanchard, Simon 654
Blank, Ben 1009
Block, Martin P. 1101
Blum, Richard A. 1014
Blume, Dan 439
Blume, Keith 793, 876
Blume, Wilbur T. 780
Blumenthal, Howard J. 1220
Blumler, Jay G. 643, 794
Blythe, Cheryl 58, 547, 834, 859
Blythin, Evan 960
Bohère, G. 82
Bolling, Landrum R. 94, 220
Bonderoff, Jason 59
Bone, Jan 1049
Bonventre, Peter 61
Book, Albert C. 350, 407
Booyaketmala, Boonrak 701
Borah, Farfalla 911, 1092
Bortz, Paul I. 432, 954, 1118
Bouthilet, Lorraine 743
Bower, Robert T. 580
Boyd, Douglas A. 139, 169
Brady, Ben 1015
Brady, Tim 389
Braestrup, Peter 218
Branscomb, Lewis M. 745
Brasch, Walter M. 284
Brazier, Jan 126, 189
Brenner, Daniel L. 285, 1073
Bretz, Rudy 1106, 1153
Brey, Ronald G. 787
Breyer, Richard 963
Bridges, Nancye 442, 466
Briggs, Asa 147, 183
Briggs, E. Donald 134, 236
Brisch-Kanaba, Janyce 971
Brooks, Tim 560, 561
Brotman, Stuart N. 1042
Broughton, Irv 964
Broussard, E. Joseph 384
Brown, Charlene J. 287

Brown, Les 554, 601
Brown, Ray 647, 776
Brown, Stanley J. 278
Browne, Donald R. 459
Browne, Steven E. 1005
Bryant, Jennings 725, 752, 756
Buckman, Peter 618, 655, 835
Bukalski, Peter J. 530
Bunzel, Reed 501, 509
Burger, Richard L. 536
Burgoon, Judee K. 52, 201
Burgoon, Michael 52, 201
Burke, Jacinta 631, 757
Burke, Richard C. 100
Burrows, Thomas D. 965
Busby, Linda 498
Butterfield, David C. 1221
Byers, Susan 1176
Byron, Christopher M. 940, 1098

Caesar, Sid 60
Caiati, Carl 1222
Campbell, Karlyn Kohrs 735
Canape, Charlene 584
Cantor, José G. 701
Cantor, Muriel G. 335
Carey, John 346, 928, 1119, 1120, 1171
Carlson, James M. 726
Carr, Joseph J. 307, 511
Carroll, Sidney L. 1179, 1180
Carter, T. Barton 286
Cary, Norman D. 350, 407
Casey, Thomas J. 1078
Cassata, Mary 527, 836
Castleman, Harry 562, 704
Caton, Joseph H. 1131, 1241
Chamberlin, Bill F. 287
Chambers, Everett 966
Chancellor, John 385
Chapman, Graham 620, 700
Charren, Peggy 727
Chaudhary, Anju Grover 112
Cheen, Bruce Bishop 433
Christensen, Mark 837
Clifford, Martin 360, 1185
Codding, George A., Jr. 170
Cohen, Daniel 594, 1051
Cohen, Henry B. 1218, 1223

Cohen, Phil   148
Cohen, Susan   594, 1051
Cohler, David Keith   386
Collins, Keith S.   288
Columbe, Bob   838
Combs, James E.   231, 897
Compesi, Ronald J.   967
Connors, Tracy Daniel   15
Conrad, Jon J.   942, 968
Conrad, Peter   602, 656
Cook, Rick   1186, 1224
Cooper, Bob, Jr.   1194, 1232
Cooper, Louis F.   280
Cosell, Howard   61
Couling, Della   833
Couloumbis, Angela   502
Courtney, Alice E.   199, 341
Cox, Geoffrey   657, 705
Craig, Don   508
Cran, William   893, 934
Cremer, Charles F.   958
Crescenti, Peter   838
Crook, Frank   442, 466
Cross, Donna Woolfolk   728
Crutchfield, Ben   373
Crutchfield, E. B.   367
Cullingford, Cedric   658, 759
Cunningham, Ann Marie   234, 337
Cunningham, Don R.   353, 1100
Curran, James   149, 152, 202, 319
Curry, Jane Leftwich   101, 289
Curtis, Liz   150, 342
Czitrom, Daniel J.   185, 200

D'Agostino, Peter   603, 1121
Dassin, Joan R.   101, 289
David, Ed   1226
Davidson, Bill   60
Davidson, Emily S.   768
Davis, Dennis K.   744, 898
Davis, Henry B. O.   22, 23
Davis, James A.   910
Davis, Lenwood   4
Davis, Richard H.   910
Dawson, James   502
DeFleur, Lois B.   211
DeGooyer, Janice   911, 1092
Delson, Donn   1023, 1189, 1228

Dennis, Everette E.   95
Denny, Jon S.   1052
De Sarlo, Carmine R.   943, 1006
DeSonne, Marcia L.   434, 1122, 1190
Devol, Kenneth S.   290
Dexnis, Peter L.   1234
Diamond, Edwin   291, 795, 912
Director, Mark D.   258
Dissanayake, Wimal   99, 198
Doerken, Maurine   760, 781
Doi, T.   362
Dolan, Edward V.   1077
Dominick, Joseph R.   413, 416
Doney, Ruane L.   537, 826
Donnelly, William J.   729, 1123
Dorn, Nicholas   3, 343
Dorr, Aimée   761, 782
Downs, Hugh   62
Drake, Harold L.   517, 518
Drucker, Malka   969
Drummond, Phillip   674, 698, 788
Ducey, Richard V.   374, 435
Dudek, Lee J.   404
Duffy, Dennis J.   447, 467
Duncan, James H., Jr.   425, 468
Dunkley, Christopher   659, 730
Durkin, Kevin   762

Eargle, John   368
Eastman, Susan Tyler   351, 410, 929, 1099, 1116
Easton, Anthony T.   1191, 1229
Eberly, Philip K.   469
Edelstein, Alex S.   102
Edgar, David   1016
Edgar, Patricia   103, 320
Editors at Knowledge Industry Publications, Inc., The   996
Editors of Consumer Guide   577
Editors of the Associated Press, The   709, 844
Ehrlich, Eugene   25
Eicoff, Alvin   352
Eisner, Joel   563
Eliot, Marc   604
Elliott, Bob   486
Elliott, Geoff   970

Elliott, Philip 684
Ellis, John 605
Ellmore, R. Terry 253
Emeritz, Robert E. 280
Ensign, Lynne Naylor 533
Eron, Leonard D. 622, 764
Esslin, Martin 606
Ettema, James S. 83, 766, 916
Etter, Terry 815
Eugster, Ernest 699
Everest, F. Alton 369

Falcione, Raymond L. 85
Fang, Irving E. 387
Farrell, Nigel 160
Fejes, Fred 460, 470
Ferris, Charles D. 1078
Feuer, Jane 840
Firestone, Charles M. 816, 1192
Fischer, Stuart 564, 706, 827
Fisher, Desmond 321
Fishman, Joshua H. 26
Flaherty, David H. 1058, 1079
Fletcher, James E. 413, 525
Flowe, Carol Connor 278
Floyd, Beth 1114
Floyd, Steve 1114
Foster, Eugene S. 45
Fowles, Jib 731
Francois, William E. 254
Frank, Peter 1173, 1174
Frank, Ronald E. 581, 930
Franklin, Marc A. 255, 286
Franks, Don 538
Fratrik, Mark R. 435
Frederick, Howard H. 461,
   484
Fricker, Maria 631, 757
Friedberg, Ardy 68
Fukada, J. 362
Fuller, Barry J. 971
Furse, David H. 747
Fury, Kathleen 878

Gach, Stephen 972
Galvin, Katherine M. 256
Ganley, Gladys 750, 869, 939
Garay, Ronald 707, 796
Garcia, Mario 1009

Gardner, Carl 148
Garrick, Lucy E. 1131, 1241
Garvey, Daniel E. 388, 417,
   418, 1111
Gates, Gary Paul 76
Gaynes, Martin J. 267
Gee, Robyn 575
Geis, Michael L. 732
Gerald, J. Edward 292
Gerbner, George 104, 172
Gerrold, David 841
Gertner, Michael H. 26
Gherardi, Thomas 928, 1120
Gianakos, Larry James 565
Giangola, Andrew 487, 503, 510
Gibbons, Arnold 142, 1124
Gilbert, Bob 389
Gillmor, Donald M. 257
Ginsburg, Douglas H. 258
Gitlin, Todd 842
Glasgow University Media Group
   660, 914
Glasser, Jeffrey 972
Glenn, Robin Day 644, 817
Godfrey, Donald G. 27, 131,
   151
Goldberg, Joel 1193, 1230
Goldstein, Fred 708
Goldstein, Stan 708
Goodale, James C. 259
Goodman, Evelyn 1017
Goodwin, H. Eugene 390
Gould, Peter 620, 700
Goulding, Ray 486
Graaf, Janny de 206
Graber, Doris A. 221, 222
Graff, Robert D. 143
Gragert, Steven K. 488
Graham, Margaret B. W. 585,
   1231
Grant, William 1107
Greenberg, Bradley S. 52, 201
Greenberg, Marshall G. 581,
   930
Greenberg, Martin Harry 854
Greenfield, Jeff 223
Greenfield, Patricia Marks 733
Gregory, David N. 1209, 1250
Griffin-Beale, Christopher 575
Griffiths, Trevor 1016
Gronbeck, Bruce E. 1018

Gross, Lynne Schafer 46, 1125
Grote, David 843
Groves, Seli 709, 844
Grube, Joel W. 724
Guback, Thomas 701
Gunter, Barrie 661, 734, 797
Gurevitch, Michael 152, 202
Gutierrez, Felix 825, 1141

Hall, Jim 710, 944
Hallin, Daniel C. 879
Hamburg, Morton I. 79, 1044,
    1080
Hamelink, Cees J. 173, 177,
    330
Hand, Raymond, Jr. 25
Hannikainen, Lauri 176, 329
Hare, David 1016
Harrell, Bobby 1108
Harrington, Thomas P. 1194,
    1232
Harris, Robert 153, 224
Harrison, Martin 662, 880
Harrop, Martin 168, 243
Harry, Keith 109, 215
Hartley, Ian 154, 187
Hartley, John 663
Harvey, Robert V. 1209, 1250
Harwell, Ernie 64
Hausman, Carl 521
Havick, John J. 322
Hawes, William 711
Hawkridge, David 105, 214,
    783, 1126
Hays, Kim 784
Hazlett, Thomas W. 881
Head, Sydney W. 47, 106, 410,
    1116
Hedebro, Göran 144
Heidt, Erhard U. 649
Heighton, Elizabeth J. 353,
    1100
Hellweg, Susan A. 85
Hess, Robert 746
Hetherington, Alastair 664,
    882
Hewitt, Don 883
Hiber, Jhan 526
Higgins, C. S. 443
Higham, Charles 65

Hill, Alison 754, 1219
Hill, Anne 18
Hill, Doug 712, 845
Hill, George H. 4, 188, 245,
    528
Hill, Sylvia Saverson 528
Hilliard, Robert L. 419, 499,
    621, 785
Himmelstein, Hal 607
Hind, John 450
Hobson, Dorothy 665, 846
Hoggart, Richard 155, 323
Holgate, Jack F. 384
Hollander, Richard 1069
Hollingsworth, T. R. 595
Hollins, Timothy 666, 1061
Hollowell, Mary Louise 1035
Hon, David 1114
Honeyman, Steve 397
Hood, James R. 391
Hood, Stuart 667
Hooper, Alan 156, 225
Hooper, Richard 668, 1155
Hoover, Stewart M. 807, 1127
Horsfield, Peter G. 808
Hosley, David H. 471
Howard, Herbert H. 358, 411,
    586, 1026, 1045, 1179, 1180
Howe, Michael J. A. 763, 786
Howell, W. J., Jr. 107, 324
Howitt, Dennis 203
Howkins, John 157, 1128
Hudson, Heather 1195
Hudspeth, DeLayne R. 787
Huesmann, L. Rowell 622, 764
Hughes, Colin A. 127, 242
Hughes, Patrick 669, 1062
Hulteng, John L. 392
Hutchison, Earl R., Sr. 420
Huxford, Marilyn 10
Hyde, Stuart W. 405

Iezzi, Frank 973
Iga, A. 362
Inglis, K. S. 126, 189
Ingram, Dave 950
International Institute of Communi-
    cations 1196
Intintoli, Michael James 847
Irvin, Patrick M. 1221
Irvine, Ian 864

Jackson, Anthony W. 915
Jackson, Charles L. 1177
James, Elizabeth 969
Jamieson, Kathleen Hall 190,
    226, 735
Jansky, Donald M. 1198
Janus, Noreene 141, 159
Jennings, Antony 1209, 1250
Jeruchim, Michel C. 1198
Jesuale, Nancy 1036, 1081
Jewell, Geri 66
Johnnson-Smaragdi, Ulla 645,
    765
Johnson, Catherine E. 558
Johnson, Jeffrey 620, 700
Johnson, Leland L. 308, 309,
    318, 1041
Johnson, Tim 1169
Johnston, Jerome 766, 916
Jones, Kensinger 1101
Jones, Maxine Holmes 1093
Josephson, Larry 516
Joslyn, Richard 227
Juilliard, Ahrgus 334

Kaatz, Ronald B. 1102
Kahn, Frank J. 260
Kaid, Lynda Lee 798
Kalbfeld, Brad 391
Kalisch, Beatrice J. 917
Kalisch, Philip A. 917
Kalter, Suzy 848, 849
Kaminsky, Stuart M. 608
Kanaba, Steve 971
Kandil, Hamdy 138
Kaplan, E. Ann 609
Kappes, Harold 928, 1120
Karnow, Stanley 884, 931
Katzman, Natan 493, 936
Katzman, Solomon 493, 936
Kaufman, Milton 951
Kay, Tommy 1261
Kaye, Anthony 109, 215
Keating, Jeffrey 1199, 1238
Keith, Michael C. 500, 504, 519
Kelleher, Brian 852
Keller, Barbara Berger 596
Kelley, Michael R. 767
Kellough, Patrick Henry 1022
Kelly, Richard Michael 850

Kenney, Brigitte L. 1029
Kent, Jacqueline 444, 472
Kern, Montague 799, 885
Kerr, Paul 840
Kessler, Ronald C. 770
Kievman, Michael S. 411
King, Larry 67
Kirkley, Donald H., Jr. 513
Kiver, Milton 951
Klein, Harrison J. 512
Klein, Lewis 410, 1116
Klein, Robert A. 351, 929,
    1099
Knapton, Robyn Eileen 533
Kolehmainen, John I. 462, 473
Korzenny, Felipe 52, 201
Kostrich, Leslie J. 806, 901
Kowet, Don 886, 975
Krasnow, Erwin G. 80, 273,
    310, 375
Krattenmaker, Thomas G. 821
Kraus, Sidney 228
Krause, Joseph M. 500
Krinsky, David 563
Kuhn, Raymond 110, 326
Kuralt, Charles 927
Kurland, Philip B. 1088
Kurtis, Bill 597, 887
Kybett, Harry 1234

Labib, Saad 138
Lacy, Dan 745
LaGuardia, Robert 851
Lahav, Pnina 111, 261
Lambert, Stephen 671
Lamparski, Richard 578
Lang, Gladys Engel 800, 801
Lang, Kurt 800, 801
Langley, Graham 370
Lanzendorf, Peter 1235
Larson, James F. 802, 888
Lashner, Marilyn A. 889
Lattimore, Dan 394
Lawler, Philip F. 890
Lazar, Joyce 743
Leapman, Michael 672
LeBaron, John 976
Lenk, John D. 1236, 1237
Lent, John A. 5, 6, 30, 122
Lerner, Mark 441

LeRoy, David 932, 1070
LeRoy, Judith M. 932, 1070
Lesher, Stephan 736, 891
Levey, Jane Freundel 31
Levine, Larry S. 1042
Levine, Pamela 972
Levinson, Richard 977
Levy, Mark R. 744, 898
Lewis, Carolyn Diana 955
Lewis, Raymond J. 32
Lichter, Linda S. 737, 892, 918, 933
Lichter, S. Robert 737, 892, 918, 933
Liebert, Robert M. 768
Link, William 977
Linsky, Martin 803
Lipinski, Hubert 1164
Lloyd, Frank W. 1078
Local Radio Workshop 451, 452
Lockhart, Ron 354, 361, 408
Lodziak, Conrad 738
Logan, Tom 945, 961
Long, Mark 1199, 1238
Longley, Lawrence D. 310
Look, Hugh Evison 673, 1157
Lowry, Esther G. 26
Lukas, Christopher 978
Lunden, Joan 68
Lusted, David 674, 788
Lyman, Peter 638, 1129, 1239

McCartney, Neil 669, 1062
McCarty, John 852
McCavitt, William E. 7, 376, 1109, 1130, 1240
McCrum, Robert 893, 934
MacDonald, J. Fred 739, 853, 894, 919
McEntee, Patrick 1114
McGee, William L. 1131, 1241
McGuire, Bernadette 53, 229, 514
McKenna, George 204
McKerns, Joseph P. 8
McLean, Mick 624, 1132
McLoone, Martin 648, 920
MacMahon, John 648, 920
MacNeice, Jill 375
McNeil, Alex 566

MacNeil, Robert 69, 893, 934
McNitt, Jim 1242
McNulty, Sally 979
McQuail, Denis 205, 625, 823, 1133
McQuillin, Lon 980, 981
McVoy, D. Stevens 1034
Madsen, Axel 895
Mahan, Jeffrey H. 608
Malsbary, Robert W. 574
Maltin, Leonard 567
Mansell, Gerard 453, 463, 474
Mansfield, Michael W. 115, 232
Manzella, Ray 599, 870
Marc, David 610
Marcus, Norman 377, 1110
Marill, Alvin H. 568
Marsh, Earle 560, 561
Martel, Myles 230
Martin, James 1158
Martin, L. John 112
Martin, Robin B. 436
Martinez, Larry 1200
Masterman, Len 675, 789
Mathias, Harry 983
Matte, Nicolas Mateesco 313, 1201
Mattelart, Michèle 140, 344
Matthews, Arthur C. 520
Mattingly, E. Grayson 1243
Mattos, Sérgio 636, 740
Matusow, Barbara 896
Maxa, Kathleen 77
May, Annabelle 158, 327
Mayeux, Peter E. 421
Mears, Walter R. 385
Medoff, Norman J. 984
Meehan, Diana M. 921
Mendel, Robin 493, 936
Mendelsohn, Harold 432, 1118
Meppen, Adrian J. 400
Mercurio, James P. 1088
Merrill, John C. 95, 114
Metzger, A. Richard, Jr. 821
Meyer, Manfred 529, 769
Meyrowitz, Joshua 741
Michalove, Edwin 1023, 1189, 1228
Mickelson, Sig 464, 475
Milam, Lorenzo Wilson 494
Milan, William G. 26

Milavsky, J. Ronald 770
Miller, Abraham H. 295
Miller, Jerome K. 818
Miller, Nicholas P. 1081
Miller, Philip 976
Millerson, Gerald 985, 986,
  987, 1010, 1011, 1012
Millington, Bob 676, 988
Mincer, Deanne 33
Mincer, Richard 33
Mitchell, Julian 1016
Mitchell-Kernan, Claudia 755
Moller, Peter 963
Moorfoot, Rex 1134
Moran, Albert 632, 989
Morgan, Janet 155, 323
Morley, David 654
Mosco, Stephen 450
Mosco, Vincent 96, 174, 328,
  1159
Moss, Mitchell 928, 1120
Moss, P. D. 443
Moulds, M. J. 677
Mowlana, Hamid 175
Mueller, Milton 291
Mullan, Bob 163, 207
Müller, Werner 529
Muraro, Heriberto 701
Murdock, Graham 141, 159, 684
Murphy, Brian 1059, 1135
Murray, Catherine A. 639, 1202
Murray, John P. 771
Muscio, Winston T. 445, 476
Mytton, Graham 119

Nadel, Mark 587, 1046, 1172,
  1175, 1181, 1203, 1217, 1244,
  1245
Naficy, Hamid 559
Nakajima, H. 362
Negrine, Ralph M. 1060
Nelson, Carole 70
Nelson, Harold L. 263
Nelson, Lindsey 71
Nelson, Robin 676, 988
Neustadt, Richard M. 1081,
  1082, 1160
Nevins, Francis M., Jr. 854
Newcomb, Horace 611, 990
Newsom, Doug 393

Newsom, Iris 34
New York University School of
  Law 819
Nicol, Andrew G. L. 161, 297
Nimmo, Dan 115, 231, 232, 798,
  897
Nisbett, Alec 363
Niven, Harold 86
Noam, Eli 587, 1046, 1172,
  1175, 1181, 1203, 1217, 1244,
  1245
Noam, Eli M. 588
Noll, Edward M. 306, 371
Nordenstreng, Kaarle 176,
  329, 345
Norman, Bruce 678, 713
Nown, Graham 679, 714, 855
Nugent, Gwen 1161
Nyhan, Michael 1164

Oakey, Virginia 534
Oberdorfer, Donald N. 809
O'Bryan, Kenneth G. 1114
O'Connor, John E. 612
Oderman, Mark 1204, 1246
O'Donnell, Lewis B. 521
O'Keefe, Garret J. 53, 229
Oringel, Robert S. 364, 991,
  1115
Orlik, Peter B. 422
Orton, Barry 1084
Overbeck, Wayne 264
Ozanich, Gary W. 1149

Paiva, Bob 523
Palmer, Patricia 633, 772
Parenti, Michael 742
Parish, James Robert 541
Parker, Bruce 160
Parker, Donald 498
Parks, Rita 922
Partridge, Simon 454, 495
Passingham, Kenneth 542, 680
Pasternak, Bill 1247
Paterson, Richard 543, 626,
  698
Patrick, W. Lawrence 1176
Patten, David A. 1138
Patterson, Richard 983

Patton, Phil 810
Pavlič, Breda 177, 330
Pearl, David 743
Pegg, Mark 455, 477
Pelton, Joseph N. 1183
Pember, Don R. 265
Penney, Edmund 17
Pepper, Robert 1071
Perkins, Geoffrey 448, 485
Perloff, Richard M. 228
Perry, George 681, 856
Perry, Jeb H. 569
Perry, Larry 274, 389, 508
Peters, P. J. 1161
Pillai, N. N. 141, 159
Pingree, Suzanne 335
Ploghoft, Milton E. 790
Ploman, Edward W. 178, 266, 1205
Plude, Frances Ford 92, 1057
Podrazik, Walter J. 562, 704
Poltrack, David 946, 1103
Pool, Ithiel de Sola 296, 1085
Poole, Mike 1019
Postian, Charles W. 1207
Postman, Neil 613, 773
Powell, Jon T. 314, 1206, 1248
Powers, Ron 811
Pragnell, Anthony 646
Pratt, Timothy 1207
Prentiss, Stan 365, 952, 1208, 1249
Price, Monroe E. 1073
Prince, Peter 1016
Pringle, Peter K. 376, 1109
Prone, Terry 406
Pullen, Rick D. 264

Quale, John C. 273

Rader, Benjamin G. 812
Rahim, Syed A. 103, 320
Rainger, Peter 1209, 1250
Rancer, Andrew S. 92, 1057
Ranney, Austin 233, 804
Rasmussen, Bill 1067, 1094

Reed, Maxine K. 598, 1054
Reed, Robert M. 544, 598, 937, 1030, 1054, 1139, 1251
Reiss, David S. 857
Renner, Louis L. 478
Research Group, The 505
Reymer and Gersin Associates, Inc. 430, 431, 506, 507
Rice, Jean 1087
Rivers, William L. 285, 388, 417, 418, 1111
Roberts, Geoffrey K. 135
Robertson, Geoffrey 161, 297
Robertson, Tom 647, 776
Robinson, John 105, 162, 191, 214, 216
Robinson, John P. 744, 898
Robinson, Michael J. 233, 805, 899
Robinson, Richard 992
Rockwell, Lee 1161
Rogers, Everett M. 116
Rojas, Gloria 701
Rokeach, Milton 724
Roman, James W. 1037
Romanow, Walter I. 134, 236
Roper, Burns W. 54
Rose, Brian G. 545, 546, 715, 858
Rosen, Frederic W. 993
Roth, M. Patricia 303
Rothman, Stanley 737, 892, 933
Rouverol, Jean 1020
Rowan, Ford 276, 282
Rowan, Kathryn 158, 327
Rowland, Willard D., Jr. 614, 824
Rubens, William S. 770
Rubin, Bernard 336
Rubin, David M. 234, 337
Rudell, Michael I. 277
Rutkowski, Anthony M. 170
Ryan, Michèle 449

Sabin, Louis 48
Sackett, Susan 58, 547, 834, 859
Sadashige, Ernie 956
Salomon, Gavriel 771

Salomonson, Terry G. G.   427,
    482
Samovar, Larry A.   960
Sanders, Coyne Steven   868
Sanders, Keith R.   798
Sandler, Martin W.   727
Sandler, Norman   291
Sanford, Bruce W.   304, 381
Sapan, Joshua   1055
Savage, Bob   508
Savitch, Jessica   72
Saxton, Judith   414
Schement, Jorge Reina   825,
    1141
Schemering, Christopher   555,
    860
Scheuer, Steven H.   579, 1039
Schlesinger, Philip   684
Schmid, Alex   206
Schmidbauer, Michael   1106,
    1153
Schmuhl, Robert   97
Schnapf, Abraham   1212
Schneller, Paul   780
Schreibman, Fay C.   530
Schuman, Howard   1016
Schwarz, Meg   774
Schwarz, Michael   1114
Scobey, Margaret   917
Seaton, Jean   149, 319
Seigerman, Catherine   502, 515
Self, David   685, 861
Selvidge, Barry   274
Sendall, Bernard   686, 687, 716,
    717
Settel, Irving   718
Shackleford, John   1174
Shaffer, Wm. Drew   1095
Shaheen, Jack G.   923
Shales, Tom   615
Shane, Ed   524
Shang, Anthony   652
Shanks, Bob   994, 1021
Shapiro, George H.   1088
Shaw, Donald Lewis   118
Shearer, Benjamin F.   10
Sheehan, Margaret A.   805, 899
Sherriffs, Ronald E.   967
Shestakov, V. P.   141, 159
Shetter, Michael D.   1007
Shook, Frederick   394, 957

Shooshan, Harry M., III   1177
Short, K. R. M.   479
Shosteck, Herschel   1150
Siefert, Marsha   104, 172
Siegel, Arthur   132, 235
Sigel, Efrem   627, 745, 1162
Signorielli, Nancy   531, 924
Silverstone, Roger   688, 995
Simpson, Steven D.   316, 382
Singer, Benjamin D.   133
Singleton, Loy A.   1142, 1252
Singsen, Michael   283
Sinofsky, Esther R.   791, 820
Sirbu, Marvin A., Jr.   825,
    1141
Siune, Karen   625, 823, 1133
Skill, Thomas   527, 836
Sklar, Rick   480, 483
Slide, Anthony   36, 481, 548
Smart, James R.   428
Smart, Samuel Chipman   192
Smeyak, G. Paul   395, 1112
Smith, Anthony   745
Smith, Charles H.   349
Smith, F. Leslie   49
Smith, Marvin   50
Smith, Myron J., Jr.   532
Smith, Nelson   117, 338
Smith, Ralph Lee   1036
Smith, V. Jackson   412
Smolla, Rodney A.   305
Snorgrass, J. William   11
Soderlund, Walter C.   134, 236
Sommer, Peter   1163
South, Nigel   3, 343
Spear, Joseph C.   237
Spencer, Susan   123, 181
Sperber, A. M.   73
Spigai, Fran   1163
Sprafkin, Joyce   746
Sprafkin, Joyce N.   768
Sreberny-Mohammadi, Annabelle
    345
Stamberg, Susan   489, 497
Stauth, Cameron   837
Steenland, Sally   925
Steinberg, Cobbett   549, 719
Stephens, Mitchell   396
Sterling, Christopher H.   12,
    13, 37, 47, 179, 331, 1031
Stevens, John D.   298

Stevenson, Robert   345
Stevenson, Robert L.   118
Stewart, David W.   747
Stewart, Donald E.   635, 926
Stewart, John   651
Stipp, Horst H.   770
Stokes, Judith   996
Stoppard, Tom   456, 490
Stover, William James   145, 1143
Straczynski, J. Michael   423
Strange, Robert G., Jr.   574
Strauss, Lawrence   1104
Strong, William C.   270
Stueart, Robert D.   745
Sutphin, S. E.   1214, 1253
Sutton, Shaun   862
Svennerig, Michael   661, 797
Swearer, Harvey F.   307
Swerdlow, Joel L.   900
Swift, Carolyn   746
Syfret, Toby   628, 1144

Taft, William H.   42
Tannenbaum, Percy H.   806, 901
Tannenbaum, Stanley I.   350, 407
Tanquary, Tom   984
Taylor, Laurie   163, 207
Taylor, Leslie   332, 1215
Teague, Bob   902
Teeter, Dwight L., Jr.   263
Terrace, Vincent   541, 556, 557, 570, 571, 1033, 1097
Terry, Herbert A.   310
Theberge, Leonard J.   117, 338, 904, 905
Thomas, David   864
Thompson, Kenneth W.   193, 238, 239, 240
Thorpe, Kenneth E.   1090
Toll, Robert C.   194
Toner, Amy   1184
Tourigny, Patrick   640, 938
Tracey, Michael   74, 164
Traister, Robert J.   1216, 1254, 1255
Trautman, James M.   954
Trethowan, Ian   75, 165
Trimble, Bjo   865

Tulloch, John   690, 866
Tumber, Howard   691, 749
Turner, Kathleen J.   195, 241
Turow, Joseph   208
Tydeman, John   1164

Udelson, Joseph H.   720
Ugboajah, Frank   345
Ugboajah, Frank Okwu   120
Ullmann, John   397
Ulloth, Dana R.   284
Utz, Peter   1256, 1257, 1258

Vahimagi, Tise   840
Vahl, Rod   89
Van Alstyne, William W.   299
Van Wormer, Laura   867
Varis, Tapio   701
Vaughan, Frank   1186, 1224
Veith, Richard H.   629, 1165
Veljanovski, C. G.   692, 1064
Voort, T. H. A. van der   775

Wade, Graham   693
Wagenberg, Ronald H.   134, 236
Walker, Savannah Waring   601
Wallace, Mike   76
Ward, Hiley H.   398
Ward, Scott   647, 776
Warner, Charles   355, 1105
Wasko, Janet   96, 174
Waters, Dennis P.   1178
Watkins, Bruce   614
Watson, James   18
Wattenberg, Ben J.   98
Watterson, Ray   125, 248
Weaver, David H.   90, 694, 1168
Weaver, J. Clark   356, 399, 424
Webb, G. Kent   1047
Weber, Kathleen   311, 347, 348
Webster, James   415
Webster, James G.   582, 1072
Webster, Lance   349
Wedell, George   14, 136
Weiner, Stewart   66
Weingrad, Jeff   712, 845
Weinstein, Bob   91, 1056
Weinstein, Stephen B.   1038, 1146

Weissman, Dick   354, 361, 408
Weissman, Ginny   868
Wenham, Brian   695, 1147
Wersky, Gary   669, 1062
West, W. J.   457, 458, 491,
   492
Western, J. S.   127, 242
Westin, Av   907
Wheelwright, Richard   1095
Wheen, Francis   696, 721
Whipple, Thomas W.   199, 341
White, Gordon   953
White, Hooper   947, 997
White, Ted   400
White, Thomas   750, 869, 939
Whitemore, Hugh   1016
Whitley, Dianna   599, 870
Whitney, D. Charles   83
Wiegand, Ingrid   998
Wiese, Michael   948, 999, 1003
Wilhoit, G. Cleveland   90
Wilkins, Joan Anderson   777
Williams, Frederick   196, 209,
   1148
Williams, Gene B.   1261
Williams, Martin   616
Williams, Tannis Macbeth   641,
   751
Wimmer, Roger D.   416
Win, P. P. de   141, 159
Windschuttle, Keith   128, 210
Winfield, Betty Houchin   211
Winn, Marie   778
Wober, Mallory   661, 797
Wolfe, Kenneth M.   167, 197,
   246
Wollert, James   515
Wollert, James A.   393
Wolverton, Mike   401
Wood, Donald N.   965
Woodbury, John R.   821
Woodman, Kieran   137
Woodrow, R. Brian   642, 1065
Woodruff, Judy   77
Woodside, Kenneth B.   642,
   1065
Woodward, Walt   357, 366, 409
Woody, Gloria T.   11
Woolery, George W.   572, 573,
   829, 830
Woollacott, Janet   152, 202

Woolley, Lynn   574
Worcester, Robert M.   168, 243
Wright, Gene   41, 43
Wright, Jay B.   286
Wulfemeyer, K. Tim   402, 403
Wurtzel, Alan   1000
Wyche, Mark C.   954
Wyver, John   1019

Yoakam, Richard D.   958
Yoffe, Emily   67
Young, Steve   400
Yurow, Jane H.   180, 333

Zacharis, John C.   92, 1057
Zeigler, Sherilyn K.   358
Zeller, Susan L.   93
Zettl, Herbert   1001, 1002
Zicree, Marc Scott   871
Zillmann, Dolf   725, 752
Zuckman, Harvey L.   267
Zwimpfer, Laurence   1164

TITLE INDEX

Access to Political Broadcasting in the EEC   135
Acoustic Techniques for Home and Studio   369
Acting in the Million Dollar Minute: The Art and Business of Per-
    forming in TV Commercials   945, 961
Actors' Television Credits.   Supplement II: 1977-81.   541
Advertising Age Yearbook   19
Advertising in the Broadcast and Cable Media   353, 1100
Aerospace Law: Telecommunications Satellites   313, 1201
Age of Television, The   606
Ah! Mischief: The Writer and Television   1016
AIM Report   1262
Airwaves   1277
Airwaves to the Soul: The Influence and Growth of Religious Broad-
    casting in America   188, 245
Alfred Hitchcock Presents: An Illustrated Guide to the Ten-Year
    Television Career of the Master of Suspense   852
All About Cable: Legal and Business Aspects of Cable and Pay Tele-
    vision   1044, 1080
All About Home Satellite Television   1186, 1224
All for Love: A Study in Soap Opera   618, 655, 835
Alternative Influence, The: The Impact of Investigative Reporting
    Groups on America's Media   890
AM Stereo and TV Stereo: New Sound Dimensions   365
American History/American Television: Interpreting the Video Past
    612
American Journalist, The: A Portrait of U.S. News People and Their
    Work   90
American Telecommunications Market, The: Commercial/Public TV,
    Cable, STV, MDS, LPTV, Home Video   544, 937, 1030, 1139,
    1251
American Television Drama: The Experimental Years   711
American Television Genres   608
America's Other Voice: The Story of Radio Free Europe and Radio
    Liberty   464, 475
Amusing Ourselves to Death: Public Discourse in the Age of Show
    Business   613
Analysis of the Federal Communication Commission's Group Ownership
    Rules, An   308, 318
Anchorwoman   72

Andy Griffith Show, The   850
Art and Science of Radio, The   498
As Good As Any: Foreign Correspondence on American Radio,
     1930-1940   471
Assessment of Low-Power Television for the Nonprofit Community, An
     1171
Associated Press Broadcast News Handbook, The   391
Audience Ratings: Radio, Television, and Cable   51
Audience Research   415
Audience Research Workbook   414
Audiences for Public Television   581, 930
Audio Control Handbook For Radio and Television Broadcasting   364
Audio in Advertising: A Practical Guide to Producing and Recording
     Music, Voiceovers, and Sound Effects   354, 361, 408
Audio in Media   359
Australian Radio: The Technical Story, 1923-1983   445, 476
AVMP.   Audio Video Market Place: A Multimedia Guide   20

Balance in Broadcasting: Report on a Seminar Held 16-17 January,
     1981 in Hull, Quebec   129, 339
Basic Issues in Mass Communication: A Debate   95
Basic TV Staging   1012
Battle for Public Opinion, The: The President, the Press, and the
     Polls During Watergate   800
Battle Lines: Report of the Twentieth-Century Fund Task Force on
     the Military and the Media.   Background Paper by Peter Brae-
     strup   218
BBC, The: The First Fifty Years   147, 183
Beginning Broadcast Newswriting: A Self-Instructional Learning Ex-
     perience   402
Behind the Scenes: Practical Entertainment Law   277
Bellaire Guide to TV Commercial Cost Control, The   583
Better Broadcasts News   1263
Beyond Broadcasting: Into the Cable Age   666, 1061
Beyond Debate: A Paper on Televised Presidential Debates   900
Bibliography of CRTC Studies   1, 130
Bilko: The Fort Baxter Story   864
Bill Kurtis on Assignment   597, 887
Birth of Electronic Publishing, The: Legal and Economic Issues in
     Telephone, Cable and Over-the-Air Teletext and Videotext   1082,
     1160
Black Families and the Medium of Television   915
Blacks and Media: A Selected, Annotated Bibliography, 1962-1982
     11
Blacks and White TV: Afro-Americans in Television since 1948   919
Blacks on Television: A Selectively Annotated Bibliography   528
BM/E--Broadcast Management Engineering   1264
Books, Libraries and Electronics: Essays on the Future of Written
     Communication   745
Boys from the Blackstuff: Making a TV Drama   676, 988

Breaking into Communications 91, 1056
Breaking the TV Habit 777
British Television Revealed: An Economic Study 677
Broadcast Advertising: A Comprehensive Working Textbook 358
Broadcast Advertising and Promotion: A Handbook for Students
   and Professionals 349
Broadcast and Cable Management 377, 1110
Broadcast and Cable Selling 355, 1105
Broadcast/Cable Programming: Strategies and Practices 410, 1116
Broadcast Copywriting 422
Broadcast Copywriting as Process: A Practical Approach to Copy-
   writing for Radio and Television 356, 424
Broadcast Engineering 1265
Broadcast Fairness: Doctrine, Practice, Prospects. A Reappraisal
   of the Fairness Doctrine and Equal Time Rule 276, 282
Broadcast Investor 1266
Broadcast Journalism: A Guide for the Presentation of Radio and
   Television News 386
Broadcast Journalism 1979-1981: The Eighth Alfred I. du Pont/
   Columbia University Survey 874
Broadcast Law and Regulation 250
Broadcast Lending: A Lender's Guide to the Radio Industry 436
Broadcast News 396
Broadcast News Process, The 394
Broadcast News Writing 395, 1112
Broadcast News Writing, Reporting, and Production 400
Broadcast Newswriting: A Workbook 403
Broadcast Newswriting as Process 399
Broadcast Programs in American Colleges and Universities 86
Broadcast Radio and Television Handbook 371
Broadcast Regulation: Selected Cases and Decisions 249
Broadcast Television: A Research Guide 530
Broadcast Writing 417
Broadcast Writing Workbook 418
Broadcasters and Political Debates: An Outline for Election Year
   Use 271
Broadcaster's Handbook on State and Local Taxation, A 316, 382
Broadcaster's Legal Guide for Conducting Contests and Promotions,
   The 268
Broadcasting 1267
Broadcasting and Society, 1918-1939 455, 477
Broadcasting and Telecommunication: An Introduction 44
Broadcasting Bibliography: A Guide to the Literature of Radio and
   Television 2
Broadcasting/Cablecasting Yearbook 21, 1024
Broadcasting Chronology, 1809-1980, The 123, 181
Broadcasting in America: A Survey of Television, Radio, and New
   Technologies 47
Broadcasting in Education: An Evaluation 213
Broadcasting in the Arab World: A Survey of Radio and Television
   in the Middle East 139, 169

Broadcasting Law and Policy in Australia   124, 247, 317
Broadcasting Law and Regulation   253
Broadcasting Research Methods   413
Build a Personal Earth Station for Worldwide Satellite TV Reception
    1216, 1254
Business Opportunities For Broadcasters in MDS Pay Television   1174
Buying or Building A Broadcast Station: Everything You Want--and
    Need--to Know, But Didn't Know Who to Ask   80

Cable Advertiser's Handbook   1102
Cable Advertising: New Ways to New Business   1101
Cable/Broadband Communications Books, The. Vol. 3:   1982-1983
    1035
Cable Communication   1034
Cable for Information Delivery: A Guide for Librarians, Educators
    and Cable Professionals   1029
Cable Mania: The Cable Television Sourcebook   1037
Cable Television   1107
Cable Television: An Assessment of Critical Issues in Washington,
    DC   1068
Cable Television and Censorship: A Bibliography   1022
Cable Television and Other Nonbroadcast Video: Law and Policy
    1073
Cable Television and the Cities: Local Regulation and Municipal
    Uses   1084
Cable Television and the Future of Broadcasting   1060
Cable Television Business   1289
Cable Television in a New Era   1043, 1074
Cable Television Law: A Video Communications Practice Guide (3
    vols.)   1078
Cable Television, Market Power and Regulation   1090
Cable Television: Retrospective and Prospective   1075
Cable Television Technical Handbook, The   1108
Cable TV Investor   1290
Cable TV Renewals and Refranchising   1087
CableAge   1291
"Cablespeech": The Case for First Amendment Protection   1088
CableVision   1292
Campaign '84: Advertising and Programming Obligations of the Elec-
    tronic Media   272, 279
Canada's Video Revolution: Pay-TV, Home Video and Beyond   638,
    1129, 1239
Candidate's Guide to the Law of Political Broadcsating, A   273
Capital: Local Radio and Private Profit   451
Career Opportunities in Television, Cable, and Video   598, 1054
Careers in Cable   1050
Careers in Cable TV   1052
Careers in Radio   440
Careers in Television   593
Careers with a Radio Station   441

Cases and Materials on Mass Media Law   255
CATACable   1293
CBS Benjamin Report, The: CBS Reports "The Uncounted Enemy:
    A Vietnam Deception":   An Examination   875
Cellular Radio: A Business Assessment for Broadcasters   1149
Changes, Challenges and Opportunities in the New Electronic Media
    1131, 1241
Changing Channels: Living (Sensibly) with Television   727
Changing Television Audience in America, The   580
Channel Four: Television with a Difference?   671
Channels of Power: The Impact of Television on American Politics
    804
Child and Television Drama, The: The Psychosocial Impact of Cumu-
    lative Viewing   758
Children and Families Watching Television: A Bibliography of Re-
    search on Viewing Processes   529
Children and Television   658, 759
Children and the Formal Features of Television: Approaches and
    Findings of Experimental and Formative Research   769
Children, Television and Food   631, 757
Children's Television: The First Thirty-Five Years, 1946-1981.
    Part I: Animated Cartoon Series   572, 829
Children's Television: The First Thirty-Five Years, 1946-1981.
    Part II: Live, Film, and Tape Series   573, 830
Children's Understanding of Television: Research on Attention and
    Comprehension   756
Chilling Effect in TV News, The: Intimidation by the Nixon White
    House   889
Chilton's Guide to VCR Repair and Maintenance   1261
Choice by Cable: The Economics of a New Era in Television   692,
    1064
Chronology of Telecommunications and Cable Television Regulation in
    the United States   251, 1076
Churches and the British Broadcasting Corporation, 1922-1956, The:
    The Politics of Broadcast Religion   167, 197, 246
Classroom Combat: Teaching and Television   760, 781
Close Encounters   76
CNN vs. The Networks: Is More News Better News?   877
Collector's Guide to TV Memorabilia, A   548
Commercial FCC License Handbook   307
Commercial Television and European Children: An International Re-
    search Digest   647, 776
Communicating Effectively on Television   960
Communicating to Voters: Television in the First European Parlia-
    mentary Elections   643, 794
Communication and Social Change in Developing Nations: A Critical
    View   144
Communication Booknotes   1268
Communication Policy in Developed Countries   103, 320
Communication Satellites in the Geostationary Orbit   1198
Communication Satellites: Overview and Options for Broadcasters
    1212

Communication Satellites: Power Politics in Space   1200
Communications and Society: A Bibliography on Communications Tech-
    nologies and Their Social Impact   10
Communications and the Law   1269
Communications for National Development: Lessons from Experience
    143
Communications in a Changing World.   Vol. 2:   Issues in International
    Information   171
Communications in Canadian Society   133
Communications Law 1985:   A Course Handbook.   Vol. 1   259
Communications Policy and the Political Process   322
Communications Revolution, The   196, 209, 1148
Community Cable for and by Children: An ACT Handbook   1113
Community Television Handbook for Northern and Underserved Com-
    munities   640, 938
Comparative Broadcasting Systems   100
Comparative Communication Research   102
Comparative Mass Media Systems   112
Competition in Local Distribution: The Cable Television Industry
    1071
Complete Book of Dallas, The: Behind the Scenes at the World's
    Favorite Television Program   848
Complete Book of M*A*S*H, The   849
Complete Book of Script-Writing, The   423
Complete Dictionary of Television and Film, The   533
Complete Directory to Prime Time Network TV Shows, 1946-Present,
    The   560
Complete Guide to Laser/Videodisc Player Troubleshooting and Re-
    pair   1236
Complete Guide to Satellite TV, The   1185
Complete Guide to Videocassette Recorder Operation and Servicing
    1237
Complete Handbook of Home Video System   1234
Complete Home Video Book, The: A Source Book of Information Es-
    sential to the Video Enthusiast   1256
Computers in Video Production   980
Confetti Generation, The: How the New Communications Technology
    Is Fragmenting America   729, 1123
Congressional Television: A Legislative History   707, 796
Connections: Reflections on Sixty Years of Broadcasting   184
Continuous Wave, The: Technology and American Radio, 1900-1932
    465
Copyright Book, The: A Practical Guide   270
Coronation Street: 25 Years, 1960-1985   679, 714, 855
Countdown II: Jockeying at the DBS Starting Gate   1187, 1225
Creating Effective TV Commercials   941, 1013
Creating Original Programming for Cable TV   1095
Credibility of Institutions, Policies and Leadership, The.   Vol. 5:
    The Media   238
Critical Communications Review, The.   Vol. 1:   Labor, the Working
    Class and the Media   96

Critical Communications Review, The. Vol. 2: Changing Patterns
    of Communications Control 174
"Crossroads": The Drama of a Soap Opera 665, 846
CTIC Cablebooks. Vol. 1: The Community Medium 1036
CTIC Cablebooks. Vol. 2: A Guide for Local Policy 1081
Cuban-American Radio Wars: Ideology in International Telecommuni-
    cations 461, 484
Cultivating the Wasteland: Can Cable Put the Vision Back in TV?
    1091
Cultural Autonomy in Global Communications: Planning National In-
    formation Policy 173
Culture, Society and the Media 152, 202
Cultures in Collision: The Interaction of Canadian and U.S. Tele-
    vision Broadcast Policies. A Canadian-U.S. Conference on Com-
    munications Policies 637, 822
Current Developments in TV and Radio 252
Current Trends in the Direct Broadcast Satellite Industry 1204,
    1246

Dallas: The Complete Ewing Family Saga, Including Southfork Ranch,
    Ewing Oil, and the Barnes-Ewing Feud, 1860-1985 867
DBS News 1294
DBS Summit Conference, The 619, 1188, 1227
Dear 60 Minutes 878
"Death of a Princess" Controversy, The 750, 869, 939
Delson's Dictionary of Cable, Video and Satellite Terms 1023, 1189,
    1228
Demographic Vistas: Television in American Culture 610
Development of Communication in the Arab States: Needs and Pri-
    orities 138
Dick Van Dyke Show, The: Anatomy of a Classic 868
Dictionary of Communication and Media Studies, A 18
Dictionary of Film and Television Terms 534
Dictionary of Media Terms, A 17
Digital Audio Technology 362
Dimensions of Television Violence 734
Directing for Film and Television: A Guide to the Craft 978
Directing Television and Film 962
Directory of Broadcast Archives, A 27, 131, 151
Directory of Cable Education and Training Programs 1053
Directory of Religious Broadcasting, The 24
Disappearance of Childhood, The 773
Do-It-Yourself Video: A Beginner's Guide to Home Video 1257
Doctor Who: The Unfolding Text 690, 866
Documents of American Broadcasting 260
Duncan's Radio Market Guide 425
Dynasty: The Authorized Biography of the Carringtons 63, 839

Early Window, The: Effects of Television on Children and Youth 768

Earth Station Planning and Construction 1190
Economic Analysis of Mandatory Leased Channel Access for Cable
    Television, An 1041
Economics of Cable Television, The 1047
Economics of Cable Television (CATV), The: An Anthology 1046
Economics of Direct Broadcast Satellites (DBS), The: An Anthology
    1203, 1244
Economics of Low Power Television (LPTV), The: An Anthology
    1172
Economics of Multipoint Distribution Service (MDS), The: An An-
    thology 1175
Economics of Physical Distribution, The--Video Cassettes/Discs, and
    Movie Theater: An Anthology 1245
Economics of Satellite Master Antenna Television (SMATV), The: An
    Anthology 1181
Economics of Subscription Television (STV), The: An Anthology
    1217
Economics of Traditional Broadcasting (VHF/UHF), The: An An-
    thology 587
Editor's Guide to Telecommunications Buzzwords, Terminology, Acro-
    nyms and Abbreviations 16
Edward R. Murrow Heritage, The: Challenge for the Future 211
EEO Handbook: A Practical Guide for Broadcasters 278
Effective Television Advertising: A Study of 1000 Commercials
    747
Effective TV Production 985
Election Year 1984: NAB-Roper Poll 53, 229
Electrical and Electronic Technologies: A Chronology of Events and
    Inventors from 1900 to 1940 22
Electrical and Electronic Technologies: A Chronology of Events and
    Inventors from 1940 to 1980 23
Electronic Christianity: Myth or Ministry 809
Electronic Cinematography: Achieving Photographic Control over the
    Video Image 983
Electronic Epoch, The 182
Electronic Estate, The: New Communications Media and Australia
    630, 1117
Electronic Giant, The: A Critique of the Telecommunications Revo-
    lution from a Christian Perspective 807, 1127
Electronic Information Publishing: Old Issues in a New Industry
    1154
Electronic Marketing: Emerging TV and Computer Channels for Inter-
    active Home Shopping 1104
Electronic Media: A Guide to Trends in Broadcasting and Newer
    Technologies, 1920-1983 37, 1031
Electronic Media Management 376, 1109
Electronic Publishing: A Snapshot of the Early 1980s 673, 1157
Encyclopedia of Television. Vol. 1: Series, Pilots and Specials,
    1937-1973 556, 570
Encyclopedia of Television. Vol. 2: Series, Pilots and Specials,
    1974-1984 557, 571, 1033, 1097

Encyclopedia of Twentieth-Century Journalists 42
End of Comedy, The: The Sit-Com and the Comedic Tradition 843
Energy Coverage--Media Panic: An International Perspective 117,
    338
ENG One: A Practical Guide to Electronic News Gathering 956
ENG: Television News and the New Technology 958
Entertainment Machine, The: American Show Business in the
    Twentieth Century 194
ETV Newsletter 1282
Evening Stars, The: The Making of the Network News Anchor 896
Every Night at Five: Susan Stamberg's "All Things Considered"
    Book 489, 497
Expanding the Orbital Arc 332, 1215
Expert Techniques for Home Video Production 1243
Exploring Careers in Broadcast Journalism 89
Exploring Careers in Cable/TV 592, 1048
Exploring Careers in Communications and Telecommunications 92,
    1057

Fair Market Value of Radio Stations: A Buyer's Guide 433
Fanciest Dive, The: What Happened When the Media Empire of Time/
    Life Leaped Without Looking into the Age of High-Tech 940,
    1098
Fast Forward: The New Television and American Society 601
Fighting TV Stereotypes: An ACT Handbook 913
Film and Radio Propaganda in World War II 479
Film and Video Budgets 1003
Film, Tape and TV: Where Do I Fit In? 596
Film, Video and Television: Market Forces, Fragmentation and Tech-
    nological Advance 693
First Amendment and the Fourth Estate, The: The Law of Mass
    Media 286
First Amendment Reconsidered, The: New Perspectives on the Mean-
    ing of Freedom of Speech and Press 287
First 50 Years of Broadcasting, The: The Running Story of the
    Fifth Estate 186, 1066
FM Subcarriers and Broadcast Data Transmission 1178
Foreign and International Communications Systems: A Survey Bib-
    liography 12
Foreign News and the New World Information Order 118
Foreign News in the Media: International Reporting in 29 Countries
    345
Four Plays for Radio 456, 490
Framing Science: The Making of a BBC Documentary 688, 995
Free but Regulated: Conflicting Traditions in Media Law 285
From Approximately Coast to Coast ... It's The Bob and Ray Show
    486
Future of Broadcasting, The: Essays on Authority, Style and Choice
    155, 323
Future of Children's Television, The: Results of the Markle

Foundation/Boys Town Conference 771
Future of Videotext, The: Worldwide Prospects for Home/Office
    Electronic Information Services 627, 1162

General, The: David Sarnoff and the Rise of the Communications
    Industry 57
General Radiotelephone License Handbook 306
Geri 66
Getting the Picture: A Guide to CATV and the New Electronic
    Media 1038, 1146
Global Journalism: A Survey of the World's Mass Media 114
Good Morning, I'm Joan Lunden 68
Good News Is the Bad News Is Wrong, The 98
Goodnight Children ... Everywhere 154, 187
Gotcha! The Media, the Government and the Falklands Crisis 153,
    224
Government and the News Media: Comparative Dimensions 115, 232
Graphics for Television 1008
Great American Values Test, The: Influencing Behavior and Belief
    Through Television 724
Great Expectations: A Television Manager's Guide to the Future
    954
Great Radio Personalities in Historic Photographs 481
Great Television Race, The: A History of the American Television
    Industry, 1925-1941 720
Groping for Ethics in Journalism 390
Group and Cross-Media Ownership of Television Stations 586
Guide to Electronic Publishing: Opportunities in Online and View-
    data Services 1163
Guide to Innovative Children's Programs for Television 537, 826
Guidelines for Broadcast Internship Programs: Minorities, Women,
    College Students 84
Guidelines for Radio: Copywriting 501, 509
Guidelines for Radio: Promotion II 502
Guinness Book of TV Facts and Feats, The 542, 680

Handbook of Interactive Video 1114
Hello Everybody, I'm Lindsey Nelson 71
Here's Looking at You: The Story of British Television, 1908-1939
    678, 713
Hibernetics: A Guide to Radio Ratings and Research 526
Hidden Signals on Satellite TV, The: The Secret Signals on Satellite
    TV 1194, 1232
Hiring Guidebook for Broadcast Technical Personnel, The 373
Hitchcock in Prime Time 854
Holy Mackerel!: The Amos 'n' Andy Story 334
Home Satellite TV Book, The: How To Put the World in Your Back-
    yard 1191, 1229
Home Video and Broadcast Television: Impacts and Opportunities 1221

Home Video and Cable Yearbook, 1982-83, The   1025, 1233
Home Video Book, The   1218
Home Video Sourcebook, The   1242
Home Video Survival Guide, The   1223
Horrorshows: The A-to-Z of Horror in Film, TV, Radio and Theater
    41
How Sweet It Is: The Jackie Gleason Story   55
How to Capitalize on the Video Revolution: A Guide to New Busi-
    ness Enterprises   584
How to Get Started in Video   594, 1051
How to Produce Effective TV Commercials   947, 997
Humanistic Radio Production   517, 518
Hunt on Cable TV: Chaos or Coherence?   669, 1062

"I Love Lucy" Book, The   832
I Never Played the Game   61
If You Want Air Time   31
Images of Life on Children's Television: Sex Roles, Minorities, and
    Families   753, 909
Images of Nurses on Television   917
Imagine Please: Early Radio Broadcasting in British Columbia   447,
    467
Impact of Cable and Pay Cable Television on Local Station Audiences,
    The   582, 1072
Impact of Television, The: A Natural Experiment in Three Communi-
    ties   641, 751
Impact of the Cable Television Industry on Public Television, The
    932, 1070
Impact of the 1964 Revolution on Brazilian Television, The   636, 740
Imperialism, Media, and the Good Neighbor: New Deal Foreign Policy
    and United States Shortwave Broadcasting to Latin America   460,
    470
In Its Own Image: How Television Has Transformed Sports   812
In the Public Interest--III: A Report by the National News Council,
    1979-1983   293
Independent Film and Videomakers Guide, The   948, 999
Independent Television in Britain.   Vol. 1:   Origin and Foundation,
    1946-62   686, 716
Independent Television in Britain.   Vol. 2:   Expansion and Change,
    1958-68   687, 717
Individuals in Mass Media Organizations: Creativity and Constraint
    83
Information Explosion, The: The New Electronic Media in Japan and
    Europe   624, 1132
Information, Ideology and Communication: The New Nations' Per-
    spectives on an Intellectual Revolution   142, 1124
Information Systems Report   623, 1156
Information Technology in the Third World: Can I.T. Lead to Hu-
    mane National Development?   145, 1143
Inside BBC Television: A Year Behind the Camera   670, 974

Inside Information: British Government and the Media   158, 327
Inside Prime Time   842
Inside Radio   1278
Insider's Guide to Advertising Music, An   357, 366, 409
Instructional Development for Videotex: Flowcharts and Scripting
    1161
Instructional Telecommunications: Principles and Applications   787
Instructional Television Fixed Services: An Analysis of ITFS Opera-
    tions   779
Intelligent Idiot's Guide To Getting The Most Out of Home Video
    Equipment, The   1226
Intelsat Global Satellite System, The   1183
Interactive Cable TV Handbook, The   1027
International Broadcasting by Satellite: Issues of Regulation, Bar-
    riers to Communication   314, 1206, 1248
International Film, Radio, and Television Journals   36
International Flow of Information: A Global Report and Analysis
    175
International Issues in Communication Technology and Policy   108,
    325
International Law Governing Communications and Information: A
    Collection Of Basic Documents   178, 266
International Radio Broadcasting: The Limits of the Limitless Medium
    459
International Satellite Directory   28, 1197
International Satellite Television: Resource Manual for the Third
    Biennial Communications Law Symposium   816, 1192
International Telecommunication Union in a Changing World, The   170
International Telecommunications and Information Policy   179, 331
International Television Almanac   539, 1028
International TV and Video Guide   543, 626
International Videotex Teletext News   1295
Internships in the Communication Arts and Sciences   85
Interplay of Influence, The: Mass Media and their Publics in News,
    Advertising, Politics   735
Interpretations of the First Amendment   299
Interpreting Television: Current Research Perspectives   614
Interviews That Work: A Practical Guide for Journalists   383
Introduction of Pay-TV in Canada, The: Issues and Implications
    642, 1065
Inventing Reality: The Politics of the Mass Media   742
Iran Media Index   559
Ireland: The Propaganda War. The British Media and the "Battle
    for Hearts and Minds"   150, 342
Issues in International Telecommunications Policy: A Sourcebook
    180, 333
It Ain't Half Racist, Mum: Fighting Racism in the Media   148

Juror and the General, The   303
Just a Few Words: How to Present Yourself in Public   406

Keys to Writing for Television and Film, The   1015
Kids' Stuff: A Resource Book for Children's Television Programming
    540, 828
Kids' TV: The First 25 Years   564, 706, 827
KNOM/Father Jim Poole Story, The   478
Knowledge Industry 200, 1983 Edition, The: America's Two Hundred
    Largest Media and Information Companies   29

Ladies of the Evening: Women Characters of Prime-Time Television
    921
Language of Television Advertising, The   732
Language Resources in the United States II: Guide to Non-English-
    Language Broadcasting   26
Largest Theatre in the World, The: Thirty Years of Television
    Drama   862
Larry King   67
Law and the Television of the '80's   819
Law of Mass Communications: Freedom and Control of Print and
    Broadcast Media   263
Learning from Television: Psychological and Educational Research
    763, 786
Learning over the Air: 60 Years of Partnership in Adult Learning
    162, 191, 216
Legal Issues Affecting Licensing of TV Programs in the European
    Economic Community from the Perspective of the U.S. Exporter
    644, 817
Leonard Maltin's TV Movies, 1985-86   567
Les Brown's Encyclopedia of Television   554
Let Truth Be Told: 50 Years of BBC External Broadcasting   453,
    463, 474
Libel and Privacy: The Prevention and Defense of Litigation   304,
    381
License Renewal Kit for Television Stations   815
Life of Python   681, 856
Life on Daytime Television: Tuning-In American Serial Drama   836
Listening to the Future: Cable Audio in the 80s   1040
Live and Off-Color: News Biz   902
Lively Audience, The: A Study of Children Around the TV Set
    633, 772
Longman Dictionary of Mass Media and Communication   15
Lotteries and Contests: A Broadcaster's Handbook   269
Low Power Television: Development and Current Status of the LPTV
    Industry   1170
LPTV   1283
Lucy: The Real Life of Lucille Ball   65
Lyndon Johnson's Dual War: Vietnam and the Press   195, 241

Made for Television: Euston Films Limited   651
Main Source, The: Learning from Television News   744, 898

Major Principles of Media Law 264
Make Your Own Professional Home Video Recordings 1255
Makeup for Theatre, Film, and Television: A Step-by-Step Photographic Guide 959
Making a TV Series: The "Bellamy" Project 632, 989
Making It in Cable TV: Career Opportunities in Today's Fastest Growing Media Industry 1055
Making It in Radio: Your Future in the Modern Medium 439
Making Millions in Telecommunications: The New Way to Get Rich in the Eighties 79
Making Money with Subcarriers 1176
Making of The Jewel in the Crown, The 935, 982
Making Television Programs: A Professional Approach 963
Managing Diversity: Federal-Provincial Collaboration and the Committee on Extension of Services to Northern and Remote Communities 639, 1202
Mary Tyler Moore 59
M*A*S*H: The Exclusive, Inside Story of TV's Most Popular Show 857
Mass Communication and Electronic Media: A Survey Bibliography 13
Mass Communication, Culture and Society in West Africa 120
Mass Communication in Africa 119
Mass Communication Law: Cases and Comment 257
Mass Communication Theory: An Introduction 205
Mass Communications and the Advertising Industry 141, 159
Mass Communications in Western Europe: An Annotated Bibliography 14, 136
Mass Communications Law in a Nutshell 267
Mass Media and American Politics 221
Mass Media and Elections 227
Mass Media and Political Thought: An Information-Processing Approach 228
Mass Media and Social Problems, The 203
Mass Media and the Supreme Court: The Legacy of the Warren Years 290
Mass Media Declaration of Unesco, The 176, 329
Mass Media in Australia, The 127, 242
Mass Media in Campaign '84, The: Articles from Public Opinion Magazine 233
Mass Media Law 265
Mass Media Law and Regulation 254
Mass Media Research: An Introduction 416
Matter of Honor, A: General William C. Westmoreland Versus CBS 886, 975
Media, The: A New Analysis of the Press, Television, Radio and Advertising in Australia 128, 210
Media Abuses: Rights and Remedies. A Guide to Legal Remedies 312
Media and Elections in Canada 134, 236
Media and the American Mind: From Morse to McLuhan 185, 200

Media Control in Ireland, 1923-1983   137
Media Crisis, The ... A Continuing Challenge   113, 294
Media Elite, The   737, 892, 933
Media for Interactive Communication   1106, 1153
Media Industries: The Production of News and Entertainment   208
Media Industry Reporter   1270
Media Insurance and Risk Management, 1985   378
Media Insurance: Protecting Against High Judgments, Punitive Dam-
    ages, and Defense Costs   301, 379
Media Law: A Legal Handbook for the Working Journalist   256
Media Law in Australia   125, 248
Media Law: The Rights of Journalists and Broadcasters   161, 297
Media Monopoly, The   78
Media Politics: The News Strategies of Presidential Campaigns   217
Media Power   723
Media Power in Politics   222
Media Revolution in America and Western Europe, The   116
Media Room, The: Creating Your Own Home Entertainment and In-
    formation Center   1220
Media Unbound: The Impact of Television Journalism on the Public
    736, 891
Media Voices: Debating Critical Issues in Mass Media   204
Media: Wasteland or Wonderland.   Opportunities and Dangers for
    Christians in the Electronic Age   244
Media Writing: News for the Mass Media   393
Mediaspeak: How Television Makes Up Your Mind   728
Mediated Political Realities   231
Meeting Learners' Needs through Telecommunications: A Directory
    and Guide to Programs   32
MegaRates: How To Get Top Dollar For Your Spots   505
Message in a Bottle: Theoretical Overview and Annotated Bibliogra-
    phy on the Mass Media and Alcohol   3, 343
Messenger's Motives, The: Ethical Problems of the News Media   392
Method to the Madness, The: Radio's Morning Show Manual   522
Mexican Americans and the Mass Media   52, 201
Microcomputers in TV Studios   996
Microphone Handbook, The   368
Microphones   360
Mighty Minutes: An Illustrated History of Television's Best Commer-
    cials   710, 944
Military and the Media, The   156, 225
Mind and Media: The Effects of Television, Video Games and Com-
    puters   733
Minute by Minute...   883
Misregulating Television: Network Dominance and the FCC   821
Modern Radio Production   521
Modularization and Packaging of Public Television Programs   928,
    1120
Modulation, Overmodulation, and Occupied Bandwidth: Recommenda-
    tions for the AM Broadcast Industry   512
Movies Made For Television: The Telefeature and the Mini-Series,
    1964-1984   568

MTM "Quality Television"   840
Multichannel MDS: New Allocations, New Systems and New Market
    Opportunities   1173
Murrow: His Life and Times   73
Music in the Air: America's Changing Tastes in Popular Music,
    1920-1980   469

NAB Computer Primer for Radio Broadcasters, The: A Beginner's
    Guide to Computers   515
NAB Legal Guide to FCC Broadcast Regulations   262
NAB Today/Radio   1279
NAB Today/Television   1284
National Association of Broadcasters Engineering Handbook   367
NBC Handbook of Pronunciation   25
New Audio Marketplace, The: Challenges and Opportunities for
    Broadcasters   435
New Directions in Satellite Communications: Challenges for North
    and South   1195
New Era in CATV, The: The Cable Franchise Policy and Communica-
    tions Act of 1984   1083
New Information Technology in Education   783, 1126
New International Economic Order, The: Links Between Economics
    and Communications   177, 330
New Media Developments: Satellite TV   617, 1182
New Media Politics: Comparative Perspectives in Western Europe
    625, 823, 1133
New Perspectives on Political Advertising   798
New Program Opportunities in the Electronic Media   1136
New Technologies, The: Changes and Challenges in Public Relations--
    A Sourcebook of General Information   1137
New Technologies, New Policies?   A Report from the Broadcasting
    Research Unit   157, 1128
New Television Technologies, The   1125
New World and International Information Order, The: A Resource
    Guide and Bibliography   5, 30
New World Information and Communication Order, The: A Selective
    Bibliography   9
New York Times v. Sullivan: The Next Twenty Years   302
News Business, The   385
News Media and Public Policy: An Annotated Bibliography   8
News Media and the Law, The   1271
News Media in National and International Conflict, The   99, 198
News, Newspapers and Television   664, 882
News of Crime: Courts and Press in Conflict   292
News: The Politics of Illusion   219
Newspapers and New Media   1138
Newswatch: How TV Decides the News   907
Newswriting for the Electronic Media: Principles, Examples, Applica-
    tions   388, 1111
Nightly Horrors: Crisis Coverage by Television Network News   897

1983 Supplement to Regulation of Broadcasting: Law and Policy towards Radio, Television and Cable Communications 258
No Sense of Place: The Impact of Electronic Media on Social Behavior 741
Norman Corwin and Radio: The Golden Years 56
Not the BBC/IBA: The Case for Community Radio 454, 495
Nothing Local About It: London's Local Radio 452
Nukespeak: The Media and the Bomb 146

Off-Air Videotaping in Education: Copyright Issues, Decisions, Implications 791, 820
Off Camera: Conversations with the Makers of Prime-Time Television 977
Official Honeymooners Treasury, The: To the Moon and Back with Ralph, Norton, Alice and Trixie 838
On Camera: My 10,000 Hours on Television 62
On Television 667
On the Air! 615
On the Good Ship Enterprise: My 15 Years with Star Trek 865
On the Road with Charles Kuralt 927
101 Ways to Cut Legal Fees and Manage Your Lawyer 375
Operational Guidelines and Accounting Manual for Broadcasters 380
Opportunities in Cable Television 1049
Opportunities in Communications Law 87
Opportunities of Channel Leasing, The: Strategic Considerations for Broadcasters 1042
Or Your Money Back 352
Organizing Educational Broadcasting 105, 214
Original Hitchhiker Radio Scripts, The 448, 485
Orwell: The War Broadcasts 457, 491
Orwell: The War Commentaries 457, 492
Out of the Bakelite Box: The Heyday of Australian Radio 444, 472
Outlet Story, 1894-1984, The 192
Over the Wire and on TV: CBS and UPI in Campaign '80 805, 899
Ownership Trends in Cable Television: 1985 1026, 1045

Packaging the Presidency: A History and Criticism of Presidential Campaign Advertising 190, 226
Parents' Guide to Television, A: Making The Most Of It 767
Perry's Broadcast News Handbook 389
Perry's Broadcast Promotion Sourcebook 508
Perry's Broadcast Regulation Political Primer 274
Perry's Broadcasting and the Law 1272
Perspectives on Media Effects 725
Perspectives on Radio and Television: Telecommunication in the United States 49
Pictorial History of Television, A 718
Picture Improves, The: A Look at the 1984 Television Season 925
Pike and Fischer's Desk Guide to the Fairness Doctrine 280

Plug-In Drug, The: Television, Children, and the Family 778
Policy Research in Telecommunications: Proceedings from the
    Eleventh Annual Telecommunications Policy Research Conference
    328
Political Broadcast Catechism 275, 281
Political Campaign Debates: Images, Strategies, and Tactics 230
Political Communications: The General Election Campaign of 1979
    168, 243
Politics and Television Re-Viewed 801
Politics and the Media in Canada 132, 235
Politics of Broadcast Regulation, The 310
Politics of Broadcasting, The 110, 326
Politics of TV Violence, The: Policy Uses of Communication Research
    824
Popular Television and Film: A Reader 600
Portable Video: A Production Guide for Young People 976
Portable Video: ENG and EFP 984
Positive Images: Breaking Stereotypes with Children's Television
    766, 916
Post 1285
Potential International Business Opportunities for U.S. Broadcasters
    81
Power of Television, The: A Critical Appraisal 738
Power Without Responsibility: The Press and Broadcasting in
    Britain 149, 319
Powerplays: Trevor Griffiths in Television 1019
Practical Guide to the Cable Communications Policy Act of 1984, A
    1086
Presidential Election Show, The: Campaign '84 and Beyond on the
    Nightly News 793, 879
Presidents and the Press: The Nixon Legacy 237
Press and Television Interests in Australian Commercial Radio 446,
    634
Press and The State, The: Sociohistorical and Contemporary Studies
    284
Press Control Around the World 101, 289
Press Law in Modern Democracies: A Comparative Study 111, 261
Prestel, Escher, Bach: Changes Within Changes 668, 1155
Primal Screen, The: How to Write, Sell, and Produce Movies for
    Television 994, 1021
Prime Time Crime: Criminals and Law Enforcers in TV Entertainment
    918
Prime Time Law Enforcement: Crime Show Viewing and Attitudes
    Toward the Criminal Justice System 726
Prime-Time Television: A Pictorial History from Milton Berle to "Fal-
    con Crest" 708
Proceedings of the Annual Broadcast Engineering Conference 372
Process of Electronic News Gathering, The 957
Producers, The: A Descriptive Directory of Film and Television Pro-
    ducers in the Los Angeles Area 536
Producer's Medium, The: Conversations with Creators of American TV
    990

Producers on Producing: The Making of Film and Television 964
Producing TV Movies 966
Production in Format Radio Handbook 504, 519
Profession: Journalist. A Study on the Working Conditions of
    Journalists 82
Professional Broadcast Announcing 404
Professional Newswriting 398
Professionals Video Graphic Design 1009
Professional Video Production 998
Program Director's Handbook, The 523
Programming Dynamics: Radio's Management Guide 524
Programming for Radio and Television 412
Progressive Video Programming: A Strategy for Making Informational
    Video on Location 972
Protecting Privacy in Two-Way Electronic Services 1058, 1079
Public Attitudes Toward Television And Other Media In a Time of
    Change 54
Public Broadcasting Report 1273
Public Radio Programming Content by Category: Fiscal Year 1982
    493
Public Radio Stations' Educational Services, 1982-83 496
Public Television and Radio and State Governments. Vol. 1: Rela-
    tionship by State 347
Public Television and Radio and State Governments. Vol. 2: State
    Statutes 311, 348
Public Television Programming Content by Category: Fiscal Year
    1982 936
Pushbutton Fantasies: Critical Perspectives on Videotex and Informa-
    tion Technology 1159

Radio and Television: A Selected, Annotated Bibliography. Supple-
    ment One: 1977-1981 7
Radio and Television Commercial, The 350, 407
Radio and TV Programming 411
Radio Broadcast Log of the Western Drama Program, A: The Lone
    Ranger 427, 482
Radio Broadcasting: An Introduction to the Sound Medium 499
Radio Broadcasts in the Library of Congress, 1924-1941: A Catalog
    of Recordings 428
Radio Broadcasts of Will Rogers 488
Radio Copy Book: Ideas and Inspiration for Radio Copywriters 487,
    503, 510
Radio Employee Compensation and Fringe Benefits Report 437
Radio Financial Report 438
Radio in Search of Excellence: Lessons from America's Best-Run
    Radio Stations 514
Radio in the United States, 1976-1982: A Statistical History 468
Radio Is... 426
Radio New Technology and You 434, 1122
Radio News 1280

Radio Only 1281
Radio Papers, The: From KRAB to KCHU. Essays on the Art and
    Practice of Radio Transmission 494
Radio Production Handbook: A Beginner's Guide to Broadcasting
    and Cablecasting 520
Radio Station, The 500
Radio Subcarrier Services: How to Make Dollars and Sense Out of
    New Business Opportunities 1177
Radio Today--and Tomorrow 432, 1118
Radio, TV and Cable: A Telecommunications Approach 50
Radio W.A.R.S.: How to Survive in the '80s 430, 506
Radio W.A.R.S. II: How to Push Listeners' "Hot Buttons" 431, 507
Razzle-Dazzle: The Curious Marriage of Television and Professional
    Football 810
RCA and The VideoDisc: The Business of Research 585, 1231
Re:ACT 1286
Real Campaign, The: How the Media Missed the Story of the 1980
    Campaign 223
Reality on Reels: How to Make Documentaries for Video/Radio/Film
    401
Really Bad News 660, 914
Rebel Radio: The Full Story of British Pirate Radio 450
Reckless Disregard: Westmoreland v. CBS et al; Sharon v. Time
    300
Regarding Television: Critical Approaches--An Anthology 609
Regulation of Media Ownership by the Federal Communications Com-
    mission: An Assessment 309
Regulation of Transnational Communications: 1984 Michigan Yearbook
    of International Legal Studies 315, 1210
Religious Broadcasting 1274
Religious Broadcasting, 1920-1983: A Selectively Annotated Bibliogra-
    phy 4
Religious Television: The American Experience 808
Report from the Working Party on the New Technologies, A 682,
    1140
Report on Cable Systems 683, 1063
Reporter's Handbook, The: An Investigator's Guide to Documents and
    Techniques 397
Reporters Under Fire: U.S. Media Coverage of Conflicts in Lebanon
    and Central America 94, 220
Reporting for Television 955
Responsibilities of Journalism, The 97
Responsibility and Freedom in the Press: Are They in Conflict?
    288
Right Place at The Right Time, The 69
Right to Communicate, The: A Status Report 321
Rocking America: How the All-Hit Radio Stations Took Over 480,
    483
Role of Technology in Distance Education, The 212
Role Portrayal and Stereotyping on Television: An Annotated Bib-
    liography of Studies Relating to Women, Minorities, Aging,

Sexual Behavior, Health and Handicaps   531, 924
Rx Television: Enhancing the Preventive Impact of TV   746

Satellite Broadcasting   1209, 1250
Satellite Communications   1207, 1208, 1249
Satellite Directory, The   35, 1211
Satellite Television Reception: A Personal User's Guide   1193, 1230
Satellites Today: The Complete Guide to Satellite Television   1184
Saturday Night: A Backstage History of Saturday Night Live   712,
   845
Say Goodnight, Gracie! :   The Story of Burns and Allen   58, 834
Scholarships in Radio and Television   88
Science Fiction Image, The: The Illustrated Encyclopedia of Science
   Fiction in Film, Television, Radio and the Theater   43
Scramble to Scramble, The: A Satellite Television Dilemma   1213
Script for Success.   Carole Nelson: Her Story   70
See, Hear, Interact: Beginning Developments in Two-Way Television
   1093
See It Happen: The Making of ITN   657, 705
Selective Exposure to Communication   752
Series TV: How a Television Show Is Made   969
Sex Stereotyping in Advertising   199, 341
Shakeout: The Year in Cable Programming   1096
Shaping the First Amendment: The Development of Free Expression
   298
Shooting Video   993
Shut Up and Listen!   Women and Local Radio: A View from the In-
   side   449
Sign-Off: The Last Days of Television   912
Single-Camera Video Production: Techniques, Equipment, and Re-
   sources for Producing Quality Video Programming   971
60 Minutes: The Power and The Politics of America's Most Popular
   TV News Show   895
Small Format Television Production: The Technique of Single-
   Camera Television Field Production   967
SMATV: A Changing Environment for Private Cable   1179
SMATV: Strategic Opportunities in Private Cable   1180
Soap Opera, The   335
Soap Opera Encyclopedia, The   555, 860
Soap Stars: America's 31 Favorite Daytime Actors Speak for Them-
   selves   599, 870
Soap World   851
Soaps: A Pictorial History of America's Daytime Dramas   709, 844
Sounds Real: Radio in Everyday Life   443
Space, Earth and Communication   1205
Speaking of Soap Operas   831
Split Screen   75, 165
Sports Junkies Rejoice! :   The Birth of ESPN   1067, 1094
Spot, The: The Rise of Political Advertising on Television   795
Squeezing Profits Out of Ratings: A Manual for Radio Managers,

Sales Managers and Programmers 525
Station Policy and Procedures: A Guide for Radio 513
Story of English, The 893, 934
Strategies for Higher-Definition Television 1169
Strategies in Broadcast and Cable Promotion: Commercial Television,
    Radio, Cable, Pay-Television, Public Television 351, 929, 1099
Structure of Television, The 620, 700
Suing the Press: Libel, the Media, and Power 305
Super Official TV Trivia Quiz Book, The 576
Supertube: The Rise of Television Sports 811
Sweeps, The: Behind the Scenes in Network TV 837
Syndicated Radio Programming Directory 429

TAB Handbook of Radio Communications, The 511
Taking Soaps Seriously: The World of Guiding Light 847
Talk Show Book, The: An Engaging Primer on How to Talk Your
    Way to Success 33
Talking Back 283
Teaching Critical Television Viewing Skills: An Integrated Approach
    790
Teaching the Media 789
Technique of Lighting for Television and Motion Pictures, The 1010
Technique of Television Production, The 986
Technologies of Freedom 296, 1085
Telecom Factbook 38
Telecommunications: An Introduction to Radio, Television, and Other
    Electronic Media 46
Telecommunications Facilities Survey 374
Telecommunications in Crisis: The First Amendment, Technology,
    and Deregulation 291
Telecommunications in the Information Age: A Nontechnical Primer
    on the New Technologies 1142, 1252
Telecommunications Policy Handbook 825, 1141
Telecommunications Primer 370
Telecommunications Technologies and Public Broadcasting 346, 1119
Teletext and Videotex in the United States: Market Potential,
    Technology, Public Policy Issues 1164
Televising "Terrorism": Political Violence in Popular Culture 684
Television 979
Television: A Guide to the Literature 527
Television: A History 696, 721
Television and Adult Education 621, 785
Television and Aggression: A Panel Study 770
Television and Behavior: Ten Years of Scientific Progress and Impli-
    cations for the Eighties. Vol. 1: Summary Report 748
Television and Behavior: Ten Years of Scientific Progress and Impli-
    cations for the Eighties. Vol. 2: Technical Reviews 743
Television and Cable Factbook (2 vols.) 550, 1032
Television and Children: A Special Medium for a Special Audience
    761, 782

Television and Irish Society: 21 Years of Irish Television   648, 920
Television and Middle East Diplomacy: President Carter's Fall 1977
    Peace Initiative   799, 885
Television and Radio   48
Television and Radio Announcing   405
Television and the Aggressive Child: A Cross National Comparison
    622, 764
Television and the Performing Arts: A Handbook and Reference
    Guide to American Cultural Programming   545, 715, 858
Television and the Presidential Elections: Self-Interest and the
    Public Interest   803
Television and the Red Menace: The Video Road to Vietnam   739,
    853, 894
Television and the Riots: A Report for the Broadcasting Research
    Unit of the British Film Institute   691, 749
Television and the Socialization of the Minority Child   755
Television Broadcast Communications   1287
Television Comedy Series: An Episode Guide to 153 TV Sitcoms in
    Syndication   563
Television Coverage of International Affairs   722, 872
Television Coverage of the 1980 Presidential Campaign   792, 873
Television Coverage of the 1983 General Election: Audiences, Appre-
    ciation and Public Opinion   661, 797
Television Drama: An Introduction   685, 861
Television Drama Series Programming: A Comprehensive Chronicle,
    1980-1982   565
Television Electronics: Theory and Service   951
Television Employee Compensation and Fringe Benefits Report   589
Television Engineering Handbook   949
Television Family, The: A Content Analysis of the Portrayal of
    Family Life in Prime Time Television   635, 926
Television Financial Report   590
Television: From Analog to Digital   952
Television in a Multiracial Society: A Research Report   652, 908
Television in Europe: Quality and Values in a Time of Change   646
Television in Singapore: An Analysis of a Week's Viewing   649
Television in the Eighties: The Total Equation   1134
Television in Transition: Papers from the First International Tele-
    vision Studies Conference   698
Television Looks At Aging   863, 903
Television Market Analysis   591
Television Marketing: Network, Local, and Cable   949, 1102
Television Myth and the American Mind   607
Television Mythologies: Stars, Shows, and Signs   675
Television News, Radio News   387
Television News: Whose Bias? A Casebook Analysis of Strikes, Tele-
    vision and Media Studies   662, 880
Television Operations Handbook   991, 1115
Television Piracy   1089
Television Production   1000
Television Production: Disciplines and Techniques   965

Television Production Handbook   1001
Television Production Workbook   1002
Television Programming Across National Boundaries: The EBU and
    OIRT Experience   699
Television/Radio Age   1275
Television/Radio Age International Newsletter   1276
Television, Sex Roles and Children: A Developmental Social Psycho-
    logical Account   762
Television Technology: Alternative Communication Systems   1130,
    1240
Television: The Critical View   611
Television: The Medium and its Manners   602, 656
Television Today and Television Tomorrow: A Guide to New Elec-
    tronic Media and Trends in Commercial Television in Western
    Europe   628, 1144
Television Today and Tomorrow: Wall-to-Wall Dallas?   659, 730
Television Viewers vs. Media Snobs: What TV Does for People   731
Television Violence: A Child's-Eye View   775
Television Writing: From Concept to Contract   1014
Television's Guardians: The FCC and the Politics of Programming,
    1958-1967   703, 814
Televisions: One Season in American Television   604
Television's Teletext   629, 1165
Television's Window on the World: International Affairs Coverage on
    the U.S. Networks   802, 888
Telling the Story: The National Public Radio Guide to Radio Journal-
    ism   516
Ten Presidents and the Press   193, 239
Terrorism: The Media and the Law   295
Third Age of Broadcasting, The   695, 1147
"This is Judy Woodruff at the White House"   77
This Is the ABC: The Australian Broadcasting Commission, 1932-
    1983   126, 189
Three Press Secretaries on the Presidency and the Press   240
Tonight   689
Tony, Grammy, Emmy, Country: A Broadway, Television and Records
    Awards Reference   538
Total Television: A Comprehensive Guide to Programming from 1948
    to the Present   566
Toward International Tele-Education   780
Transmission   603, 1121
Transnational Communication and Cultural Industries   701
Treachery?   The Power Struggle at TV-am   672
Tube of Plenty: The Evolution of American Television   702
Tune In to a Television Career   595
Tuned to Baseball   64
Turned-On TV/Turned-Off Voters: Policy Options for Election Pro-
    jections   806, 901
TV and Radio: Everybody's Soapbox   160
TV and Schooling   674, 788
TV and Teens: Experts Look at the Issues   774

TV and Video   575
TV Arab, The   923
TV Commercial Film Editing: Professional Motion Picture Pre- and
    Post-Production Including Animation, Rotoscoping, and Video
    Tape   943, 1006
TV Commercial, The: How It Is Made   942, 968
TV Coverage of the Oil Crises: How Well Was the Public Served?
    Vol. 1:   A Qualitative Analysis, 1973-74/1978-79   904
TV Coverage of the Oil Crises: How Well Was the Public Served?
    Vol. 2:   A Quantitative Analysis, 1973-74/1978-79   905
TV Coverage of the Oil Crises: How Well Was the Public Served?
    Vol. 3:   An Economist's Perspective, 1973-74/1978-79   881
TV Facts   549, 719
TV Genres: A Handbook and Reference Guide   546
TV Guide Index: 1978-1982 Cumulative Supplement   558
TV Lighting Methods   1011
TV or CATV? A Struggle for Power   1077
TV Schedule Book, The: Four Decades of Network Programming from
    Sign-On to Sign-Off   562
TV, Science, and Kids: Teaching Our Children to Question   784
TV Technology   1288
TV: The Casual Art   616
TV Trivia: Thirty Years of Television   577
TV Use and Social Interaction in Adolescence: A Longitudinal Study
    645, 765
TV's Greatest Hits: The 150 Most Popular TV Shows of All Time
    561
TV's Image of the Elderly: A Practical Guide for Change   910
Twilight Zone Companion, The   871

"Uncensored War," The: The Media and Vietnam   879
Understanding Broadcasting   45
Understanding News   663
Understanding Satellite Television Reception   1214, 1253
Understanding Television Production   973
Uninvited Guests: The Intimate Secrets of Television and Radio
    163, 207
Universal Television: The Studio and Its Programs, 1950-1980   569
Update Cellular Radio: Its Economic Feasibility for Smaller Markets
    1150
U.S. Television Network News: A Guide to Sources in English   532
Use of Microphones, The   363
Use of Satellite Communication for Information Transfer, The   1196
Using Copyrighted Videocassettes in Classrooms and Libraries   818
Using the Media for Adult Basic Education   109, 215

Variety of Lives, A: A Biography of Sir Hugh Greene   74, 164
VCR Explosion, The   1259
Video Age, The: Television Technology and Applications in the 1980s
    1145

Video Camera Techniques 987
Video Cassette Recorders: Buying, Using and Maintaining 1247
Video Cassettes: Production, Distribution and Programming for the
     VCR Marketplace 1260
Video Democracy: The Vote-from-Home Revolution 1069
Video Editing and Post-Production: A Professional Guide 1004
Video Electronics Technology 950
Video Guide, The 535
Video Media Competition: Regulation, Economics, and Technology
     588
Video Nasties, The: Freedom and Censorship in the Media 653, 813
Video Primer, The: Equipment, Production and Concepts 992
Video Production Guide, The 981
Video Production in Education and Training 970
Video Production--The Professional Way 1222
Video Register, The 551
Video Source Book, The 552
Video Tape Post-Production Primer, The: A Professional "Overview"
     of Electronic Editing 1005
Video Taping Handbook, The: The Newest Systems, Cameras and
     Techniques 1235
Video Techniques 953
Video User's Handbook 1258
Video Violence and Children 754, 1219
Video Week 1296
Videotape Editing: Communicating with Pictures and Sound 1007
Videotex Journalism: Teletext, Viewdata, and the News 694, 1168
Videotex: Key to the Wired City 650, 1152
Videotex Marketplace, The 1166
Videotex/Teletext Bibliography, A 553, 1167
Videotex/Teletext: Principles and Practices 1151
Vietnam: A History 884, 931
Viewdata and the Information Society 1158
Violence as Communication: Insurgent Terrorism and the Western
     News Media 206
Visible Fictions: Cinema, Television, Video 605
Voice of America Calling Finland 462, 473
Voices and Values: Television Stations in the Community 906

War, Peace and the News Media: Proceedings 234, 337
Warner Bros. Television: Every Show of the Fifties and Sixties
     Episode-by-Episode 574
Watching Dallas: Soap Opera and the Melodramatic Imagination 833
Watching TV: Four Decades of American Television 704
Western Hero in Film and Television, The: Mass Media Mythology
     922
Whatever Became of...? 578
What's This Channel Fo(u)r? An Alternative Report 654
What's Wrong with This Picture? A Look at Working Women on Tele-
     vision 911, 1092

When Information Counts: Grading the Media   336
Where Have I Been? An Autobiography   60
Who's Who in Broadcasting   166
Who's Who in Television and Cable   579, 1039
Who's Who on Television: A Fully Illustrated Guide to 1000 Best
    Known Faces on British Television   697
Women and Mass Media in Asia: An Annotated Bibliography   6, 122
Women and Media: Analysis, Alternatives and Action   121, 340
Women, Media and Crisis: Femininity and Disorder   140, 344
Wonderful Inventions: Motion Pictures, Broadcasting, and Recorded
    Sound at the Library of Congress   34
Wonderful Wireless: Reminiscences of the Stars of Australia's Live
    Radio   442, 466
Working Press of the Nation, The. Vol. 3: TV and Radio Directory
    39
World Broadcasting in the Age of the Satellite: Comparative Sys-
    tems, Policies, and Issues in Mass Telecommunication   107, 324
World Broadcasting Systems: A Comparative Analysis   106
World Communications: A Handbook   104, 172
World of Satellite Television, The   1199, 1238
World of Star Trek, The   841
World Radio TV Handbook   40
World Wired Up, The: Unscrambling the New Communications Puzzle
    1059, 1135
Writing and Reporting Broadcast News   384
Writing for Mass Communication   420
Writing for Television and Radio   419
Writing for the Broadcast Media   421
Writing for the Soaps   1020
Writing Television and Motion Picture Scripts That Sell   1017
Writing Television Criticism   1018

You Can Be a Game Show Contestant and Win   547, 859
Your Career in Radio and Television Broadcasting   93